AL ILLICH'S
HOW TO PICK WINNERS

Albert George Illich

arco

New York

Published by ARCO PUBLISHING COMPANY, INC.
219 Park Avenue South, New York, N.Y. 10003

Copyright © Albert George Illich, 1971

Library of Congress Catalog Number 72-161211

ISBN 0-668-62472-0

Printed in the United States of America

Contents

Introduction

FOR NEARLY HALF a century I have had the rare distinction and pleasure of being a leader in the field of education. Though the subject I have specialized in might not be included in the curriculum at Harvard or Yale, I can testify with indisputable authority that many a candidate for a baccalaureate at these and similar schools of higher learning expressed a keen, if extracurricular, interest in my field. Though my name as the author of this book will no doubt be recognized by countless thousands of my pupils—and by probably an even greater number of persons who never enrolled for my courses—I hasten to add to one and all I operated a successful correspondence school designed to broaden appreciation and knowledge of the art of Horse Racing and to develop skill at picking winners.

Although a far cry from such cultural disciplines as the humanities, the popular response to my treatment and presentation of the subject was incredible in magnitude and truly representative of a broad cross-section of our American Society. I counted among my customers people in all walks of life—workingmen, barbers, garage mechanics, waiters and waitresses, factory hands, housewives, society matrons, merchants, bankers, industrial tycoons, doctors and lawyers and, believe it or not, members of the clergy, who have the same right as anyone else to partake of the stimulation and excitement the sport affords.

My sense of modesty somewhat rebels when I repeat some of the grandiose terms in which I have often been described by sports editors and others connected with the sport: "Mr. Phi Beta Kappa of the Turf"—"The Einstein of Racing"—and "The Old Professor." The latter epithet was regularly applied to me in his column by that dean of sports editors, the late great Dan Parker. Bill Corum, the nationally syndicated sports editor of the New York Journal-American mentioned me on numerous occasions. On the eve of a dramatic race like the Kentucky Derby certain sports columnists would telephone to ascertain my choice as to the probable winner. Needless for me to add, not all of my predictions came through as I had predicted.

Occasionally my fame as an educator branched out of the narrow confines of the sporting page and spilled over into other departments of the paper, as, for instance, when Ralph Hendershot, the distinguished financial editor of the lamented *New York World-Telegram*, allotted his entire by-lined space to the unique success I achieved in my field of activity.

At one time or another during my career every conceivable system and formula, every newly developed technique applied in the handicapping of races has landed on my desk. Men who had laboriously worked out what they regarded as infallible and fool-proof systems came to see me to discuss and prove their miraculous findings. From all this exposure and from my own exhaustive researches and experience, I distilled the facts and substance that became the foundation for my correspondence courses which, incidentally, brought me fees of as high as $100 for a few of my treatises.

For a number of years I maintained my own stable of racing thoroughbreds and had the honor of having some of the country's leading jockeys ride in my silks. This experience as a race horse owner afforded me a keen insight into racing that later proved invaluable to me as well as to my student-clients. In the heyday of my turf operations my stable of thoroughbreds numbered as high as 14 and such well-known jockeys as Ted Atkinson, Johnny Longdon, Alfred Robertson, Sammy Renick—to name only a few—rode in my white and gold silks. My horses competed on every major track in the East and getting into the winner's circle became a regular experience for me. With the start of World War II I retired from racing to concentrate on my publishing enterprise.

I had already been operating my turf counseling enterprise for some time when I started to purchase thoroughbreds and enter them in major competition. The mere fact that my over-all credentials were immediately okayed by Major Daingerfield, Secretary of the Jockey Club and other eligibility committees, testifies to the legitimate character of the mail order and correspondence business I was conducting on a national scale.

Picking winners in racing is very much like trying to buy the right investment securities. The element of luck and chance occasionally upsets the best and soundest of calculations. However, in the long run and over a period of a given time a sound and competent security analyst will surmount these setbacks and on balance end up with a sizable profit. It is simply a case where knowledge pays off. The same principle holds true for picking winners in racing.

With leisure rapidly becoming a way of life for most Americans, and with the volume of betting reaching astronomical figures—the pari-mutual turnover for thoroughbred racing in New York State alone last year was in excess of *one billion dollars*—it is obvious that horse race betting is of gigantic proportions and of sufficient magnitude to qualify it as one of the major industries in dollar volume in the country. What the illegal, off-track volume may run to can at best only be guessed, but enough is known of such operations to warrant the statement that there are few industries in the United States whose total dollar volume exceeds the amount of money that is wagered by racing fans. In the light of these statistics, a handy and practical guide based on expert knowledge and experience should prove helpful to all racing fans, novice and veteran alike.

Over the years thousands of racing devotees have importuned me to put my teachings and knowledge—the series of lessons and other data they received from me—into a book. The public will readily appreciate why I have hesitated to do so up to now. It was a difficult adjustment to make since the price for some of my courses was $100 each. As the time-worn adage goes about "leaving well enough alone," I was reluctant to discard lightly a proved and successful method for selling my services in favor of a new and untried approach. But time inexorably works its change. I am now past the biblical age of three score years and ten and am beginning to find the daily routine of conducting courses by mail a little too irksome for my physical powers. I am therefore bowing to the earnest wishes of my racing friends, fully confident they will be pleased with my decision. Whether it be flat or harness races, I am certain all who read this book will learn something about the sport and profit from my advice.

ALBERT GEORGE ILLICH

1

How and Why I Started Playing the Races

I WAS BORN and went to school in the northeast section of the Bronx when it was undeveloped and considered country. In those days automobiles were a rarity and the rich maintained stables of horses. They employed grooms, coachmen, and footmen. During the hot summer months they journeyed to the far corners of the earth for their vacations.

In the summer it was the custom to send their horses to what was called a stock farm. This consisted of many acres of pasture and stables. The carriage and riding horses of the rich were sent to these farms during the time their owners were away from the city.

George McCrain was one of my schoolmates and his father owned and operated a stock farm. It consisted of about 60 acres of land and many stables and was located four or five miles from my home. Every opportunity I had, and this was several times a week and week-ends, I visited George. Our usual diversion was to go into one of the large pastures where the boarded horses were grazing. We'd get upon the back of a horse with nothing on the horse but a halter. Galloping around the field, narrowly escaping being scraped off the horse's back by the many shade trees therein, we were lucky enough not to get seriously injured. Thus was my first introduction to the horse. And the high regard and affection I have for them today originated in this fashion.

My next introduction to horses was when I joined the 105th Field Artillery, National Guard, located at 166th Street near Morris Avenue. There we were taught riding by getting on a horse with nothing but a blanket and surcingle to hold it on the horse's back and a snaffle bit bridle. And by the way, if you ever want your children to be given riding lessons insist they be started bareback as I have just explained. There is no substitute for this manner of starting riding lessons.

We soldiers used to play mounted basketball in the large arena of the Armory. We rode with only a bridle and blanket on the horse. The ball could only be passed or shot at the basket from horseback. When the ball fell to the ground, the nearest player would quickly dismount and attempt to throw it from where it was picked up to a member of his own team and then grasp his horse's mane and jump onto its back. This was how I acquired more knowledge of horses and horsemanship.

At the start of World War I, I volunteered and was assigned to the Remount Service located in Spartanburg in the Carolinas. The purpose of a Remount Station is to buy and issue all Cavalry (Cavalry was used at the time) and Artillery horses. A regular Army Lieutenant Miller was in charge of the purchase and approval of all horses shipped to the station from all over the United States. He selected me as his assistant, probably knowing I had had some contact with horses since I had served a "hitch" in the Artillery. When a shipment of newly purchased horses would arrive we would go to the isolation corral. The Lieutenant would examine them carefully, their teeth, bone structure, search for defects, and the like. I would stand by and copy down his observations on each examined horse.

In this way some of the knowledge of a horse's condition and conformation must have rubbed off on me.

One day the Lieutenant said to me, "Illich, you should take the competitive examination for officer rank."

It seems, at that time at least, the Army once a year offered enlisted men a chance to take examinations for an officer. They had to be recommended by their commanding officer or secure letters of high recommendation from well-known persons. This notice was supposed to be posted on the bulletin board so that any enlisted man could apply. The Remount Station was commanded by a Colonel who did not post the notice but selected his top sergeant and a couple of other pets of his. They were sent to Officer's Training School at night long before examination time.

When the Lieutenant spoke to me it was a short time before the examinations were to be held and I had to rush to get the required letters of recommendation. I did so under the deadline, took the examination without any preparation, and passed high up among those taking the examination.

This may give the idea I think highly of myself, but to deflate any such idea let me say that while in the Artillery my commander was a captain of a happy-go-lucky nature whose interest was more in conviviality than in his military duties. I was a corporal and his office clerk. Voluminous detailed reports had to be filled out every day. I'd ask the Captain how to handle them. He'd shrug his shoulders and walk off. Fortunately, the Adjutant of the Regiment was an exceedingly competent officer and I would go to him and he'd explain how to handle the matter. This was exceedingly valuable to me.

The examinations were held one or two each night on a different subject for seven days. One was on Hippology. This covered about everything pertaining to a horse, shoeing, caring for it, riding and saddling it, and so on. Few who took the test were more versed in this subject than I. So I was commissioned a lieutenant.

When I came back from the war, I became engaged to a famous concert violinist. She lived in Queens Village within a short walking distance of the Belmont Park Race Track. She had as a neighbor, and knew well, the wife of the famous horse trainer Max Hirsh. My sister attended the Ursuline Academy in the Bedford Park section of the Bronx and her best chum was the daughter of Tom Healy, another famous trainer who was training for Jock Whitney at the time.

All racing stables of any size have what are called "work-horses." These are used by the trainer or stable help to lead a race horse onto the track with a lead rein and exercise the horse; or for the trainer to watch a charge's workout from horseback. I can't recall which, but either my fiancee asked Max Hirsh or I asked Tom Healy if we could ride work horses on Sunday when there was no racing. In any event, we started to ride these horses every Sunday on the main or training track at Belmont Park.

This track is located in Elmont which is adjacent to Queens Village. When we arrived at each of the two different stables the horse was saddled and we'd go to the other stable for the second mount. One Sunday when we arrived the horse I was going to ride was out. An exercise boy of the stable had ridden it to the Post Office in Elmont to pick up the mail. When he returned he dismounted and offered me the horse. I told one of the men to lengthen the stirrups. Naturally, the exercise boy rode the usual jockey way with short stirrups.

It was suggested that I ride with the short stirrups and I told those present I'd never be able to stay on the horse's back riding that way. But they kept after me telling me it was better and easier. They showed me how to cross the reins over the horse's neck holding both joined as one in both hands. I tried it and found it interesting. I could stand up in the stirrups as jockeys do and balance myself by each fist on either side of the neck resting down with the crossed reins. I proceeded thusly to the track, slowly at first and then gaining confidence started to trot and gallop.

What I learned from this ride is the basis of all my horse racing enthusiasm to the present time. It was what caused me to make my first bet on a horse.

Bert Mulholland, who died about the time I am writing this, was the stable foreman for the George D. Widener establishment and later became its trainer. He and his sister in particular were avid fans of classical music and never failed to attend a concert of my fiancee when she appeared, many times, in Carnegie Hall. Because of this acquaintance we never failed after finishing our ride to visit Bert at his stable.

As far as I know Bert was not a betting man. But he'd tell me about certain horses that he thought might soon win when raced. I knew absolutely nothing about betting horses and paid no attention to what he told me. I had never seen a past performance or racing paper and did not even know how to follow up any horse even to see how it ran if I wanted to do so.

But on the first Sunday I had ridden with short stirrups I thought I had discovered a great secret about playing the horses. Whether I did or not, you can be the judge after reading this book.

The *only* thing I did know about racing was that all handicapping was based upon the weight a horse carried in a race. I had up to this point never seen a past performance chart or a racing paper.

It is important that I tell you the difference between riding a horse as every equestrian does compared to the style of jockeys. The former rides horseback through the use and application of both a grip and balance. He sits with his legs hanging down the barrel of a horse. The stirrups are adjusted so that the top of the stirrup is about two to four inches (depending on the preference of the rider) higher than the ball of the foot when hanging down loosely. The calves of his legs grip the horse fairly firmly and the insides of his kneecaps grip the horse as firmly as possible. From his knees the upper portions of his legs (the thigh) are almost parallel with the ground and his trunk being upright it forms a sort of reversed L position. It is perfectly obvious that practically all a rider's weight is placed back of or behind the kneecaps. Because of the grip of the calves and the knees and the ball of the foot being higher than the stirrup a rider can press hard with his knees and raise himself in the stirrups so that his seat is above the saddle and not resting on it. This position gives a rider the necessary grip and balance.

Now the jockey has balance but has no gripping power. Both are necessary to the equestrian. Only balance is necessary to a jockey. In the case of the jockey the knees are much *above* the horse's backbone. With the equestrian the knees are much *below* the backbone.

I tell you this now to whet your appetite for the fascinating coverage of this subject in Chapter 6.

After discovering the secret about weight as explained herein, I then became interested in betting on the horses. I consulted acquaintances who played the horses about past performances, and their meaning and how to use them. Thus, I started my career as a turf operator, and later as the author of racing "know-how" material that has been in demand and sold in practically every country that conducts horse racing. Requests for my writings have come from Europe, Japan, and even as far away as Australia.

2

My First Period of Horse Playing

THE TIME HAD come, I thought in my innocence, for me to start playing the horses and acquire all the spending money for which I had any desire. I took a bankroll of a few hundred dollars and entrained for Saratoga where racing was being held at the time. At this time, there was no such thing as pari-mutuel wagering. The wagering was done between the player and the bookies at the track. Most have probably seen pictures of old-time betting. Each bookie had a stand. The bookie would have a slate on a staff so that it was exposed high above the crowd and could be seen the length of the betting ring. The names of the horses and the odds the bookie was offering on it were written in chalk. (The expression chalk-player originated because of the chalked prices. It means playing the favorite or short-priced horses.)

A horse might be quoted at 6 to 1 on practically every slate in the ring. Some player would make a large bet on it and the bookie who accepted it would rub out the 6 to 1 and make it 5 to 1 or some lesser figure. Each bookie had a runner who watched the prices other bookies were quoting. When a price was cut on some horse he would rush back to his own bookie giving him the news so that this bookie could, if he wanted, cut his own price. If a bookie at one end of the line cut the price, you'd see a rubbing of the slates all down the line. If a cut was made by a bookie in the middle of the line you'd see the changes being made to his right and to his left.

Of course not every bookie changed his price every time another one did. It would depend upon whether he had enough action on the horse whose price was changing. This resulted in the rushing about of players to get the best price quoted because the same horse might be 6 to 1 with one bookie and 5 to 1 or 4 to 1 with another.

In those days it was difficult for any secrecy to be maintained. A successful, winning operator was known to all the bookies and to all professional plungers. When he was known to wager on a certain horse it attracted thousands of additional dollars to be bet on his horse. Most of the real big plungers hired what was known as "betting commissioners" who did the wagering for their employers. "Pittsburgh Phil" was of course the most famous plunger of all times. He used extreme measures to prevent anyone from knowing what horses he was wagering on. He hired and kept changing his betting commissioners. He even went as far as betting as much as thousands on a horse purposely to throw the public off and then secretly wagered many additional thousands on the horse he favored. This attempt to fool the public sometimes failed. But mostly it succeeded in its purpose.

These heavy plungers would have large sums wagered with bookies all across the nation. And when these bookies tried to lay off more wagered money than they cared to accept with fellow bookies, it often became evident to the bookies that a possible "killing" was in the making and—when pari-mutuel betting started—they would send large sums to the track to be bet in the machines. This served them two purposes. It knocked down the price of the horse and it relieved them of too heavy a commitment on one horse. This is how the term "come-back-money" came into being.

These plungers and/or their commission men would try to be cagey and instead of calling out a bet to the bookie might hand the bookie's clerk a slip with the bet shown on it or step up and whisper into the ear of the bookie.

The bookie stands were lined up in front of the grandstand. Whenever a known operator entered the ring players looking for tips would converge on him and follow him from bookie to bookie in an effort to learn on what horse he was placing a bet. Most of the time a plunger would not bet all his money with one bookie who might not want to take it all but only a portion. Also on an extra large wager, where the board quoted 6 to 1 the bookie might offer only 4 to 1 if the bettor insisted on his taking the full bet. So to help keep the price up the plunger would scatter his bets among different bookies.

In the meantime, the crowd following the operator would increase. Sitting in the grandstand above the bookie ring this is what you would see: A crowded arena with little space between heads and bodies. All at once your eye would be drawn to a movement of people. The leader would be the plunger or a known betting commissioner followed by the crowd. You could easily follow the crowd as it moved in a snakeline sinuously from bookie stand to bookie stand.

Those were the days! Racing has never been the same in excitement, shopping for price, in the fascination of this mode of procedure since when the days of bookies were in flower. All this was 90 percent of the enjoyment of attending a race track.

Now to get to my own betting. In the beginning I was most successful. So much so that at the hotel where I stayed, residents began to ask me what horses I was going to play. And, believe me, I became moderately well known as a successful operator. People would follow me in a small snake line when I approached a bookie to learn which horse I was betting on.

Political acquaintances I knew would consult me daily. Judge McGeehan never failed to watch for me when I arrived at the track and would ask me about horses. One incident I'll never forget because I made one of my biggest wins. Senator John Dunnigan was a very good friend of mine. Incidentally, he is known as the father of racing since it was mainly through his efforts that pari-mutuel betting became legal and brought such enormous tax income to the State of New York.

Dunnigan and McGeehan used to look for me every day. One day, they introduced me to Charley Buckley, who later became County Chairman and Boss of the Democratic party of the Bronx. Incidentally, I was always a Republican in one of the strongest Democratic counties in the United States. Buckley had a most engaging personality, and liking him, I decided to see if I could give him a real good winner so he'd remember me. I guess by this time my success had given me an inflated opinion of my ability— little did I then know time was running out and that I was coasting along on borrowed time. I forget its name except that it was a filly or mare whose name started with an "S." I figured the horse would win and should be rightfully 5 or 6 to 1. Instead it was 20 to 1 or more with some bookies. I knew the public was not playing this horse only because it was picking up 15 pounds. I was applying what I had first discovered when riding jockey-fashion—that it was not the weight that counted but how it was distributed. In any event I convinced Buckley to play this horse and I won one of my largest wagers I had made up to this point in my career.

The Saratoga season ended. Racing returned to New York City. And I returned with winnings of over $5,000. I was practically a kid at the time and this amount was an astronomical sum for me. I felt I was riding on the top of the world. Keep in mind that about forty days before my return to the City I did not even know what a racing paper was, nor what past performances meant.

With confidence I started to bet much heavier than I had at the start of my wagering career. Where $20 had been a good-sized bet I did not hesitate to make $50 and $100 wagers. There is one incident at this period that is so vivid in my mind that I can even recall the name of the horse involved although it was only a cheap claiming horse. I spotted for play a horse named Austrilitz. I first made a bigger-than-usual bet on it. It was an ordinary horse, its record was poor and it lost. Then one night I had a dream in which Austrilitz won at an enormous price. I never previously believed or paid any attention to dreams. Unluckily for me between the combination of figuring this horse to win and the dream I was convinced that it was going to win.

For the next four or five races it ran I bet heavily on it. Each time with a larger wager. I bet as much as $1,000 on it in one wager. One day my bookie, who was Vic Lehman, said to me, "Al, do you know something about this horse that you continue to bet it?" Later Lehman confessed to me that because I was betting so heavily and because the horse's record was poor that I was holding out on him and knew something about the horse that warranted such confidence on my part. The horse never won any race to my knowledge and I had lost the major portion of my bankroll. But this experience taught me a lesson that the reader might well consider. This is: *Never buck your head against a stone wall in racing. Learn to know your mistakes and admit them.*

The lesson was well learned for me because to this day I never thereafter stuck with a horse figuring it just had to win.

Shortly thereafter I had lost my entire bankroll. Some players at this stage would have started to plunge and ended up compulsive gamblers. But I analyzed things. I determined that my original success was not due to any ability of my own but that I simply had had beginner's luck.

I decided that what I had learned about past performances was superficial and that there was much more to them than I had figured. This started me on a self-taught regime of selecting horses to play and making small $2.00 bets on them. Whether this horse would win or lose I would look at its race chart. I would try to reason out why it had lost or won. I would go back to the past performance chart of each such horse and try to reason out why, how and where I was correct or wrong in my analysis. *It was then that I learned the know-how of how to play the races successfully.*

Where I reasoned that a played horse lost because of my own faulty analysis, and not because my reasoning was faulty, I would make a card on this horse and watch for it when entered again and if placed right would again play it. No two races are the same and many a horse loses that should on the basis of every factor win. This is part of racing. There are innumerable good reasons why in the actual running of a race the best horse does not always win.

What I was now unconsciously doing was to treat playing the races as a most specialized field of endeavor, a field that required specialized knowledge. I keep at trying to acquire this required specialized know-how. I now strongly advise every player to secure every book on racing he can because he is certain to benefit by such reading.

3

My Second Stage
of Horse Playing

IT WAS NOW my daily habit to get the *Racing Form* each day and glance over all entries. In those days, we had two racing papers here in the East—the same *Racing Form* available in all sections of the country and the *Morning Telegraph*. Eventually, the Triangle Publishing Company, publishers of the *Daily Racing Form*, bought out the *Morning Telegraph* and for some years continued both papers in the East. Since then they issue only the *Morning Telegraph* in the East.

I would pick a number of horses from a number of races as a starter. Then, I would go over them more carefully and make eliminations, until I had finally selected one horse in a race to play. I would make a list of the horses to be bet that day and telephone my bookie and give him the bets.

At that time, bets could be made in stationery stores, barber shops, bars, and other such public places. Of course this does not exist today because of stricter laws, and bookies are almost as scarce as hen's teeth.

My determination to beat this racing game through a sustained study of all angles started to pay off. Whereas my operations at Saratoga were little known, if not totally unknown locally, when I started to operate through local bookies my regained success became neighborhood knowledge among my business associates.

I was the sole owner of a city-wide known real estate and insurance business. I had large space. When you entered the door a very large front area had a rail toward the front. My personal office was an enclosed space, being one of three closed-in rooms.

As it became common knowledge that I was winning by playing the races, the neighboring business men started to stop in and I'd let them look over my own list of plays for the day. This continued for at least a year, possibly several years.

In those times most large bookie establishments had a wire service. The calling of a race over a loud speaker was the service rendered in addition to the price line and changes, late information, and the like. If you were on good terms with your bookie, and I was, you could phone him just about post time of any race. By hanging on to the telephone you could hear the race being called as it was run. No need to tell how interesting and fascinating this was! The neighbors would come into my private office, get the results of some desired race as it was run, and then return to their own business establishments.

Where success is involved, it does not take long for such news to spread. One would think that all this interfered with my business. But I was well established, had long-employed and competent help, these neighbors were in my private office and in this respect everything was satisfactory since they did not interfere with the office force.

I concentrated more and more on my research and playing, so a stage was reached when I could not give the necessary concentrated attention to my efforts. Like any office on a street level, visitors would just open the door and walk in. I did not deal in selling private homes. The bulk of my business was done with speculators, builders, and the sale of vacant business property. For this reason the coming in of my friends in no way affected the operation of my business. But the time came when I had to tell my friends not to come in and bother me.

I guess because we were such close friends, they failed to pay much attention to my request so they still continued to annoy me. Finally, I put a bolt on the entrance door which prevented anyone from simply turning the knob and walking in. They would come to the door, and finding they could not enter, would pound on the lower wooden panel. Naturally, after a time seeing their efforts to enter were of no avail, they stopped bothering me. That bolt put on the door over thirty years ago is still there!

Once again I was fortunate as in this matter of friends bothering me because it resulted in what became, and now is, the most important of my life's work.

Naturally, I had losing as well as winning horses, as did my friends. We got the results, occasionally through the bookies' wire service but more often by keeping the radio turned on to a station that gave the results of each race right after it was finished. This is illegal now, and the best that one can get is the total results at the end of a day's racing. We would discuss among ourselves the pros and cons of this or that winner or loser.

One day, something happened that ended up with my starting a handicapping school by mail. As far as I know, I was the first. Many books on how to handicap had been written, but nothing in the way of lessons.

This day started off with rain and it continued to rain heavily the day long. A famous stake race was to be run in the highest purse bracket. A large percentage of horse players will not play a horse unless it is running on a fast track because it is a well-known fact that the largest percentage of racing upsets occur when a track changes its condition overnight or between races. It being a dull day with nothing much to do, after I had placed my wagers for the day, I picked up the *Racing Form* and began to study this coming stake race. There was a horse quoted in the morning line at a high figure—it may have been 20 to 1, as that was about the limit price shown on any horse, even though it might be a 50 to 1 chance. I noticed that all its best races (it was a 2-year-old filly race) had been run on an off track. I decided to take a chance on it and called back my bookie and bet this additional horse.

One of those who used to come into my office was a doctor who lived nearby and was a friend of all the business owners in the immediate neighborhood. In my opinion, he did not know much about horses or racing. But he was lucky and he won more often than most of the others. He happened to come in just about the time I had the radio on to get the results of the stake race. Consider yourself in my position when the results were given and the horse I had bet on won, paying over 100 to 1. I had big payoffs before and after. My own horse, Who Calls, on October 12, 1942, with Ted Atkinson riding at Jamaica, won at odds of 54.25 to 1 or a mutuel of $110.50. But, never anything like this for a thrill! The doctor rejoiced with me when the result came in and he was as excited as I was, as I had told him the name of this horse while we were waiting for the results.

After settling down, the doctor looked over the past performances for the entries in this race. He said to me, "Al, how could you possibly bet this horse?" I then went over the past performances of this horse with him. I explained that the horse's races clearly demonstrated its best running was on off tracks. And that its picking up of considerable more weight meant nothing to me. The distance of the race was longer than these 2-year-old fillies had ever been asked to go. I explained that the breeding of this horse would indicate it could go a long distance. I reasoned the pros and cons in detail.

I do not want you to draw any false conclusions from this anecdote. Had this horse been shown on the pricemaker's line at odds of 10 to 1, or less, I never would have played it. When a horse is quoted at 20 to 1, as it was, it could pay any price. Only because I figured this horse indicated it could possibly win, although it was a remote possibility, I took a chance because of high price. While it is valuable and will assist you to figure a horse's liking for an off track, and the same is true of its breeding, these things should be considered only in relationship to other of its possibilities. What I am trying to say is that such factors may, at times, be used to turn the scales in your favor.

Often, when I had a winner at a good price, my associates would raise the same question of how was it possible to figure it. Then a discussion of its past performance record would take place.

These acquaintances had been playing horses long before I had ever looked at a racing paper. It continually amazed me that during talks about horses played, they proved from their talk that they did not know how to interpret past performances. They could read the print, of course, but they misinterpreted what the figures actually intended to portray of the running of the races.

This group of men were much above the average in intelligence. All of them owned successful businesses. I reasoned that if these men did not know how to interpret past performances and charts and analyze them so that they could select winners, then the average horse player would be even more deficient in this respect.

I decided to put into lesson form the things I had been explaining to my friends. With this in mind, I wrote a ten-lesson course entitled "Now You Can Pick Your Own Winners."

These lessons consisted of a well-grounded practical racing "know-how," without which one could have small expectations of winning at playing the races. There are many different approaches to the objective of selecting winners. All are good in themselves. Which approach to use for the racing fan depends upon the personality, the willingness or lack of willingness to learn, the time available for playing.

My lessons were an immediate success. Continued requests by my readers for additional material resulted in further publications that covered separately every known possible approach. These now total over 40 publications.

Undoubtedly, the most successful and the best internationally successful horse player was "Pittsburgh Phil." He left an estate of over three million dollars—all of which was gleaned from his wagering on the horses. Long after I had published my lessons and was selling them, I was fortunate enough to secure a book about "Pittsburgh Phil." It was written by his close friend Edward W. Cole, who was at the time Turf Editor of the *New York Evening Telegram*. The only person to whom this famous plunger entrusted his winning secrets was Cole. He revealed them with the proviso that they were not to be divulged until after the operator's death. The book was published in 1908.

That the same kind of common sense must be applied to racing as to any endeavor and that it is the predominant factor for success is proved by the saga of Phil. Let me quote him:

"I have been accused by some of having what they term 'an ace in the hole,' that is, they have accused me of having had jockeys pull a horse in one race to make a killing in the next, when it was nothing in the world but my close observation *after* the previous race had been run.

During the running of the race my glasses never leave the horses engaged. I see every move they make. I can see that this one is not in stride, or is running unnaturally, or is being ridden poorly. I can see if a horse is sulking, what horse is fit, what horse is unfit. After the race is run, it is sometimes said a horse has had a bad ride, or that the trainer has sent him to the post in unfit condition, or anything and everything, except the truth."

Read this quote over again. Burn the words into your mind because if you get the significance of what it tells, you will be rewarded to the extent of thousands of dollars. These words disclose the most important factor in the millions won by this plunger.

You may reason that you cannot be at the race track every day as he was. True as this may be, you still can gain the same "ace in the hole" available to him.

Let me demonstrate by taking an example from my lessons. On July 15, 1940, in the 6th race at Arlington Park, the horse Swell Chance ran 4th, beaten by $8\frac{1}{4}$ lengths, running at odds of 11 to 1.

Then on July 23rd, eight days later, it ran in the 4th race at Arlington Park at odds of 38 to 1 and won, paying $78.00.

The conditions of the two races were identical in all respects as to fast track, distance, and conditions of the race. How many of you readers would think of betting on this horse in its second race after it had been beaten by $8\frac{1}{4}$ lengths? Well, my students would have bet it and here is why. In its race of July 15, if Phil or you had watched the race you would have seen—quote from the chart caller—"*Swell Chance, never far back and in close quarters early, closed well when clear.*"

Unlike Phil you would not have to be at the track. The chart caller can be your eyes. You'd have noted this horse and played it in its next race, under certain qualifications that you'll later learn, and been rewarded with a winner paying $78.00. This is not an isolated example. You'll find such plays almost every racing day.

Phil made notes every day of such facts. In his day, there were no such things as racing papers with charts and past performances. He had to make his own and he is actually the inventor or originator of past performances and charts as we know them today.

One thing I want to impress upon readers. I will be giving you examples of races that may have been run many years in the past. The reason for this is that I have this data at my finger tips in my published works. Now remember this. Thoroughbred horses have long since reached their peak of evolution to their present conformation. Races have been run in the past and at the present and will be in the future under the same conditions: starting point, distance, and finish line. Obviously, whether a race was run 10 or 50 years in the past or is run in the present or will be run in the future, the element of time will in no way affect any sound method of picking winners.

I received the book on "Pittsburgh Phil," which is of incalculable value, many years after I had written my first lessons. From answering questions posed by my students, it was at least 10 to 15 years after publication that I became aware that my method of playing the races is based upon Phil's secrets. And I had arrived at many of the same conclusions he did from my own personal observations since, as I have stated, I did not read about his secrets until many years after I had published my lessons.

4

Basic Requirements for Successful Horse Playing

BEFORE WE DIG into the mechanics of learning how to pick winning selections, it is necessary to understand that there are certain basic requirements to the sport. In practically every profession I can think of it is impossible to function without the tools incident to that endeavor. In order to make a success at racing, so too, it is necessary to use the proper tools and to build on a solid foundation.

The tools of racing consist of charts and past performances. Without them, lacking in a proper interpretation of them, it is *impossible* to win. This does not mean that a constant analysis of them is required as you will later learn. But you *must* understand what they represent! You must know how to interpret them, you must know when and what can safely be disregarded.

That the vast majority of players do not utilize the potentialities of these racing tools is evidenced by the fact that while untold millions play the races every day, at or away from the tracks, the total circulation, I understand, of the two official racing papers, the *Daily Racing Form* and the *Morning Telegraph*, is only between 300,000 and 400,000.

Both of these papers are published by the Triangle Publications, Inc. The *Daily Racing Form* and the *Morning Telegraph* each cover various sections of the country through different editions. The *Morning Telegraph* is available only in the eastern part of the United States and the *Daily Racing Form* in other sections of the country. Originally, the *Morning Telegraph* was under different ownership and both papers were available in the East. After change of ownership both papers were procurable in the East, but subsequently the *Form* was taken out of eastern circulation.

The data given in charts and past performances is the same in both papers. The only difference is the arrangement in the printing format. There is one exception to this and that is that the *Telegraph* uses, in certain distances, one additional running position for some races.

Before any player, seasoned devotee or novice, makes another wager he should write to either of the named racing papers and ask for their booklet

"How to Read Charts and Past Performances." They constantly run an offer in the papers to send you this booklet free. Write to them.

In all areas of specialized fields, and racing is a most specialized field, there are those who succeed in it and those who completely fail. Take law, or medicine; one group that earns a degree in the field will become eminently successful and the other abject failures. Yet, in both groups may be those who have studied the same subjects at the same universities. They have qualified through exams or they would not have been awarded their degrees.

What then is the reason for this difference? The reason is the adaptation of knowledge. The degree of success in any field is influenced by the personality and/or characteristics of the individual. One must possess certain inclinations to get the most out of any effort.

It is therefore important to consider the personality, characteristics, and inclinations of each individual. Some are aptly suited to given aims, some are not. However, let it be said that necessary aptitudes can be acquired where they are lacking, provided one is willing to make the effort to gain them.

Requirements for a Successful Player

First of all, a horse player should make an examination of himself and determine what his primary interest in playing the races is. Is he out solely for profits or for thrills and enjoyment? Or is he out for a combination of both? Undoubtedly, the vast majority are seeking both objectives.

A player must have a realization of the imperative necessity of constantly seeking to learn all there is to learn about racing. A mystery that I have never been able to explain is why any person, otherwise most intelligent, will play the races possessing such a lack of understanding of the simplest fundamental knowledge of the sport. Those who watch a football, baseball, or basketball game know all the angles—the rules, something about the players and their abilities, the standing of leagues, and players, and the like. They have acquired this knowledge without effort from childhood, having either played the game or been vitally interested in it. It is but natural that such contact over many years should give these fans an intimate knowledge of all phases of the sport.

But contrast this with the horse player. Usually he has never owned nor does he know anything about horses. He has never ridden a horse in a race. The race horse as such and the mechanics of the sport are an unknown quantity to most players, and few are willing to overcome this deficiency by adequate research.

The average horse player has never participated in any phase of horse racing, except as an outside spectator, whereas the baseball fan has actually performed the mechanics of that sport.

I have never known of a course of instruction prepared for those who wish to wager on baseball or other participant sports. I am sure such a course would fail to sell because practically every fan knows all the answers.

A horse player must use the same kind of common sense, apply his reasoning power and logic the same as he has to do in his business. It is not enough to have all the know-how available if he neglects to apply his common sense. The knowledge is not so important. After all, once a player knows *all* the angles, then it becomes only a matter of simple horse sense to profit therefrom by making potentially winning selections.

Most important is that the player must realize that losing is as important as winning. Winnings derive from the losses of those who do not have the know-how. Since out of all money bet, an average of 15 percent is deducted from the total wagered on each race, it is apparent that there has to be more losing players than winning players. Otherwise racing could not exist. Therefore, be prepared to appreciate that *every* player will lose more times than he will win. This does not imply that profits cannot be made if you have more losing plays than winning plays. *By a judicious method of betting one can be a winner if right only 5 percent, 10 percent, 33 percent, or 40 percent of the times.*

This may have happened to you. If it has not, at least you have known of it happening. Two players can go to a race track. Both have the exact same selections they intend playing. At the end of the day, one will come out a small, medium, or big winner, whereas the other ends up a poor loser. Obviously, the answer to this is in the different methods of wagering of the two players.

Few realize that knowing how to wager is just as important as being able to pick winners. This matter of wagering will be the subject of a later chapter.

A race consists of these important components: First the horse. Second the trainer. Third the jockey. Fourth the racing secretary who sets up the conditions under which each race is run. The purpose of this official is to attempt to make equal the chances of every horse to win. This denotes how important it is for the player to know all about this angle. Yet few players, even the most experienced, give any heed to this subject. Fifth the jockey's agent. Sixth the owner.

All of these have a bearing on whether or not a horse will win. In certain races one or the other of these must be given consideration. At other times it is irrelevant.

Lastly, a player must be cold-blooded. This does not mean a player should not root his horse in. What I mean is one must have patience to wait for a proper spot to play. One must be able and willing to pass up a play, if conditions are not right, as he is to make a play. Phil might go for days on end without making a single wager. When he wagered, whether he won or lost the bet, at least conditions were in his favor.

Incidentally, do not feel badly if you should have a losing streak. "Pittsburgh Phil," the world's most renowned winning plunger, had as many as twenty-six straight losing bets.

What to do when you hit a losing streak and how to prevent loss of your bankroll and how to handle the other features mentioned in this chapter will appear in their proper sequence.

5

Do Not Follow the Crowd or Accepted Theories

I HOPE THAT every reader will have previously read books on playing the races and has bought systems.

If he has he will find that 90 percent of my approach and the knowledge I impart is completely different in concept and in the results he will achieve in his playing.

Before I go into more detailed and explicit demonstrations of how to pick your own winners, let me illustrate what I mean by my approach being different. I want to give you two examples of what it means, and I'll wager you never heard anything like this, or if you have it has been taken from one of my works.

First-Time-Starter Pattern

Probably 98 percent of all bets made on a horse results from two sources. First, from the selector's page in the *Form* and *Telegraph*. On this page is given a price line and the public selections of from five to six handicapping experts. Later on in this book, you'll be given data concerning these experts that will be of incalculable winning worth to both seasoned and novice players alike. Next from the price line whether in a morning line or from other sources.

Now consider this: A horse that is running for the very first time—it may be a maiden 2- or 3-year old—wins the race at a very small price—you'll find it mostly a favorite and frequently at odds-on like 80¢ to $1.00.

Since this is the horse's first race, it means that the past performances give *only* this data: Its name and breeding, owner and trainer. If it has any workouts, this too will be shown. There is nothing else to go by.

Every situation such as this, which creates a dilemma for the player, should be investigated. The first several times I noticed this situation I sought to find out why and how it was possible to go off at such short odds. I tried to find out the answer and turned to the selector's page. In some instances I found this winner was not selected to run even in the money. I also looked over the Graded Handicaps, giving the approximate odds. With the price line given in the *Morning Telegraph* alongside each price is some comment such as "Can do better," "Expected to improve," "Last race not true," "First time starter."

When these pricemakers give the biggest odds they show it 20 to 1 even if the horse had not a chance in a million. But 20 to 1 is the biggest odds given. I do not know why this is so, but I reason that in the days of the bookies their limit odds were 20 to 1.

More than one letter from one who had learned the secret about this horse from me called it a *miraculous* play. So to make it easier for you to understand what I am discussing, let's call this horse Miraculous.

The only reason these experts would give a first time starter any notice at all would be for the following:

1. Horse was well bred, sired by some famous producer.
2. It had been purchased as a yearling at some extra big price.
3. It was owned by some great stable such as Calumet, Greentree, or the like.
4. It had shown out of the ordinary good workouts.

Under these conditions the horse might be picked by some of the experts, or if not picked, shown at a price of 5 to 1 or some price less than 15 or 20 to 1. If either of these two conditions prevailed, the expert must have some reason of his own not to ignore the horse and price it at 20 to 1. Generally, when the odds are 20 to 1 a comment "First time starter" appears.

If the horse was listed at all as having a chance, or if its odds were less than 15 or 20 to 1, then I forgot it and ignored any consideration of it.

But, if the price shown was 15 or 20 to 1 and if no one mentioned it, I reasoned thusly: The public would not bet this horse with nothing to base an option on; then who had bet on this horse?

And mind you, to make it a short-priced favorite or an odds-on play, a tremendously large wager had to go through the machines to make this possible. A figure in the thousands was the only thing that could do it.

And the fact that the horse won proves conclusively that those betting were right in their judgment of this horse Miraculous.

The answer comes to you, undoubtedly, as it did to me. *It was possible for only the horse's connections*, owner or trainer, to know how good this horse really is.

The natural question coming to mind is—since Miraculous has run and already won, what benefit is this research and analysis? But wait! What further does our conclusion reveal?

In view of the fact that the connections bet many thousands on Miraculous in its initial race before they ever saw it in a race, and since their judgment of this horse was actually confirmed by its winning, who can say just how really good this horse is?

No one knows, so the horse-sense thing to do is to watch for it in its next few races and wager on it no matter how or where entered. List this type of horse and watch for it in its coming races. Do not be afraid to bet and follow it.

Here is what will happen. It will be entered, and win or lose, will continue to be entered in higher class and it *will* win races. Stick with them until their prices become too short to make them interesting as a wager. You'll find that this is a solid horse to follow in play.

But that is not all there is to this secret. How about the horse or horses that were not beaten too badly by Miraculous?

We do not know how good this horse is. It may be a potential Man O' War, or a Kelso. Therefore, I would also list Miraculous' keen competition and watch for them to run. How many times to follow them in play would depend upon their future showings. I have won many, many wagers on both of these two examples given in this chapter.

From the time I first started to play the horses, I have come up with new and different winning approaches of my own invention, if the process might be called that. Many were contrary to accepted theory. But they have survived the test of time and have been profitably used by other operators. Of all these I am most proud of this foregoing particular discovery.

Imported-Horse Pattern

When I was racing my own stable of horses before the start of World War II, very few—in fact, I can recall no horses—were imported and raced in this country. There was considerable importation of horses from England and France but they were for breeding purposes. But of late years you will constantly see them entered and running on American tracks.

I believe the vogue of importing horses started like this. One day at New York, I think the track was either Jamaica or Aqueduct, two horses that had been bred in Argentina were entered by an Argentinian trainer. They were entered for their initial starts in America in claiming races, if I correctly remember, not exceeding $2,500 or $3,000 in value. Both won and it was rumored that a small fortune was made by their connections. This was in the days when bookies of the ilk of Tom Shaw would accept $10,000, $50,000, and higher bets without the blink of an eye.

Be that as it may, it happened that Hirsh Jacobs claimed one of these horses. Probably being afraid of losing it himself by being claimed the first time he ran it he placed it in a nonclaiming race, probably an allowance race, which it won. From then on it continued to be raised in class and earned a considerable amount of money for Jacobs.

Thereafter, a few importations of Argentinian-bred horses were made. But they were of a cheap claiming class and failed to attract attention, as they seldom won a race. The temporary fad seemed to die out. So for years after, few were imported.

Toward the end of the year 1960 I noticed that there seemed to be a new influx of imported horses from France, Italy, England, Argentina, and other countries. What drew my attention to them was the fact that they were winning races from claimers up to the highest classes.

Often a look at their past performances showed maybe no races or two or three at the most run in this country. The balance of their past performances listed where they had finished in their originating country which, of course, was of no value in handicapping here. Yet they were winning races and at real long-shot prices.

This presented to me the same kind of dilemma as with Miraculous and I sought to seek the answer as to how I could use these imported horses in my playing.

I forgot to mention that also in the past performances of these horses their total earnings was given. Research indicated that their past winnings was the key that would open the treasure chest they represented.

The value of a race horse is determined upon its earning capacity just the same as any stock listed on the Stock Exchange. Therefore, the amount of purse money a horse earns is a most important consideration.

Let us consider the 5th race at Aqueduct on October 8th, 1960. Seven horses were entered in this race. The winner was Scotland, but this horse was disqualified for fouling and Wolfram, the declared winner, paid $35.80. Here are the chart comments: "Wolfram, outrun early, moved up fast at the mile, was caught between Scotland and Bergamot near the three-sixteenths mile post and, after being forced to check, closed gamely."

Let me show how and why Wolfram stood out like a beacon light to a qualified player possessed of racing know-how. Turning to the past performances for this race we find, *Wolfram. The asterisk (*) preceding the name denotes it was an imported horse. This mark appears before the names of all imported horses and is the only way to know they are foreign-bred horses. The horse had run only one race in this country. It was the 7th race at Saratoga run August 20, 1960. This was an allowance and the horse ran 6th, beaten by 28 lengths. Previous to this race the record shows it ran six times in France and in stake races and finished as follows:

			FINISH
August 27, 1960	Saratoga	Allowance	6 beaten 28 lengths
November 8, 1959	France	Stake	1 WON by 2½ lengths
October 15, 1959	France	Stake	2 beaten 3 lengths
September 19, 1959	France	Stake	2 beaten 3 lengths
August 9, 1959	France	Stake	1 WON by 2½ lengths
August 2, 1959	France	Stake	1 WON by 2 lengths
July 26, 1959	France	Stake	1 WON by 3 lengths

The worst it had finished in six stake races was 2nd, beaten only by a few lengths. The highest odds it ran at was 2.40 to 1 and the shortest at odds of 0.30 to 1. And get this! In only three of these seven stake races was it a favorite, this indicating that it was running against France's best stake quality horses.

Its money earned record showed:

Races Run		Win Finish	Place Finish	Show Finish	MONEY EARNED
1960	1	0	0	0	—
1959	10	6	3	0	$23,196

You can disregard the fine finishing record of this horse. You'll find many imported horses showing meritorious records and yet they do not win in this country.

The secret involved here is the earned money record, as you'll learn.

The favorite in the race was Scotland, going off at odds on of 0.60 to 1. This horse is a native (U.S.) bred horse. Its earning record showed as follows:

1960	11	1	2	2	$20,850
1959	20	5	3	1	$79,698

On the basis of 1960 earnings, it is impossible to make a comparison between these two horses because Scotland had raced 11 times and Wolfram had raced but 1. And this was the first out for Wolfram in this country.

They must be compared on their 1959 record.

In this country the purse money is many, many times higher in value than a comparable race in any other part of the world. Also the value of the U.S. dollar is considerably more than its comparable value any other place in the world.

By purse money value I mean this: In this country purses of $50,000 up to several hundred thousands are almost a semi-weekly occurrence. The same comparable race in any other country might be, and is, from $10,000 to $75,000.

I do not know, and I doubt if any reader will know, exactly what the difference in value of purses and the dollar is. Therefore the only way I know to handle this dilemma is to set an arbitrary value figure to them. I have found that by figuring the combined purse and dollar value the differential is about 10 to 1. In other words, if a horse in this country wins $10,000 it is the same as a horse earning $100,000 in another country.

Following this reasoning, since Wolfram earned in a foreign country the total sum of $23,196, it really represents ten times that amount or $231,960 compared to Scotland's earnings of $79,698.

In support of my contention, let me present these facts. Outside of America the most money won by any horse in 1967 was, in France, $274,000; in England, $260,000; in Argentina $89,757.

In other countries, it was so much less there is no point in listing the amounts. Now contrast this to money earned by horses in America.

There were, in 1967, over 200 horses that won $300,000 or more. Many won over $400,000—Damascus leading with $817,941.

True, there are fewer races run in foreign countries but to offset this the number of horses racing are but a small percentage of the number racing here. But no matter how you analyze it, an imported horse that has won $2,000 in the originating country has presumably performed with equality to a horse here having won $20,000, possibly more.

All I can say is that if I should be wrong, I'm lucky to have won many wagers based upon the premise involved.

Don't you agree that this is common-horse-sense reasoning? If you do not, I can tell you if you look for these spots and notice results, you'll find the analysis confirmed time after time.

There is another consideration to which one must give thought. In foreign countries the aim of breeding horses is more for stamina and distance than it generally is in this country. The fetish here seems to be for speed and more speed. Hence the construction and maintenance of race tracks here is based upon this aim to get more speed. Naturally, the surface upon which a horse races influences its speed. The same is true of humans. Slower time is made when running in the sand on a beach than it is on turf or on a specially constructed running track.

This being true, a foreign horse accustomed to racing on turf or average dirt tracks when performing on our tracks can better its speed average on our tracks. This must be considered and thought about.

The two examples given in this chapter are types of play that do not appear every day. There may be a considerable time lapse between their appearances and you have to keep your eyes open and watch for them. Since no handicapping, as such, is involved—I mean you select them not based on speed figures, weights, or the usual handicapping aides but upon unrelated factors—I call them Spot Plays and I'll devote space to Spot Plays later on.

When one stops to think about it, the selection of these two types as good prospective winners at a price is nothing more than the groundwork performed by detectives in solving a case. In reality, it is horse racing detective work. I do not know, but maybe my use of racing detective work comes naturally. My father was a very famous New York City detective who solved many murder crimes and has been well publicized in books and magazines, not to mention newspapers at the time the crimes occurred. As a matter of fact, when I was of high school age, when a young man was required in detective work—one such case being a printer's devil in a printing establishment where a grown man could not function—I was hired for the purpose.

Anyone doing detective leg work would have spotted Wolfram as a most likely winner at most satisfactory odds. He would have been right and collected a wager at $35.80. This horse ran thereafter and continued to win, but never again at such odds. In order to be a successful player, one must be able to keep ahead of the public. There are many such plays as these which I shall go into later. Different from handicapping as such, is it not?

Briefly what I want to emphasize in this chapter is: That in this book you will find methods that *actually do produce winners*. That they are unique and different from anything that has previously appeared in print. Look for a first time starter that has won as a favorite, or a very short-priced winner. If not more than one selector has picked this horse to win and if the morning price line was 10 to 1 or more, list this horse as a good future winner. And also list any horse that finishes second or third not beaten by more than three lengths. Look for imported horses and compare their total earnings with that of their competition. *Multiply the foreign earnings ten times in order to make a meaningful comparison.*

6

Weight, the Villain of Handicapping

THE MOST PREVALENT fetish of *everyone* connected with racing is that concerning weight carried by horses when racing. It is the cause of more money being lost than any other factor.

With this chapter in particular, I recommend that players read carefully and think about it. I guarantee that, whether or not you agree with my conclusions, you'll always remember what I have said and make good use of it in the future.

When one considers how racing started in this country and how it developed, it is no mystery why the weight question became the fetish it is today.

When the early American settlers cleared the forests, they started to bring in horses from England. The development of the present-day thoroughbred originated in England. The original three Arabian and Barb horses imported into England are the progenitors of every thoroughbred, since they were used for stud purposes. They were crossed with the then existing English mares and thus started a new breed of horses, the thoroughbred.

Many among those brought to this country were of thoroughbred stock. As young America developed, roads were constructed and it was natural for owners of horses to boast of their speed and to pit one against the other since competition in sports is a natural trait in man.

Inevitably, from one horse being pitted against another, the time came when a number of horses competed in the same race. In this way, racing as it exists today had its start in the United States. In these competitions when one horse had demonstrated his superiority over all others, the system of handicapping originated. The dictionary definition of the word handicap is:

1. Handicap race or contest in which, in order to equalize chances of winning, an ARTIFICIAL *disadvantage* is imposed on a supposedly superior contestant or an *artificial advantage* is given to one supposedly inferior; also, the advantage given or the disadvantage imposed.

2. Figuratively, any disadvantage that renders success more difficult.

My own definition for the word with reference to racing:

An attempt to equalize the winning chances of all horses in the SAME race.

This purpose in the beginning was to make the most superior entrant run a *greater* distance than the next best horse, a lesser distance for the third best, a lesser distance for the fourth best, etc. Let us set up the starting points of an imaginary race run in those days.

START   **FINISH LINE**

Horse A*_____|

Horse B*_____|

Horse C*_____|

Horse D*_____|

As the sport increased in popularity, more and more horses were entered in race meets. In the early days, cups and plates were the prizes competed for. When purse money was substituted for awards of cups and plates, it became impractical to have a number of horses start from a different starting point. It was only then that handicapping was invoked as a method of equalizing the chances of all entrants by adding or deducting the weight a horse had to carry in a race.

This method adequately served its purposes for many years. And then one day, behold! across the firmament, like a meteor, came a jockey who caused the efficacy of weight assignment to change. He was jockey Tod Sloan, the father of what is referred to as "monkey-riding" and it is still known by that term.

He started racing back in the late nineties and earned undying fame and fortune on two continents as the most successful jockey of all times. It poses an interesting question: If he were riding today in competition with such greats as Ted Atkinson, Eddie Arcaro, and others of their skill, how would he rank? In my opinion, they would rank in the same class since all would be using the same type of riding.

There is an immeasurable difference in the style and effect of riding a horse as an equestrian compared to that of riding as a jockey. In Chapter I I have shown what this difference is, but in order to illustrate more clearly the all-importance of this weight question, I am going to show charts taken from my original lessons.

The first chart shows the skeleton of Sysonby, one of the great immortals known in racing history. It is on display in the New York Museum of Natural History.

Please turn your attention to Chart No. 1 on page 29.

Chart 1. 29

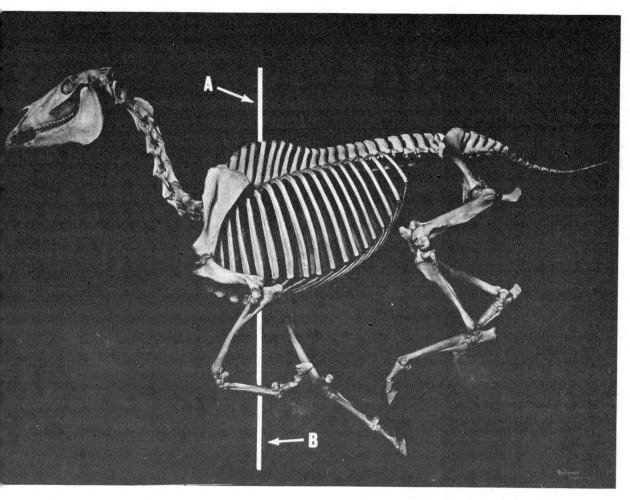

Figure 1
Skeleton of the great *Sysonby* in Museum of Natural History

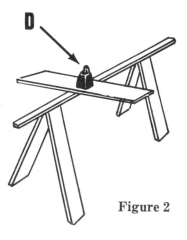

Figure 2

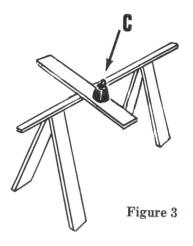

Figure 3

The running action of a horse consists of a series of bones and muscles operating in the manner of a series of levers, with the proper correlation, of course. Now, in order to appreciate the value of my theory about weight, it is necessary to understand that a race horse does not actually *run*. A trotting horse runs, but a race horse *leaps*. Each stride of a race horse in full motion is a *leap*. What happens is that the horse lifts its front feet in the air and then *drives* with his hind feet, the drive propelling him through the air until the force of gravity exerts its influence by bringing the body down closer to the ground. As the front feet touch the ground, the horse actually rests its full weight on its front feet while he draws his rear feet up under him. The rear feet then strike the ground and the horse propels himself forward again through the drive of his rear legs.

Now, while this is taking place, contrary to what would ordinarily be expected to take place, the horse does not leap into the air to any great extent; that is, not *all* of his body rises the same distance above the surface. The horse's action may best be described as that of a see-saw, with the ends rocking up and down over a central *pivot point*, exactly as a pair of scales may be rocked up and down, without moving the central or pivot point in the slightest.

A horse's action is very similar to a see-saw inasmuch as his head will go down as the rear portion of his body goes up and, conversely, as his head goes up, the rear part of his body will go down. This action, however, takes place around a pivot point in the horse's anatomy and this particular point happens to be placed in a position with the line drawn on Chart No. 1. I have indicated this line with the letters "A" and "B."

Study this picture for a few seconds and you can see that the horse is in a position where, during the next split-second, his hind feet will strike the ground. At this time the rear portion of his body is high in the air but it will shortly come down while the horse's head will go up as his front feet go forward. But while this action is taking place, the only movement of the part of the horse indicated as the pivot point—the part with the line drawn through it—will be a forward motion and not an upward or downward motion.

To make this point clear, let me say that if you were to stick a pin through the center of the body of this horse, directly on the drawn line, and if you were to rock the picture up and down at the ends you would get a see-saw action very similar to the action that you would get if you placed a board over a saw-horse and rocked the ends of the board up and down. This is a rough illustration of a horse's action. There is a distinct rocking of the extreme ends above a central pivot point, in addition to the forward motion.

Now turn your attention to Figure 2, on the same chart. This is a crude sketch of a board, the center of which rests on a saw-horse. Now take a heavy weight, and place it directly in the center of the board so that the weight rests squarely over the saw-horse. What happens? Nothing happens, of course. The board will maintain the same *perfect* balance and it would not require any great *effort* on your part to rock the board up and down. This is because the weight is placed exactly over the pivot point and therefore has no effect.

Now place the weight just a little to one side of the saw-horse (see Figure 3) and what happens? The board will tip down, of course, on the end carrying the weight. Now, if you were to try and rock the board with the weight in this position you would have to either grab the board at the end having no weight on it and you would bear down on this end to rock the board. Or you might grab the board by the end upon which the weight rests and in this case you would have to lift the weight in order to rock the board.

Assuming that you are lifting the weight, by taking hold of the board at the end of the half upon which the weight rests, you know that the farther the weight is moved away from the pivot point, the harder it becomes for you to lift the weight.

This is precisely the same with a horse. When the weight is placed directly over the pivot point—directly over the line "A" and "B" in Figure No. 1 —this weight does *not* interfere with the see-saw action of the horse. The horse does not have to lift this weight as there is but slight upward motion of the horse at this point. Move the weight back of the pivot point, however, and the horse must necessarily lift the weight every time the rear part of his body goes up and the farther away from the pivot point this weight is placed, the more effort is required by the horse to lift this weight.

I believe this point should be perfectly clear and it remains only for me to show how the riding style of jockeys has changed since Tod Sloan first originated the "monkey style" of riding. Please turn to Chart No. 2, and I will try to show the difference between the two styles of riding. Look at Figure 1, on Chart No. 2. The pivoting point on the horse is indicated by the line "C" and, as you will note, this line is about in line with the jockey's knees. Now, in the old days the riders sat in a position very much like the rider in Figure 3 and much longer stirrups were used. The rider's knees would be only slightly bent and while riding he would simply lean forward in his seat—and consequently his weight would be firmly anchored in the saddle, meaning that the weight was carried well back of the pivot point. The horse, therefore, had to lift this weight with every upward move of the rear part of the horse's body.

Note the difference in the position of the knees of the jockeys, when comparing Figures 1 and 2 with that of Figure 3, on Chart No. 2.

Now turn to Chart No. 3 and see what happens when the "monkey style" riders go to work. Look at Figures No. 1 and No. 2, at the top of the page. Note how these riders get their weight up over the horse's withers, or pivoting point. These pictures do not illustrate the point as clearly as they might, due to the angle at which they were taken but they will serve to show the difference between this style of riding and the old style (see Figure 3, Chart No. 2) which had the weight of the rider located over the horse's back, in the saddle.

If you will look at the Figure 3 below, on Chart No. 3, you will note that I have indicated the saddle position with the letter "E" and the pivot point with the letter "F." Now note how the lines "A" and "C" point to the saddle position of the two horses above while the lines "B" and "D" point to the pivoting point of the two horses. You will then clearly realize that the two riders manage to

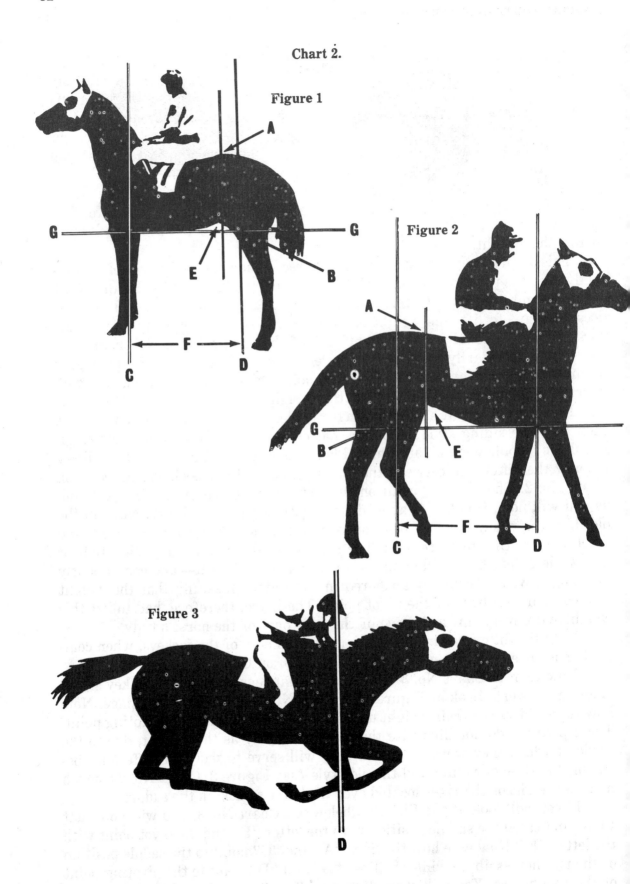

Chart 2.

Figure 1

Figure 2

Figure 3

Chart 3.

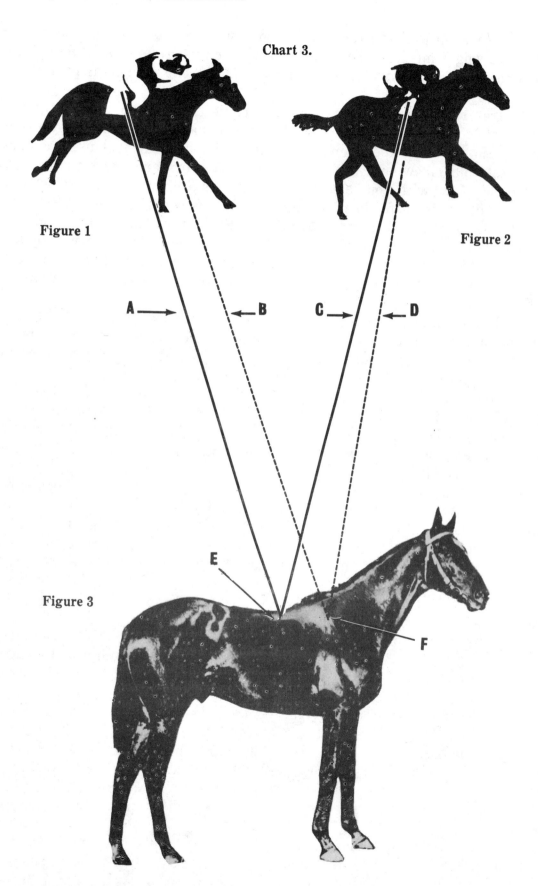

Figure 1

A → ← B

Figure 2

C → ← D

E

Figure 3

F

place their weight well over the pivoting point whereas the old-style rider would locate his weight much further back, in a position where the horse would have to lift the rider's weight with every upward movement of the rear part of the horse's body.

There are, I suppose, those who will argue that 100 pounds is still 100 pounds, no matter where it is placed. To these die-hards I can only suggest that they try the see-saw experiment or, if this be impractical, just use a clothes iron. Rest your elbow on a table, extend your forearm and grasp the iron by the handle. Now, with your elbow on the table as a pivoting point raise your forearm until it is perfectly perpendicular. In this position, you can hold the weight without effort for any length of time. But lower your forearm and still holding the iron extend it until the iron just clears the table. See how long you can hold it this way compared to when the arm is perpendicular. I am sure you'll agree that the effort required to carry weight increases or decreases in relation to the pivot point.

Tod Sloan immediately upon his appearance on New York tracks became a sensation. He outrode all jockeys, winning race after race. The term "monkey-riding" originated because other jockeys jealous of Sloan's success used to deride him saying he looked like a monkey on a stick.

No one ever figured that his style of riding offset to a great extent the effect of the weight being carried. And I have never to this day known of my theory ever being accepted that it is the riding position which determines the effect even among the few believers, like myself, that weight carried means very little in handicapping.

Be that as it may, it took a long time before jockeys started to figure maybe the "monkey-riding" position was the reason for Sloan's success, and they started to adopt it. Now, of course, this is the only method being used.

The theory of assigning weights has never changed since the day it was inaugurated. The effect of this weight has changed since the time changing the position of the jockey in relation to the pivot point took place. It is my contention, therefore, that weight as such has no such effect as assumed, except in few and rare instances and I'll give evidence to support my belief.

Within reason, of course, weight can make a difference. Unfortunately, realities prevent this. The weight a horse must carry is determined by the Racing Secretary. He is faced with the task of assigning weight in a given race. He has at his fingertips complete records of all the entries and aims to make a strictly impartial decision and at the same time to please the owners and trainers of every horse entered.

He fairly rates horse "A" as being 50 pounds better than horse "B" and he honestly believes that with such a difference in weight, the result will be a horse race and not a "walk-over" for the better horse. Now, how can he assign weights on these two horses so that there will be a difference of 50 pounds in the weights?

Were it not for a question of riders, it would be simple to assign the impost of 125 pounds to horse "A" and 75 pounds to horse "B," allowing this 50 pounds difference. But where is an owner that can find a jockey who weighs 75 pounds? A very few young apprentice riders can scale down to 90 or 95 pounds. The Secretary, for this reason, does not dare go much below 100 pounds for horse "B." Assuming he assigns 95 pounds to horse "B" he would have to assign 145 pounds to horse "A" which would result in the owner refusing to accept such a load and would scratch his horse. The chances are the Secretary would be forced to scale the weight of horse "A" down to about 130 pounds in order to get the owner to agree to run his horse. This would mean a difference of 15 pounds (145 to 130). So the realities prevent the actual culmination of the Secretary's honest belief and decision.

The Secretary knows his job, but he has so many angles to consider that rarely is he able to assign the weights in the manner that his considered judgment tells him they should be allotted. Consequently, when a Secretary assigns top weight to a horse in a stake or handicap race it does not mean, in my opinion, that this weight will slow certain horses down where they will finish in a dead-heat with the rest of the field. It merely means that the Secretary considers the highest weighted horse to be the best horse in that race.

The results of many thousands of races analyzed bring out clearly that the very horse the Secretary considered to be the best horse, by assigning it the heaviest impost, in the vast majority of races proves that it is still the best horse by winning a large percentage of all races run, in spite of the fact that weight is supposed to stop them and they often prove that weight does not bother them by cracking or equaling track records. If interested, a reading of the records of those horses who have made track records will show a great preponderance of them carried top weight in the race.

It should be understood that in handicap and stake races the weight to be carried is determined solely by the Racing Secretary. In all other races the weight to be carried is determined by the owner and/or trainer. The way this operates is that the conditions of the weights to be carried are announced in the Condition of the Race. In a number of ways the owner decides on this and though a subject little known to even the advanced player it is most important. An important chapter on this subject will appear under the title "Race Conditions."

Live and Dead Weight

Since jockeys are of different weights, it should be obvious that it has important bearing on figuring. It is seldom a jockey can be assigned to ride a certain horse and be of the same weight the horse is to carry. Let's say the horse is to carry 128 pounds. The contract rider of the stable or the rider hired to ride may weigh say 110 pounds. This difference of 18 pounds is made up by putting pieces of lead, weighing 18 pounds, in the saddle pockets. These are located under the stirrup flat of the saddle.

From what you have read, you know that the position of the saddle is *back* of the pivot point of the horse and must be *lifted* by the horse as it runs. It is not placed over the pivot point where it balances. The lead carried in the saddle is known as *dead* weight and is stationary and fixed and cannot be shifted when the horse is running to be over the pivot point where it would make little difference.

However, the amount of dead weight can be carried *only* within well defined limits. Since it can be added only to the weight of the jockey, obviously, it can be but a small fraction thereof and you can forget about it because knowing the exact weight of every jockey and deducting it from the total weight assigned to learn the small amount of dead weight is not worth the effort and really serves no useful purpose.

There is still another reason why I eliminate this consideration in my search for picking winning selections. A race horse weighs in the neighborhood of 1500 pounds. I would judge, eliminating the biggest money stake races, that a fair average of weight carried in all other races would be around 115 to 118 pounds. This represents less than 8 percent of the horse's weight.

Let us take a person weighing 180 pounds. Eight percent of that is minutely close to 14½ pounds. It is doubtful that the average paper-filled brief case carried back and forth daily by thousands of men weighs more than that and surely it does not discomfort them in any way. Then too, he is not keenly trained to perfection as is a horse for the purpose of running with weight on its back.

Look over the past performances and you'll see the addition of the reduction of from 1 to 10 pounds in at least 90 percent of all such assignments. This slight difference means as much to a strong, healthy, well-trained horse as a few flies on its skin.

In support of my contention that in the search for picking winning selections the subject of weight has the least importance of any factor except in one race out of hundreds, and had best be disregarded, I offer these observations:

1. The vast majority of track records are held by the two or three of the highest weighted horses in the race when the record was made.

2. Such a large percentage of the top-weighted horses that either win or run in the money indicates a weight penalty does not influence their efforts.

3. Most of all, time after time, you will find a horse winning a race in a certain time. This same horse within a very short period of time, running at the same distance on the same track and carrying *less* weight, will get a lower speed rating. This is one of the best indications of the worthlessness of weight assignment.

Here is an example of what I mean: The immortal Equipoise on July 9, 1932, won the Arlington Gold Cup, running the 1¼ miles in 2:02⅘ carrying 128 pounds. Two weeks later, entered in the Arlington Handicap, it ran the same distance of 1¼ miles on the same track, Arlington, carrying the neat package of 134 pounds in 2:02⅕, or ⅗ths faster despite the additional 6 pounds.

These foregoing examples are not isolated instances. They occur constantly. Hence my assessment of weight is that the player may well disregard it entirely.

I previously said that in stake and handicap races the weight is arbitrarily assigned by the Racing Secretary. I might say in passing that in some races, for instance the Kentucky Derby, weight to be carried is determined by the "Scale of Weights" as published by The Jockey Club.

It would be impossible in these days of big fields to start entries in a race from different starting points as they originally did. Undoubtedly, when adding weight to be carried was the means of handicap, this substitution for different starting points gave satisfactory results. But not because of the weight by itself, but because it was placed where the horse had to lift that weight with each stride. Undoubtedly, it slowed down the horse. But when the style of riding changed, the effect of weight became almost nil.

I'd like to tell you of an instance when this weight fetish meant $36,000 to me. I had a very popular mare named Jim's Niece. It was summer racing at Saratoga and we had waited and waited until we found a suitable spot for her. My trainer entered her and on the day she was to race I left New York City early in the morning to arrive in Saratoga about 12 o'clock noon. I found that she had an apprentice jockey riding and I was furious with my trainer. In practically every race she had run since I bought her my rider was Sammy Renick. My trainer explained that he had made the change of riders in order to get the apprentice allowance of 5 pounds and that he wanted to take every advantage, as we had planned a long time for this race and were betting a substantial sum.

The race was run. Coming into the finish Jim's Niece was lengths in the lead of the pack and on the rail. The young smart-aleck apprentice turned his head around to the *left* and stuck his tongue out at the jockeys behind him. But the race ended in a photo finish with Jim's Niece nosed out. How come after being in the lead by lengths?

Had the apprentice turned his head around over his *right* shoulder to ridicule his fellow riders, we would have won the race. What happened was this. A horse was running on the outside rail far out from the pack and so close to the outside rail that I did not see it, my attention being on my own horse. This horse was within striking distance of Jim's Niece. However, as the apprentice jockey realized he was far enough ahead of the pack, thinking nothing could stop him winning, he eased up Jim's Niece, at which time the horse on the outside rail nosed her out at the wire.

My trainer's fetish about weight meant, in this instance, a difference of $36,000. But that is the least of it. Consider the irony of this.

Hughie Fontain, trainer of the late Mrs. Isabel Dodge Sloan's Brookmeade Farms stable, was a very good friend of mine and through this connection I became acquainted with Mrs. Sloan and she often invited me into her box at the race track. Her husband was the first person to import the Schnauzer breed of dogs into this country and breed them. Later on I received my first Schnauzer from Mrs. Sloan. I mention these facts merely as a prelude to my turning down the acquisition of the horse Market Wise who ended up winning $222,140.

Millionaire stables operate for the glory. They are not interested in any horse that does not show potentialities of becoming a great handicap or stake prospect. Once a year some stables hold a public auction to dispose of this surplus stock, others sell them privately.

Prior to the Jim's Niece race, Hughie Fontain approached me and said he had three horses I could have and no payment for them.

Stabling space is at a premium for the Saratoga racing season, and naturally space is allotted first to the large millionaire stables with their top handicap and allowance horses. I had been unable to get stabling space and Mrs. Sloan graciously gave me two of her stalls so the only horse I had there was Jim's Niece.

In those days, unlike now, there was only a short racing period following the close of the Saratoga meet, and then racing was over until the following Spring season started.

When Hughie offered me the three horses, it was before racing started that day. I thanked him and immediately sought out my vanning man and told him the first chance he got to pick up these horses at Brookmeade Stables and van them to my stable located at the Jamaica race track. Naturally, there was no space for them at Saratoga.

Later in the day, Hughie and I were watching Jim's Niece race. He was most interested in this horse because it had been named for his wife. This mare was bred by that fine sportsman and gentleman William Arnold Hanger. He is a member of the most exclusive club in the world, The Jockey Club, which has full control of all racing and is strictly limited to 40 members.

Mr. Hanger still races his own stable and has several breeding farms, his main one being in Paris, Kentucky. He bred Jim's Niece and when he named this filly he chose the name of Jim's Niece because he had a friend named Jim who had an attractive niece. This was the girl that Hughie eventually married.

This is how I came to buy Jim's Niece. I was racing the first horse I owned, Dohoev, in New England. One day, trainer-owner William Martin was saddling Jim's Niece in the adjoining paddock. I liked her looks and asked Martin, from whom I originally bought Dohoev, if he would sell her to me. The horse, under Martin, would finish second and he could not seem to win with her. He agreed to sell her to me after he ran her at Empire City track because at this track the stretch was much shorter than any of the tracks around. Martin thought Jim's Niece was a quitter. He has lost a few good bets on her as she had run second. He figured that *because* of the exceptionally short stretch at Empire Jim's Niece would get to the finish line before the competition would catch if she started to quit.

Jim's Niece again ran second that day and then he raced her at Empire.

I forget how she finished, but I believe it was second again. Martin was a betting man and had lost many bets on her.

Immediately thereafter I took my money, visited Martin who lived in a hotel in Jamaica, and bought her.

His exact words about her are indelibly impressed on my mind. He said she was strictly a sprint horse and never to run her on other than a fast track as she detested mud. He said she loved to hear the patter of thundering hoofs behind her.

It was my opinion that she was running second because Martin, figuring her a speed horse, had her immediately rushed to the front in all her races. I figured this was why she was running second. She was a fast breaker, and she proved as she raced under my colors to be as fast a breaker from the gate as any horse!

The first time she raced under my colors I instructed the jockey to let her break as she wanted, and then to restrain her and keep her within close striking distance, holding her second or third if possible. She won this race and continued to win many races for me under this changed manner of racing her.

Martin was a good trainer, and acting on his advice, I scratched her several times when it rained and she would have had to run on other than a fast track. Permission to scratch is usually given when track conditions change, if the field is large. But I noticed when it rained and the track was sloppy, on her way for a workout she would paw the sloppy water and I suspected she really liked it. I decided to take a chance and ran her on a sloppy track and she won by 6 or 8 lengths. She turned out to be one of the best off-track performers to be found.

I'll never forget one day at Empire when she spread-eagled her field in the slop and won by many lengths. Tom Healy, one of the famous trainers, came to me and said, "Al, why didn't you tell me Jim's Niece ran well in the slop?" I said to him, "Mr. Healy, just go and look at her former past performances." Among her past performances that did appear that day, none showed that she had won on other than fast tracks. All her off-track races were shown in older past performances than those shown that day.

It was after Jim's Niece won for me three or four times that comments appearing alongside *Racing Form*'s price line changed from: "A notorious quitter" to "A jewel of consistency" to "Very game," etc.

She was never beaten in a race when any horse was close enough to run head and head with her. In the parlance of racing, this is called "dogging." Under such conditions, she'd always give that extra effort to win and this made her very popular with the fans.

As a matter of fact, she was so popular that when she bowed a tendon and I retired her from racing, I had requests for her photograph from all over the country from many who had wagered on her. I happily granted these requests. Generally, when a horse bows a tendon it is, by a painful process of burning holes in the leg with a red-hot firing iron for this purpose and after this process heals and forms a sheath over the tendon, continued to be raced. My trainer wanted to do this with Jim's Niece but I could not bear the thought of her running thereafter as a crippled performer who might break down in any race.

So I retired her from racing. Mr. Hanger, seeing her gameness in racing, had made me promise that when I retired her I would sell or make a trade with him because he wanted to breed her. So I had her shipped to his breeding farm and received in trade the horse Cosine. Thus, Jim's Niece returned home after finishing her contests in racing.

You'll recall that Mr. Martin told me Jim's Niece was strictly a sprinter and never to run her over 6 furlongs.

When Sam Hildreth was trainer of the great Sinclair Stable, the racing authorities invited the owner of the renowned French horse Epinard to send the latter to this country to race in three international races of big money value. Epinard ran these three races and proved its class and ability by running second on all three or running second twice and winning once. I can't recall which. But the times it lost by a slight margin it was due to most unfortunate circumstances. In other words, except for bad breaks, they did not have starting gates then but horses broke from a walk-up to a webbing stretched across the track. Epinard, in the opinion of all horsemen, should have won all three races. These races, of course, were for a route distance.

Epinard was the paternal grandfather of Jim's Niece and though I had disregarded Martin's advice and run her in a route race, the first time I did this at $1\frac{1}{16}$ miles she either won or ran second and ran a very good race throwing off challenge after challenge. So she proved herself as effectively in routes as well as in sprints.

Well, Jim's Niece's race was over and Hughie and I watched while a sure $36,000.00 (made up of bets I made plus the purse) flew out the window.

Naturally, I was disgusted and felt badly. With Jim's Niece I was stabling, I think, 14 horses. The racing season had only a short period to go, so I was faced with the prospect of having to carry these extra three horses over the winter until the following Spring. Unfortunately, I made a quick decision and told Hughie I did not want the three horses he had offered to me. I then contacted my van man and told him to forget vanning these horses for me.

Among these horses was one named Market Wise. It was being disposed of because a veterinarian had declared that it had a bad heart condition. The horse was subsequently sold and went on to win $222,140. But more important it was very successful in stud and produced many good winners. And thus run the tides of fate.

I am about to finish up this chapter concerned with the subject of weight, but want to leave it with a final observation.

When my lessons on how to pick winners were submitted to The Jockey Club, as related at the start of this book, in addition to Major Daingerfield it was analyzed by the steward of The Jockey Club, Marshall Cassidy. He was one of the sons of the most famous racing official families. His father was the great Mars Cassidy, who functioned as starter. His brother, George Cassidy, is still a starter at this time of writing and I believe there is another brother acting as starter some place in the United States.

But Marshall Cassidy was probably one of the most spectacular figures ever to appear upon the racing scene. From the time he was a very young man he participated in every phase of the sport. Starting as a jockey—not very successfully, he told me—he next performed as an assistant starter under his father. From then on he served as an official of the sport in every capacity. At the time of his death he attained the highest position possible as the secretary of the Jockey Club, which is one of the world's most coveted positions. No person in racing history influenced racing rules and procedures in many ways more than Mr. Cassidy. When my lessons had been approved and I was allowed to continue to race my horses and because of this incident I became friends with Mr. Cassidy. From then on, I consulted him continuously and even hired the last trainer I had on his personal recommendation.

One day, during one of my talks with him, I brought up the subject of the effect of weight in handicapping. He told me that at one time in his career he acted as Racing Secretary on a Canadian track. He told me how he figured the weight and admitted to me, to my surprise, that the addition of the usual weight made little or no difference in the results of the races he handicapped.

As I write I have before me the Sporting Section of the *New York Times* dated March 23, 1969. Let me quote:

"REVIEWER coming through with a remarkable performance carrying top weight of 130 pounds in the seven-furlong Bay Shore, Reviewer sped to a three-length triumph—something never before accomplished in the Bay Shore. And his time was a stakes-equaling 1:22⅘."

This was in the 7th race at Aqueduct. The chart shows Reviewer won by three lengths with only mild urging. The second horse was Hey Good Looking carrying 113 pounds, 17 pounds less than the winner.

They say weight brings them together and base all racing conditions on this premise. I'll bet all the tea in China that if the second horse carried only 90 pounds—a difference of 40 pounds—it would not bring them together, and that if the race was run over with the second horse carrying 90 pounds less, the result would be the same.

For every instance where one brings support to the theory that weight differences can effect the result of a race, I'll guarantee to produce official records to prove to the contrary.

Again, I repeat, the majority of races are won by the top-weighted horses and this occurs to a greater degree in handicap and stake races than in other races. Again, I repeat, when a track record is equaled or a new record made that it is accomplished by the top-weighted horses in the race.

Undoubtedly, by now many readers will conclude that I am a fanatic on the subject of weight. To this charge I plead guilty.

I know I am on solid ground when I say that the importance given to the addition of weight to equalize the winning chances of horses is one of the primary causes of money loss in wagering.

Unfortunately, for those players who place too much reliance on public handicappers, they as a whole make the subject of weight their leading factor in their analysis. This is evidenced by the comments they make in the process of their work.

The acquisition of Jim's Niece was one of the most memorable and satisfying acts of my life. It resulted in my acquaintance and/or close friendship with Hughie Fontain, Mrs. Isabel Dodge Sloan, and William Arnold Hanger. These friends have given me much pleasure. Mrs. Sloan has lamentably passed on, I have lost contact with Mr. Fontain, and do not know if he is still active at this time. I had lost track of Mr. Hanger until about a month ago when I contacted him and received from him the present of two newly published books on a most interesting and valuable subject.

There are many horses like Jim's Niece, always being close to the winner but seldom winning until I bought her and changed the method of racing her. What I had learned about her alerted me to watch carefully for horses rarely winning, but always close to the finish. Often, I discovered this type and watched for a change of trainer or jockey. I particularly watched for a change in its running style; by this I mean, if the horse was always rushed to the front and was in the lead in the early part of the running and the pattern changed so that instead of always being in the lead it was reserved back of the leaders. Many, many good winners were picked by my analyzing the races of such horses.

What I have written about Jim's Niece has its place in the Art of Picking Winning Selections.

In this chapter I have used the word "handicap" within its true meaning. However, the word is used with other connotations. For example: a certain class of race is called a *handicap*. Advance prediction of any given horse winning a certain race is loosely called handicapping. Those engaged in making price lines and publishing predictions are called handicappers.

The track Racing Secretary is termed by some as the Track Handicapper.

To reduce this subject of weight to its essentials, I want to say that the importance attached to it is a carry-over from the early days of racing. True, at that time it was important. But due to the shift of weight of the jockey, as I have explained, that importance has so greatly diminished it can be totally disregarded, for all practical purposes.

7

One Special Method
that Really Wins

IN THIS CHAPTER I am going to tell you about a method of play that is suitable for the novice as well as for the experienced player. It has the advantage of mainly eliminating those long strings of consecutive losers that is the fear of all players.

Since the days of "gyp" race tracks, when the sport became subject to the jurisdiction of The Jockey Club, there is one figure of percentage that remains almost constant. This is the percentage of winning favorites. This varies from 30 percent to 35 percent at times. But the never-changing percentage over any extended period of time is 33 percent.

Of course, not 33 percent win every racing day, or week, or month. But when a long enough period of time to permit the averages to assert themselves is observed it will always come up 33 percent, give or take a point or two.

But one will say there is no nourishment in playing horses at short favorite prices and they will be right to some extent. Yet, consider that transactions in the millions of dollars are based upon a *fraction* of 1 percent. A percentage of 1 percent of a million dollars represents earnings on 1 percent. Why then could not a syndicate or group with big capital make the safest kind of investment by playing favorites? It would be impractical because the large bets necessary, for reasonable profits, would defeat its own end.

I'd like to make this comment now. In my own wagering my constant aim has been to wager only on horses offering long-shot possibilties or, in other words, to get the best of the odds. A long shot to most players conjures up prices like 15, 20, 50 to 1, or higher. But a 5 to 1 can be a long shot in my book. For example, assuming a horse's *real chances*, its price should be 2 to 1. However, if its actual price is 5 to 1, *or better*, it is a long shot in my judgment. A long shot in my opinion is any price of 2 to 3 points higher than should be quoted consistent with its winning chances. Keep in mind that: Every price quoted on a horse should be determined solely upon its winning chances. This sound, mathematical, scientific conclusion is constantly being violated in a large percentage of instances.

This transgression against scientific common sense occurs because of these considerations:

1. A horse at stud is a known producer of stake winning get and because of this is favored by handicappers, and whereas one of its get, let's call it "A" for simplicity, is comparable on its record with horse "B" will be priced several or more points lower in odds between the two. Now consider this! For every horse born of a given sire or breeding that goes on to fame and fortune, that *same* breeding also produces dozens—that prove themselves perfectly useless. The champ is remembered! The scrub is forgotten!

2. Some horses become favorites of the public. I do not mean pricewise but in affection and sentiment. This can be and often is the cause for price-makers to cut the price by several points.

3. A stable is eminently successful in winning races. During the period of their success *every horse they run* is priced several points lower than their *actual winning chances*. Among the stables of this class that I recall are the Greentree Stable, the Sinclair Stable when Hildreth was its trainer and the popular Earl Sand its contract rider, Calumet Stable under Ben Jones, the elder.

4. It is not infrequent for some apprentice jockey to become a star in the firmament and to win race after race, often winning several races each day he performs. This is one of the commonest ways to attract unknowing public support and cause a price much below the *actual winning chances* of the horse involved.

There are many other such elements but these should be sufficient for you to know what to look for in this regard. Don't let the public lead you. Learn to make your own decisions based not on sentiment or wishful thinking but on expert know-how.

From my contact with thousands of students over a span of thirty or more years, I have found that their development from an embryo player to their more advanced experienced years follows the same pattern.

Almost invariably, their initial bet results from either receiving a tip and advice from a friend to play a certain horse. Or they make a selection based upon a scratch sheet, a newspaper selection, or public handicapper. I wonder how many readers will recognize this as their introduction to playing the races!

In the early stage of being a player the novice finds that he loses many wagers by reason of the favorite in the race winning, whereas he had bet on another horse. Observing so many favorites winning, often from three to six on a day's card, he then becomes imbued with the idea that in order to win he should play favorites. After wagering on favorites for a time, he discovers they offer small "nourishment" even if it were possible to keep ahead as a winner. This discourages him and thereafter he does either one of two things: He continues to play the races in hit-or-miss fashion and helplessly flounders about for the rest of his race-playing career.

Or he gets smart and realizes in order to win he must treat playing as a business or career and must proceed to gain a necessary know-how the same as is required in any effort in which success is the objective to be achieved. He buys systems and books on racing. He finds that there are systems that will win at times. He eventually realizes that whereas a system may not keep him ahead as a winner that there are certain factors therein that are strong aides in selecting a winner. The next step is for him to devise his own system. And there are many successful players today who have originated a system suitable to their own particular requirements that wins.

The former group, those who are hit-or-miss players, are the segment in racing who by their losing are necessary for the survival of the sport. It is their losses that pay the bill for the operation of race tracks, to pay the purses, and to pay the winnings awarded to the second group who make a serious study of playing the races. That many do win is attested to by the fact that approximately 85 percent of every dollar wagered at the tracks is paid back to holders of winning tickets and by the number of tax returns based upon profits from playing the races.

I do not want to leave the impression that one cannot be a winner through playing favorites or short-priced contestants. On the contrary, there are many methods of play confined to favorites that are used and produce profits year after year. More so that with any other method of play there is an element little thought about that is absolutely essential to make money-playing favorites. That element is the method of wagering.

It is strange that so few horse players ever give a thought to applying a systematic form of wagering to their efforts. When and why and how to wager $10 compared to $2 is as important to success as is the selection of a given percentage of winners. The rudiments of making profits from playing consists of the following: *A certain percentage of winners geared to amount of money wagered upon same.*

Every reader will agree that there is always a percentage operating against the player. The purpose of a systematic method of handling wagers is to *defeat the effect of this ever-present percentage against the player.*

And this purpose can be achieved as will be proved in a later chapter, which perhaps may be considered by many as the most important chapter in this book.

Using exactly the same unit of play (whether it be $2, $10 or $100), if you bet *more* money on every winner you play than you do on every loser, there can be but one result. You'd have to win. Of course, your net profits would be contingent to some extent upon the odds quoted on your winning plays. But for the time being, until you read the chapter on wagering, suffice it to say that if you are able to *bet* more on every winner you play you'll win—but good.

I ask this question: In the matter of playing favorites on the big major tracks, on which the world's best horses perform and are unquestionably more consistent, compared to the small minor tracks, where the cheapest racing material functions—and 98 percent of them doctored up cripples—where would you expect to find the highest percentage of winners?

I'm confident that you'll say on the major tracks, as I did until I became a racing detective, and through my experience learned to research the remotest factor involved in the objective of picking winning selections.

But you'd be wrong as I was! There are two reasons why playing favorites on minor tracks offers greater opportunities for profit than is possible on major tracks.

In the first place the average winning percentage of winning favorites on minor tracks is *higher* than on major tracks. But, and perhaps even more important, is the fact that for favorites on minor tracks the payoffs are higher than for comparable payoffs on major tracks. This undoubtedly will come as a surprise to most players as it did to me when I started my research.

On the following pages I will give you statistics to support this contention.

My hypothesis that minor tracks produced more profits playing the favorites, when compared to major tracks, is based upon my original research made in 1948. Intermediate checking since then supports this conclusion even to a greater degree.

For two reasons I am giving records on this research. First, that I dislike making a statement without evidence to support it. Second, I want to prove that the time element has no bearing as to the merit of a method of play. By the latter I mean provided a system is based upon sound principles, and not upon coincidence, it must and will work now and in the future equally well.

For the 1948 I made the same, but lengthier research, than I have for 1967. I want to keep this book as short as possible so I will not give the detailed information since I imagined no one would have records so far back to check it as they may for 1967. But I will give a revealing resume of part of it.

I felt that whereas averages give a true value I wanted to be more specific so I selected for three tracks an exact win payoff and compared it to the place and show comparison and a total for the three positions.

1948

	Win	Payoffs Place	Show	Total		Win	Payoffs Place	Show	Total
Sar	$5.40	$2.70	$2.10	$10.20	C.F.*	$5.40	$4.20	$3.40	$13.00
AP	7.20	3.60	2.80	13.60	"	7.20	4.80	3.00	15.00
"	3.80	2.60	2.20	8.60	"	3.80	3.40	2.80	10.00
	$16.40	$8.90	$7.10	$32.40		$16.40	$12.40	$9.20	$38.00

* C.F. denotes Cumberland which did not operate in 1967.

Winning Percentage of Favorites

MAJOR TRACKS

Purse Distribution			Percentage of Winning Favorites		Distribution per Race
	1967	1965	1967	1965	1967
Aqueduct	$12,185,510	$10,297,085	34%	34%	$8,380
Arlington	1,972,350	1,792,000	33%	31%	5,933
Atlantic	2,587,975	2,025,325	33%	29%	4,970
Belmont	4,736,765	3,849,215	35%	36%	9,677
Detroit	2,708,640	1,964,940	35%	31%	3,420
Hawthorne	1,779,350	1,591,000	26%	36%	5,392
Hazel	2,791,550	2,198,650	30%	32%	3,794
Hialeah	2,634,300	2,508,250	35%	30%	6,055
Hollywood	4,886,850	4,676,975	36%	31%	9,279
Laurel	2,497,325	3,349,240	32%	31%	6,089
Monmouth	3,186,465	2,638,039	34%	32%	5,882
Pimlico	2,787,250	2,299,005	30%	32%	4,836
Santa Anita	4,406,325	4,188,825	33%	33%	7,958
		Average	32.07%	31.00%	

MINOR TRACKS

Purse Distribution			Percentage of Winning Favorites		Distribution per Race
	1967	1965	1967	1965	1967
Berkshire	$233,425	$215,700	40%	37%	$ 844
Ferndale	20,000	20,750	56%	41%	556
Fresno	137,890	107,235	45%	45%	1,637
Hagerstown	172,520	238,000	38%	40%	1,106
Lethbridge	29,800	25,876	46%	30%	436
Marshfield	38,500	32,832	47%	33%	700
Northampton	56,950	43,200	41%	31%	1,005
Scarborough	407,336	390,584	43%	35%	928
Solano	156,030	136,150	40%	45%	1,608
Weymouth	39,200	36,100	54%	40%	700
		Average	45.00%	37.70%	

The realistic fact is that no matter how you make the comparison better opportunities exist at minor tracks.

To further enhance the value of this research for the year 1967, I selected a major and a minor track in each of the major racing sections across the country, covering the Eastern, the Central and the far Western portion. I did not want to pick spots.

The period covered is from August 1 to August 12, 1967. I decided upon twenty winning favorites as they occurred as being more than sufficient to disclose the purpose aimed at. Obviously, had I covered a longer period the discrepancy between averages would have been wider and only further prove the point. (See also charts at top of pages 49 and 50.)

	SARATOGA starting Aug. 1, 1967				ROCKINGHAM starting Aug. 1, 1967		
	Win	Place	Show		Win	Place	Show
Sar	$3.60	$2.60	$2.60	Rkm	$5.60	$3.40	$3.00
"	5.20	4.00	3.00	"	5.60	3.40	2.80
"	5.60	3.80	3.00	"	5.00	2.80	2.40
"	5.60	3.20	2.60	"	6.00	3.80	3.00
"	3.60	4.40	4.40	"	5.00	4.00	2.60
"	5.40	4.00	3.20	"	5.40	2.80	2.20
"	3.80	2.80	2.40	"	6.80	5.00	3.80
"	5.40	3.20	2.60	"	4.00	2.60	2.20
"	3.80	2.60	2.40	"	8.00	4.60	3.20
"	4.60	3.60	2.80	"	4.60	2.80	2.20
"	6.40	3.60	3.00	"	4.60	3.00	2.80
"	4.40	2.80	2.60	"	7.60	4.20	3.20
"	4.00	3.40	2.60	"	6.40	3.00	2.40
"	5.80	3.40	2.80	"	7.60	3.80	3.20
"	4.00	2.80	2.80	"	5.40	3.60	2.60
"	3.40	2.40	3.20	"	4.40	2.60	2.40
"	5.20	5.50	3.20	"	5.00	3.00	2.40
"	5.20	3.60	2.80	"	6.20	4.20	3.20
"	3.20	2.80	2.80	"	3.60	3.20	2.60
"	3.20	2.40	2.10	"	7.40	4.00	3.40
Average	$4.50	$3.30	$2.80	Average	$5.70	$3.50	$2.80

It was natural that when my inquiring mind established the fact that the winning percentage of favorites was generally higher on minor tracks than it was on major tracks, I researched the comparative payoffs for the three choices on both types of tracks. To my surprise I found that on an average the minor tracks showed a higher comparable payoff.

Many horses quoted at 8/5 which represents $1.60 to $1.00 ended up a win payoff of $5.20 on a major track. However, more often than not, on a minor track with the same odds of 8/5 the win payoff would be $7.20 or better; or

	ARLINGTON starting Aug. 1				**DETROIT** starting Aug. 1		
	Win	Place	Show		Win	Place	Show
AP	$6.60	$3.40	$2.80	Det	$7.60	$5.40	$4.80
"	7.20	5.20	2.80	"	7.80	4.40	2.80
"	6.80	4.40	3.20	"	5.60	3.60	2.80
"	6.60	4.00	3.40	"	6.80	4.40	2.80
"	4.00	2.80	2.20	"	6.20	3.40	2.80
"	5.60	3.40	2.60	"	6.60	5.00	4.20
"	7.40	4.00	2.80	"	5.80	3.40	2.60
"	5.20	3.60	3.20	"	4.80	3.40	2.80
"	4.80	3.60	3.20	"	6.40	4.60	3.20
"	4.40	3.40	2.80	"	5.00	3.60	3.80
"	4.00	2.60	2.00	"	6.20	4.20	2.80
"	4.60	2.80	2.40	"	8.80	4.40	3.40
"	3.60	2.60	2.20	"	5.80	3.60	2.60
"	5.60	3.20	2.60	"	7.80	4.80	4.00
"	6.00	5.40	3.60	"	6.60	5.00	3.80
"	5.60	3.20	2.60	"	7.60	4.80	3.20
"	6.20	4.20	3.40	"	6.80	4.20	3.40
"	7.80	4.20	3.00	"	4.20	3.60	2.80
"	4.00	3.00	2.40	"	4.40	3.00	2.60
"	4.40	3.00	2.60	"	7.20	4.40	3.40
Average	$5.50	$3.60	$2.70	Average	$6.40	$4.10	$3.20

in other words $2.60 to $1.00 compared to $1.60 to $1.00. This means of fifty such wagers you'd end up with *$50.00 more net profit*. Won't you agree this dissipates some of the "percentage against the player"?

Fortunately for me, I learned early in my playing to apply great skepticism to anything that looked like a good thing. Literally thousands of letters have come across my desk regarding what the writer thought was a winning system. Ninety-nine percent of them proved to be based upon merely a recurring incident or incidents. In my racing detective work, I have time and again detected such factors that did for a time produce the most amazing and unbelievable results. But I have never accepted any conclusion unless it was based upon sound reasoning as to *why* such incidents recurred.

After I decided that minor tracks proved to have a higher percentage of winning favorites, I wanted to know *why* this was so. If the conclusion was sound enough to be profitably applied now there had to be a reason for it, if it was to work ten or twenty years from now. And if it was sound, it would do just that!

On every race track there are hundreds of eyes constantly searching to learn something. Owners, trainers, stable help are a cagey lot. They are all of a friendly group among themselves. They stable next to one another and get a

	BAY MEADOWS starting Aug. 1, 1967				DEL MAR starting Aug. 1, 1967		
	Win	**Place**	**Show**		**Win**	**Place**	**Show**
Bmf	$5.40	$3.00	$2.60	Dmr	$5.00	$3.00	$2.40
"	6.20	3.80	3.00	"	6.60	4.20	3.00
"	4.00	3.40	2.80	"	6.00	3.60	2.60
"	5.00	3.20	2.60	"	5.20	3.60	2.80
"	3.00	3.00	2.60	"	4.80	3.00	2.60
"	3.80	3.00	2.40	"	6.40	4.00	3.20
"	3.60	2.80	2.60	"	6.00	3.00	2.60
"	8.20	3.20	2.40	"	4.20	2.80	2.60
"	5.80	3.60	2.80	"	6.00	4.60	3.00
"	3.00	2.20	2.40	"	4.40	2.80	2.80
"	4.60	3.20	2.80	"	7.60	4.00	3.40
"	6.00	3.80	3.40	"	5.60	3.60	3.40
"	7.20	3.40	2.60	"	9.20	4.80	3.60
"	7.00	3.60	2.80	"	4.00	3.20	2.60
"	4.80	2.60	2.80	"	4.40	3.40	2.80
"	6.20	4.60	3.20	"	4.20	3.00	2.80
"	3.40	2.60	2.40	"	4.20	3.40	2.60
"	3.80	2.40	2.40	"	7.20	3.80	3.40
"	4.80	3.00	2.80	"	7.60	4.00	3.40
"	4.40	2.80	2.40	"	4.80	4.60	3.20
Average	$4.80	$3.10	$2.70	Average	$5.60	$3.60	$2.90

line on each other's horses. No matter how secretive stable help may be, they can't hide the true condition of a horse. A horse must be worked and exercised and later be cooled out by being walked about until it dries after being washed off. Knowing eyes follow each move and in this way the fitness or lack of fitness is easily discerned. There are many signs to indicate the condition of a horse. If it is at the peak of its form its eyes will glisten, it is alert with its ears turning in all directions; it will prance and jump and pull on the lead rein trying to break and run away. These are but a few indications of whether or not it is at the peak of its form.

This same situation exists on both minor and major tracks. The only difference being that on the smaller tracks you might find several hundred horses quartered whereas on the major track there will be several thousand.

A player who bets small amounts like $2 is not interested in the small profits offered. Even though he may think the favorite will win, he'll still play a horse that is quoted at longer odds.

The average wager on minor tracks is considerably smaller than on major tracks. The bulk of the betting is made up of $2 wagers. One of the reasons why a horse is made favorite at small minor tracks is that insiders bet. By insiders I mean the horsemen stabled at the track: owners, trainers, grooms, exercise boys, and the like. They know the horse from personal observation and a large portion of the money wagered on favorites is bet by them. The natural result is that such *wise* money creates a truer favorite than would be created by the bets of the unknowing public. The inevitable result is for a higher winning percentage of favorites to take place, because there are fewer false favorites.

This deduction satisfied me that a higher percentage of winning favorites on minor tracks was not a matter of chance, but was based upon sound reasoning, and only then did I accept it and use it in my work.

The next problem to be solved was the higher price and payoff level. Players in a position to make large wagers do not attend minor tracks. They go to the big tracks for obvious reasons. A few bets of $500 or $1,000 put into the machines at small tracks would raise havoc with the price of the horse wagered on. It could cause a logical 6 to 10 to 1 entry and end up a false favorite. Conversely, on the big tracks wagers of $5,000 are ordinary. And bets ranging from $1,000 to $5,000 and over are mostly placed on the favorites.

Common sense tells us that the ordinary racegoer does not bet in such large sums. It is the professional player and the connections of the individual horse that sends in such huge sums, and the result is generally proportionally smaller payoffs on the favorites at major tracks.

The question might be raised why, since smart players connected with racing are the cause of higher favorite winning percentages on minor tracks, this should not be equally true for the major tracks. The key is in the proportions involved.

Naturally, the angle I have been discussing in this chapter is at my finger tips. But I want it to be clearly understandable to readers. In order to clarify it further perhaps the comparative statistics on page 52 will assist. These relate to the number of horses stabled at tracks and this affects the action of "smart" money.

But even with these discrepancies, it does not paint a true picture. At a track like Belmont Park, stable help and some minor jockeys sleep in separate jockey quarters. Stabling horses required space for feed, equipment, tack, trunks, and so on. At the better major tracks these are provided for exclusive of actual horse stalls.

But on minor tracks the possible stall accommodations are depleted by stalls that have to be utilized for track living accommodations and similar purposes. Just picture how much room is taken up by bags of feed, bales of straw for bedding and hay for feeding. Then, too, this must be considered. On major tracks there are stables composed of ten to more than fifty horses.

On minor tracks there are stables of only a few horses ranging in two, three, four, five to ten horses. Each separate stable requires the extra space being discussed. So this again results in greater discrepancies.

On the small tracks a greater proportion of employees can get a truer line on horses. This is true not only because there may be only 1,000 horses stabled

1967 Stable Accommodations

Aqueduct*	500
Arlington Park	2,069
Atlantic City	1,680
Belmont*	2,100
Beulah Park	1,000
Detroit	1,300
Ellis Park	1,089
Finger Lakes	988
Gulfstream Park	1,368
Hagerstown	600
Hazel Park	1,370
Hollywood Park	1,634
Randall Park	650
Santa Anita	1,622

* For Aqueduct and Belmont the available stalls are a total of the two, being close together. Therefore 2,600.

at one track compared to 2,000 or more at another, but also because of the acreage size difference. At Belmont, for example, you'd walk half a mile to over a mile from the stabling area to the training area. On smaller tracks in many instances a walk of one hundred yards or so will bring into focus all that is going on.

Many professionals confine their efforts to the three choices. This type of playing has many advantages over all others. The small return in profits on single wagers is offset by the accumulation of such profits over a number of races won. It requires less capital than needed with any handicapping method because the percentage of winning plays is higher.

Advantages of Playing the Choices

1. The novice player has every advantage the seasoned player has.
2. Less capital is required since consecutive losers are less.
3. Tedious time spent in the search for a play is eliminated.
4. Action in every race is possible or in as many races as preferred.

The chances of any player ending up each year a winner are infinitely greater with this way of wagering. There need be but one other factor to make a success. The lack of this factor being used is the reason for the failure of 95 percent of those who try this method. That factor is a *proper wagering method* geared to this method of play. Steep progression dooms one to failure. But there are ways of overcoming this. The subject will be covered in a chapter devoted to wagering properly.

What I have tried to convey here is that, despite the possible disinclination to play favorites, doing so offers worthwhile rewards. This is especially true on minor tracks because the majority of horses contending thereon are mostly unsound physically and do not run consistently enough to be handicapped along traditional lines. And the better payoffs and higher percentage of winning favorites at these tracks is an asset. There is an additional advantage for the player who wants plenty of action. He has a play in every race if he desires. The idea is to supplement the action of playing favorites by watching for and playing the type of plays found in Chapter 11, page 76.

8

Speed and Time

ABOVE EVERYTHING ELSE the breeding of thoroughbreds is based upon producing horses with speed first and stamina next. In foreign countries the leaning is more toward stamina combined with speed. In general more races of greater distances are conducted in Europe than in this country.

Any breeder will tell you he breeds speedy stallions to speedy mares in an endeavor to get speed horses.

It must be conceded that if it were possible to select the *one* single positive determining factor in the winning of races it would have to be *speed*. And this is true of all competition wherein the legs are used for motion such as running or skating. Given a starting point, breaking and running a given distance to a finish line *inevitably*, barring interference, the competitor with the most speed has to win. There are no two ways about it!

If this was all there is to it the art of picking winners would be within the easy grasp of all. It would be a simple matter to establish the relative speed potentiality of any horse, and when the horse was fit, it would run to its speed capability. Ratings could be established for each horse and then anyone in possession of these ratings could win.

Unfortunately, it is not as simple as all that. Probably the most costly mistake made in racing—and by the greatest number, novice and veteran alike —is the failure to realize a horse is not a machine. A watch will move a wheel 60 times and come up with the result of one minute of time. And just as long as the watch is in perfect mechanical condition, it will continue to do this every time the wheel completes its cycle until the machinery wears out with use. And there will be no variation, 60 turns of the wheel will *always* end up in one minute even after millions of turns.

Subconsciously, players expect a horse to perform like a watch. If based upon what appears, and what may be the soundest scientific judgment, they figure a horse should run in a certain time, if the horse fails to do so they attribute it to likely chicanery. They never stop to think that a horse is a warm-blooded animal as is a human being; that it is subject to ailments, that it has its days of lassitude, when it will perform below its norm and other days of vigor, when it will function above it.

A human might reasonably be expected to perform below par if he is grieving over the loss of a loved one, even though he may or may not have lost sleep the night before the contest. In this instance the deterrent is caused by a mental state.

In bygone years there was a popular and good horse named Peanuts. Its name derived from the fact that it was under the average size of a race horse. It had a pet as a companion in its stall. I am quite sure it was a goat. Peanuts was a well-behaved docile animal just as long as the goat was in the stall or near the door where it could be nuzzled and played with by a stretching of the horse's neck. While the goat was in the immediate vicinity Peanuts was happy and contented. But at one time the goat was injured and was absent for a week under care of a veterinarian. The horse fretted, went off its feed, and nervously walked its stall. In racing parlance this is known as "stall-walking." The horse just keeps moving about, never resting, and it is one of the most depleting actions a horse can take to spend its energy. A race for which Peanuts had been carefully prepped for a long time came up. It had been expected to win and went to the post a stand-out favorite. Despite having every advantage in the race it ran the worst race of its career.

Upon the return of the goat to the horse's stall, Peanuts recovered its spirits, and quickly regained its lost peak of form. This clearly indicates that the mental attitude of both the human and the horse will and does influence their physical performances.

It is not my purpose to digress from the subject matter of this chapter but I do want to comment upon this subject of "horse's pets." If the removal of a companion and playmate of a horse can influence the latter's performance, then it is obvious that this knowledge can be used to achieve the same purpose as the administration of a drug to retard or advance the speed of a horse. This subject will be discussed in one of the last chapters.

The greatest loss to players comes about because of the two most fundamental bases of racing. These two are *weight* and *speed*. And not because of these factors in themselves, but by reason of the fact that wrong values are attributed to them. The matter of weight has already been reviewed. Now let's tackle the subject of speed in its true context.

Since racing records have been carefully established the time of every race has been scientifically measured and entered in the archives of racing statistics. The time of every race run is thus maintained. The fastest time achieved becomes the track record for each individual track and for every distance run. In order to avoid the computations of differences in the time of races a quick, simple, easy reference was devised to evaluate a comparative method of approach. Thus speed ratings came into being.

The computation of speed ratings is made as follows:

Time is figured in fifths of seconds. Each length of a horse is considered equal to $\frac{1}{5}$ of a second. At Laurel race track in Maryland a new track record for the 6 furlong distance was established November 2, 1964, by Mister Judge.

The time for this race was 1:10⅖ and thereafter would rate 100 as a speed rating. The (1) means a minute; the (10) means ten seconds; the (⅖) means two fifths of a second. This figure represents 70 and ⅖ seconds.

The speed rating allotted to the track record is.................... 100

A horse winning in time of 1:10⅘ would rate ⅖ slower than the track record 98

A horse running second beaten 3 lengths behind the winner would rate   95

One running third beaten 1 length by the second horse (4 lengths behind winner) would rate...................................... 94

And so it would go down to the horse finishing last in the race.

This is a practical method of handling the subject. And as a result this is the basis applied for all time and speed considerations. This sounds logical but when you apply a searching examination of the theory you will find it "full of holes."

The fallacy of giving too much importance to speed ratings seems to be apparent when an analysis and study is made of the following facts and statistics.

Track records are not made by mediocre or even average horses. Those making records are the outstanding performers of their era. For every horse such as Man O'War, Equipoise, Citation, Swaps, Kelso, Damascus, and others, there are thousands, yes thousands not hundreds, that are just run-of-the-ordinary; and an even greater number that are very ordinary, to the extent that they cannot earn their training expenses. And keep in mind that I mean during the *same* period of time they are all racing.

The records are replete with track records being made 20 to 30 years ago. Here is an example of a few of even greater age:

Year	Horse	Track	Distance	Record
1890	Salvator	Mth., N.J.	1 Mi	1:35½ 79 years
1890	Banquet	Mth., N.J.	1¼ Mi	2:03¾ 79 years
1901	Montanic	Wash., Ill.	6¼ Fur	1:15⅘ 65 years
1920	Man O' War	Bel., N.Y.	1⅜ Mi	2:14⅕ 48 years

Dozens of records made in the 1920's, 1930's, and 1940's have never since been broken.

Now then, consider this! There can be no question but that the race courses of today are of superior construction and quality and are conducive to horses running with greater speed. Despite this, many records of long past have never been broken. This leads to a reasonable conclusion that practically all track records have been made by the most superior contestants of their era.

The owner of every race horse hopes that it will earn the maximum profits possible. With this in mind those race tracks that offer the biggest purses are able to attract the most capable performers available. Let us forget for the moment the consideration of those races in which the leading horses contest. Ninety-nine percent of all races figured with the purpose of selecting the eventual winner deals with average horses and not with the champions.

When one of the great horses, racing for a purse that may be worth more than $100,000, makes a track record it gets a speed rating of 100.

When a horse, racing for a purse of $3,500, makes a track record it gets a Speed Rating of 100.

(In reality, if a horse makes a new record it must run in a time faster than the record. So if it ran faster by $\frac{1}{5}$ of a second necessary to make a new record it really would receive a speed rating of 101; if $\frac{2}{5}$ faster, 102. But for the purpose here calling it 100 suffices becauses thereafter it will rate 100.)

Now I ask you to imagine a horse running on a leading track like Belmont and Aqueduct in New York; Santa Anita, Arlington Park, Monmouth Park, or Hialeah Park. Let's call this group (1) and the horse "A." The horse wins in a race for a purse of $50,000. It runs the race in time that is $\frac{4}{5}$ slower than the track record. It thus earns a speed rating of 96.

Now let's compare this performance with that of "B," on a track such as Beulah Park, Pimlico, Ellis Park, Hagerstown, Simonium, or Sunshine Park. Both horses run the same distance and in the same time off the track record where racing so both earn a speed rating of 96.

Obviously, the higher the purse distribution the tougher the competition. So let's examine this important factor for the year 1967. A true picture can be obtained by comparing the total distribution, the average daily distribution, and the average race distribution of purse money.

Track	Total Distribution	Average Daily Distribution	Average Race Distribution
Aqueduct	12,185,510	311,010	34,557
Arlington Park	1,972,350	53,379	5,933
Belmont	4,423,300	174,187	19,354
Hialeah Park	2,634,300	60,550	6,055
Monmouth Park	3,186,465	52,935	5,882
Santa Anita	4,406,825	143,256	15,917
Beulah Park	745,180	29,807	3,310
Ellis Park	555,015	14,605	4,713
Hagerstown	172,520	9,585	1,106
Pimlico	2,787,250	43,520	4,836
Timonium	296,900	24,741	2,749

Here we have horse "A" and horse "B" both running the same distance but on different tracks, in the same time *off* the respective track record, both getting a Speed Rating of 96.

By the widest stretch of the imagination can you conceive that if these two horses were entered in the race that "B" could offer any serious threat to "A"?

Because of a number of reasons such as drainage, temperature, and humidity, certain tracks are faster and make for better time than others. Research proved to my satisfaction that Santa Anita is the fastest track in America. I think you'll agree with me that it is the fastest, if you will compare its track records with other major tracks. If by reason of construction every horse that runs on a certain track is able to better its time than when it runs on any other track it does not mean the horse improved. The cause for the faster time must be attributed to the physical aid of the track surface. On the other side of the picture, consider Fair Grounds. I do not mean to say it is the slowest track in America as I have not researched for this purpose, but I will say it is a much slower track than Santa Anita.

I am taking three most representative distances for an equal test to show you the variation between tracks.

On page 59 are the times for races run in 1967 showing various distances. Where no time appears for any distance it means that distance was not run. The top line for each distance and track is the track record for that track and distance shown. The next-to-top line shows the best time made for the distance in 1967.

Aqueduct, Arlington Park, Monmouth, and Santa Anita should be grouped together as being among the highest-class tracks in America.

Beulah Park, Ellis Park, and Hagerstown are grouped as belonging to the minor league in racing.

Time appearing as 1:21–3 represents 1 minute, 21 seconds and three-fifths of a second.

Keep in mind that one-fifth ($\frac{1}{5}$) of a second is equal to one length and note the discrepancy between the track record and best time. Also bear in mind that not one but thousands of horses ran the distance to establish the best time.

Damascus was the leader in 1967 in the 3-year-old age group, ending up the season with winnings of $817,941. You'll note it took the leading horse of the year to make the record. Can anyone applying the master rule of reason, which is statistics, for one moment compare this horse with any other that made a new track record in 1967 or equalled any existing record? Damascus ran 1⅛ miles at Arlington Park in 1:46–4 and gets a speed rating of 100. At Ellis Park a horse running the same distance gets a speed rating of 100; to me it just does not make sense.

We now have two reasons to suspect that track records and speed ratings as used by players are of little or no value:

1. Records are mostly made by champions or the best performers of their era, whereas we mostly deal with average performers.

	6 f	6½ f	7 f	1 m	1⅛	1¼
Aqu	1:08–2	1:15–4	1:21–1	1:33–3	1:47–1	1:59–3
	1:09	1:15–4	1:21–3	1:33–4	1:48	2:00–1
A.P.	1:08–3	1:15	1:21	1:32–3	1:46–4*	—
	1:08–4	1:16	1:21–1	1:33–2	1:46–4	—
Mth.	1:08–2	—	—	1:37–4	1:52–1	2:02
	1:09–3	—	—	1:37–4	1:52–1	2:02
S.A.	1:08–2	1:15	1:20–3	—	1:46–3	1:58–2
	1:08–4	1:16–1	1:23–4	—	1:48–1	2:00–4
Beu	1:09–2	—	—	—	1:49–2	
	1:10–2	—	—	—	1:49–2	
EIP	1:10	1:17	—	1:36–2	1:50–1	
	1:11–2	1:19–3	—	1:39	1:51–1	
Hag	1:13	—	—	1:40		
	1:14	—	—	1:41–4		

* At Arlington Park, August 5, 1967, Damascus broke the old record for 1⅛ miles. So the new record and the Best Time is the same.

2. Some tracks are faster than others, therefore better time mostly may be due to this aid in racing and *not* to a better performance of the horse.

The basis of all speed handicapping is the track records and speed ratings. Over the years many methods of play have been offered founded upon these two statistics. All but one have been of the same ilk. This exception does take into consideration the weaknesses I have been talking about and attempts to adjust for them.

The usual application of track records and speed ratings tends to complicate and make more difficult the art of picking winning selections. Until these are promulgated upon the foundation of the following they will never be very effective:

1. In order to more efficiently attach a true value to a track record the class of horses competing at track where and when record was made must be figured.

2. Consideration must be given as to whether the fast time was or was not due to the composition of the record track.

For years I have been researching on the facts offered in this chapter. Shortly after the completion of this book, I expect to pass my findings through a computer to make a final test of them.

Think! Think!

The Kentucky Derby with a purse value of $119,700 was won in 1967 by Proud Clarion in the time of 2:00⅗. The track record for this race is 2:00, so Proud Clarion gets a speed rating of 97.

Every day many horses running for a claiming price as low as $2,500, for a purse of less than $2,500, earn the *same* Speed Rating of 97.

On the criterion of a speed rating figure *both* the Kentucky Derby winner and the lowly claiming horse performed exactly the same degree in value.

Is it logical? Does it make sense? You must agree with me that there is "something rotten in Denmark."

Please do not misunderstand me. It is not my purpose to convey that track record and speed rating figures are of no value to the player. On the contrary, they have their place in seeking winners, provided they are properly evaluated.

Thus far, I have been discussing certain fundamentals inherent in racing that are generally improperly appraised in their use for the search of winners.

A successful search for hidden treasure, diamonds, or gold, or winners requires first the removal of anything that *might* tend to obstruct their discovery. Unless you take into consideration the factors thus far revealed, it is foreshadowed that you will be led along a wrong trail. Up to now I have attempted to eliminate false trails. Little more of this is required before I get into the "meat" of the mechanics of the art of picking winners.

The essential point to remember and bear in mind at all times is that you should not give the importance and value to speed ratings that most in the racing game do. The acceptance of it on its face value is suicidal. Use it only as a minor guide.

9

Class

CLASS IS THE most dominant factor in racing.

Let me quote "Pittsburgh Phil": "Show me the man who can class horses correctly and I will show you the man who can win all the money he wants, and he needs only a dollar to start.

"Mike Dwyer said that to me years ago, and time has shown it to be one on the greatest truths ever uttered about horse racing. Class, that intangible thing that almost defies definition, controls almost positively the running of thoroughbreds! *Class enables one horse to beat another no matter what the physical odds imposed may be, what the conditions or what the distance.* You may say it is that which enables a light bull terrier to whip a big dog of another breed. It enables sometimes one fighter to whip another. As I said before, it is hard to define, but everybody discerns it, when it is there.

"In trying to define class in horse racing, the best I can do is to say that class in a horse is the ability possessed by it to carry its stipulated stake weight, take the track, and go the distance that nature intended it to go. It is heart, nerve, and ability combined, which ignores all ordinary rules and ordinary obstacles."

Here is my own personal theory of class in thoroughbreds, and I feel my conclusions are supported by plausibility. Since the class factor is one that is the most important in all races higher than the lower claiming grade of races, I shall discuss just what class really is, as well as why one horse has more of this quality than has other horses.

Class is invariably defined as "an indefinable something" that a horse is born with, a quality that no one can properly explain, yet a quality that enables a horse endowed with an abundance of class to defeat, in some inexplainable manner, any horse that happens to be less abundantly endowed with class.

If you were to ask anyone connected with the sport of racing, from the lowliest groom to the finest trainers, riders, and right up to the men in the judges' stands, just what constitutes class in a horse and just *why* a horse of superior class is able to defeat a horse of inferior class, you would unfailingly get the same stock answer: Class is something a horse is born with. Either it has it, or it hasn't got it. A horse of superior class defeats one of inferior class by simply pulling alongside and looking the horse of inferior class in the eye, and, presumably in horse language, orders the horse of inferior class to "get back where you belong, plug." So the inferior horse, beset as he is with an inferiority complex, obeys the order of his aristocratic superior and promptly retreats to the rear.

As proof of the truth of this line of thinking, the exponents of this generally accepted theory offered the fact that a horse of superior class would often defeat one of inferior class in *slower* time than the inferior class horse was able to make. Thus, a horse of inferior class, when running with horses of his own class, might, time and again, run the mile distance in something like 1:36.0 (one minute and 36 seconds) and yet be defeated by a horse of superior class in time as slow as 1:38.0. This sort of thing happens with such regularity that the standard explanation of what class is takes on the appearance of plausibility.

Still, as far back as 1918 when I first became seriously interested in horse racing, I could not accept this theory. I had been around horses all my life, had started riding first on farm horses and later on the finest Arabian stallions. My idea of class, in a horse, was largely a matter of *conformation*, not something vague and indefinable but something that you could *see*, something that you could put your finger on.

For example, put an Arabian stallion alongside of a farm horse, and it takes no expert eye to spot the class of the stallion. His beautiful conformation tells the story. You note at once that he was bred, through centuries of selective breeding, to "fly like the wind."

At the yearling sales, how do the prospective buyers distinguish between real class and ordinary race horses? What makes one horse bring a bid of $50,000 or more, while others are bid in for as little as $1,000? Yearlings are *untried* horses; no workout figures are available. You buy them on pedigree, action in the walking ring, and conformation. That's what makes for the difference in class, in race horses: breeding and conformation. On the whole, class is bred into a horse. Breed a Man O' War, a Citation to a champion mare and you have every right to expect offspring of real class; breed a horse who could never get out of the $1,000 claiming ranks to a mare of the same class and you'll get offspring that belong in the $1,000 claiming class. This is an immutable law, as any horseman knows.

Here is what an analysis of the 1967 Yearling Sales discloses. Forty-two yearlings were auctioned at prices ranging from $60,000 to the top price of $250,000. The latter price was paid for Majestic Prince, a colt bred out of Raise a Native. Ten of these 42 mentioned brought a price of more than $100,000 each.

A total of 3,375 brought an average of $6,373.64 per sale. The lowest price paid was $200. And I should judge that the largest percentage of sales at prices of $1,000 down to $200.

To get back to the fundamental issue, What makes a horse of superior class able to defeat one of inferior class? I began asking myself that question back in the early twenties, and after endless hours of research, digging through reams of statistics I came up with the one and only logical answer: Horses of superior class defeat horses of inferior class because they have greater *speed.* Yes, speed and nothing but speed. Not necessarily speed, as expressed in the final time of a race, but speed at the right time, speed when it is most needed.

That may sound like a contradictory statement, since I have just ack-knowledged that a horse of superior class will defeat an inferior horse, and do it in much slower time than the inferior horse has been making. In order to understand why this is so, it is necessary to understand the importance of the *pace* in a race, meaning the speed prevailing at the different stages of a race. The cheaper horses have just one burst of speed, one "run" as the horsemen call it. This "run" may be during the first quarter of a race, it may have to be used during the middle of a race, or it may have to be reserved for the stretch run. For that reason, the cheaper horses have to have a favorable pace in order to run a given distance in a given time. A horse who has an abundance of early speed, but no staying power, must go to the front and open up a long lead, if he is to win; a horse who does his best running in the stretch but lacks early speed, may be so badly outrun during the early part of a race that he falls too far back, and is unable to reach the leaders during the stretch run.

Cheap horses must have a favorable pace, to do their best. Horses of real class can handle any kind of a pace; they can go to the front, and stay there, or they can come from behind; they can turn on a tremendous spurt of speed, at *any* stage of the race, during the early part, at the halfway mark, or toward the finish.

It is this ability to turn on high speed, when needed, that makes for a difference in class among race horses. High speed, at the right moment, when-ever the rider calls for it, combined with enough staying power, is what gives a horse class. The more of this reserve power to turn on great speed, when it is needed, without "burning up," without becoming extremely fatigued, the more of this quality a horse has, the higher his class; the less a horse has of this reserve power, the lower his Class.

What happens, then, when a horse of superior class defeats one of a lesser class is this. At some stage of the race, the class horse pulls alongside of the lower class horse, and cuts loose with blistering speed for a short distance, speed that is beyond the capability of the lower class horse to cope with, without "burning out." The lower class horse tries to match strides with the better class horse, for a short distance, but this extra effort takes so much out of the cheaper horse that he has nothing more left and will therefore finish the remaining part of the race in much slower time than he customarily makes, when racing with horses of his own class.

And, right there you have the whole answer to this thing called "class." When a cheap horse is forced to go at a pace that, even for a short distance, puts an excessive strain on him, that extra effort burns up what little he has of reserve power and energy and he slows down at a far greater rate than he would through normal tiring, as is the case when he is not pushed beyond the limits of his capabilities. A horse of high class has enough of this reserve power to be able to turn out bursts of tremendous speed at *any* stage of the race without using his last ounce of energy, and thus burning himself out.

Further than that, painstaking research covering all races run over a period of years, thousands upon thousands of races, has proved beyond a shadow of doubt that speed and class, while not the one and same thing, always go hand in hand. The simple reason why a $2,500 horse, at the top of his form, does not and indeed *cannot* defeat an $8,000 horse who is also at the top of his form is because the $8,000 horse can *run* faster. And the reason why $8,000 horses do not defeat high class allowance and handicap horses is simply that the higher class horses can and do run faster *at the right time!*

Now, throughout this book, as well as any of my other works, I do not ask you to ever accept anything that I say, solely upon the strength of my word. I'll never ask you to accept anything that I say, unless I can prove to you that my statements are grounded in facts, provable facts. And you can prove to your own satisfaction that horses of higher class do run faster than horses of lower class, by simply comparing the time figures of a representative group of horses in each class range. Do so, at any one major track and only at one track at a time. And use the actual time figures, never the speed ratings. The reason for sticking to one track is that there is a difference in the speed and the very same horses run races in faster or slower time, at different tracks, owing to the difference in speed of the racing strips. So, compare the time figures of horses in the different class ranges, at any one major track (not the speed ratings, which are highly inaccurate) and this is what you will find: there will be a difference of about one-fifth of a second in the time made by horses in the different class ranges.

By different class ranges, I mean a difference in claiming price of $2,500, in claiming races. Thus, the different class ranges would run $2,500, $7,500, $10,000, and so on up to the allowance and handicap divisions. Stick to claiming races, for now, because some allowance races, even at major tracks, may be made up of $5,000 horses while others are made up of $10,000 to $25,000 horses. Use the time of a group of horses, in each class range, not just an individual horse and then figure the average time made by each group, then compare this average time of horses in one class division with the average time of horses in another class division and you'll find that for each $2,500 difference in class there will be about one-fifth difference in speed, all the way from the cheapest claimers up to the finest stake and handicap horses.

This difference in time will be less noticeable at the shorter distances, more pronounced as the distance gets longer, for it is at the longer distances that class has its most telling effect. This is because the more class a horse has, the more he is able to carry his speed over a distance of ground, the real test of class. Class always has been correctly indicated as being able to run *fast* and *far*, even by those who never could define class, itself. The real test of high class has always been, always will be, the ability to carry high speed over a distance of ground. Cheap horses cannot carry their speed, anywhere near proportionately so, beyond the *sprints*: as the distance gets longer their time figures get proportionately slower and slower.

For example, a high-class horse who can get 6 furlongs, equal to ¾ mile, in the time of 1:09.0 (1 minute, 9 seconds) should get the 1¼ mile distance in 2 minutes flat. A cheap horse who barely is able to get 6 furlongs in 1:12 (3 seconds slower) will be all out to run the 1¼ mile distance in 2:07.0. This means that the cheap horse is 3 seconds slower at 6 furlongs, but 7 seconds slower at the 1¼ mile distance. That's why, at all major tracks, where the finer horses run, while all track records for distances run by the high-class horses are held by horses of high class, it is particularly true that *all* records at distances of 1 mile, or longer, be they track records, American Records, or World Records, are invariably held by the champions and near-champions of the turf: undisputable proof that speed and class go hand in hand. And proof that the true measure of class is the ability to run *fast* and *far*.

In the *sprints*, however, the margin of speed that separates the class divisions is smaller, and the shorter the distance is, the less noticeable becomes the difference in speed. Even cheap horses can run fast for a short distance. At the 3-furlong distance, there is but a difference in time of 1 to 2 seconds between the cheapest and the finest; at 6 furlongs, there is a difference in time of 3 to 4 seconds; at the 1¼ mile distance, there is a difference between cheap claimers and stake horses of from 6 to 8 seconds. This is not a matter of mere theory, but provable facts, verified through examination of thousands of time figures of actual races.

What class in a race horse really is offers the most difficult dilemma to solve. Perhaps using one of my horses, Jim's Niece, as an instrument, class may be more readily understood.

This horse seemed to possess everything that is necessary for high class. She was well bred with Epinard, a great international horse of its time, her paternal grandsire. (Epinard was invited from France to participate here in three special races arranged for him during the Hildreth-Sinclair Stable era. He would have won all three except for bad breaks. I believe he won one of these races and ran second in the other two.) Jim's Niece had plenty of speed. She was a "jewel of consistency," running every race in fast time within ⅕ seconds of all her races. She was extremely game and *no* horse that ever tried to stay (running neck to neck) with her at any time in the race failed to be beaten by her.

It was common talk among jockeys that anyone could win on Jim's Niece. I'll never forget what one jockey said. He contended you could tie a bag of oats on her back and she would *run her own race and win*. Sammy Renick, who rode her more times than any other rider, told me she liked to run her own race and would pick her way and he always let her run the way she wanted. She seemed born to race and loved it. In the paddock when being saddled she stood erect never making a move. But her head was held high! Her ears were cocked! Her eyes without movement stared out looking at the racing strip! Watching her you'd swear she knew what was coming and eagerly wanted the race to begin.

She had every quality that is inherent in every horse of real class. Why then did she never graduate from the lower claiming class? I think I know the right answer!

Jim's Niece was "pigeon-toed." Standing in front of a horse the hooves of the front feet will be facing straight forward. Her hoofs turned in and this is known as being "pigeon-toed." She had to be carefully shod because of this. If not, in full stride she would strike her rear legs.

She possessed every ingredient necessary for class. But she just did not have it. If she did, she would have undoubtedly been one of the top-notch horses of her time. Because she possessed all the necessary potentialities of great class is the reason her breeder, Arnold Hanger, wanted her as a brood mare after she was retired from racing. I do not know how many horses she foaled but one of them had plenty of class, broke a track record in California, and won considerable money for Mr. Hanger, but for some reason had a short-lived career.

Remember about Jim's Niece being pigeon-toed because later I shall tell some informative and interesting things about it.

10

Relative Rank of Races

MOST PERPLEXING TO the vast majority of players is how to grade into relative importance the different classes of races. They are impossible to be scientifically evaluated in specific gradations. At best, they can be roughly grouped only, no matter how meticulously and methodically an attempt be made.

Before the advent of organized race meetings, sportsmen owning speedy horses would each put a certain amount of money into a pot to be contested for. This money was not divided between the three first horses but given to the winner. Such races were called "sweepstakes." This term is seldom used today. It has become shortened to "stakes" races.

Stakes are the top ranking of all races. Unfortunately for the player there are different classes of stakes. Subject to rules of The Jockey Club, handicap, allowance, special weight, scale of weight, or weight-for-age may also be classed as a stakes.

Rule 9, in the Rules of Racing of The Jockey Club, states:

A "sweepstakes" is a race in which *stakes are to be made of the owners of the horses engaged, and is still a sweepstakes when *money or other prize is added, but, within the meaning of this rule, no *overnight race, whatever its conditions, shall be considered as a sweepstakes.

*Stakes made by the owners consists of the fees paid by them to engage their horses. Other money or prize means a cup or plate and added money put into the pot by the Racing Associations. *Overnight means entries made 72 hours before race is scheduled.

I think to make it more readily comprehensible as to what this rule means, giving the actual condition of the following races will best serve the purpose.

The most fascinating race to me has always been a "Futurity." It derives its name from the fact that a horse is entered now to run in the long *future*. Just keep in mind that the age of a horse is reckoned as beginning on the first of January in the year it was foaled. Thus a horse born January 20, or March 15, or April 5 would be considered as its birth occuring January 1. This arbitrary date is, of course, used for practical purposes. In 1923 there were 2,763 foals registered with The Jockey Club. Incomplete figures for 1967 show

21,385 registered. You can imagine the confusion if the actual age of a horse had to be figured for over 21,000 foals. Hence, this sensible and practical arrangement.

On September 23, 1967, at Aqueduct, the seventy-eighth running of the Futurity took place. I am placing an asterisk (*) before certain conditions of the race. This is for the purpose of your being able to refer to them as I discuss them after concluding the conditions of the race.

1967 Conditions—Futurity Stakes

7th race, Aqu. 6½ furlongs. Scale weights.* 75,000 added.* 2-year-olds nominated to the Futurities of 1967 by a joint payment of $30 each Aug. 16, 1965.* To continue eligibility,* the following payments must be made to The New York Racing Association Inc.: by Nov. 1, 1966, $50 each; by Aug. 1, 1967, $200 each. (Fillies that have been kept eligible for the Matron* of 1967 may be made eligible for the Futurity of 1967 not later than Aug. 1, 1967, upon payment of $250 each.) Starters to pay $1,500 additional, with $75,000 added by the New York Racing Association Inc.; of which $4,000 to the nominator of the winner;* and to the nominator of the second and third horses, $2,000 and $1,000 respectively. The balance, together with one-third of the nominating fees to the Futurities of 1967 and all further eligibility payments and starting fees, to be divided 65 percent, 20 percent, 10 percent, and 5 percent to the owners of the first, second, third, and fourth horses, respectively. Weight, 122 lbs.* A Gold Medallion Trophy will be presented to the owner of the winner and trophies to the winning trainer and jockey. Closed August 16, 1965, with 1,037 nominations at $10 of which 493 remained eligible after Nov. 1, 1966, paying an additional $50 each.* On Aug. 1, 1967, 111 remained eligible after a further fee of $200; 20 fillies eligible for the Matron were nominated for the Futurity at $250 each. Value of race $146,220. Value to winner $90,493; second $27,844; third $13,922, fourth $6,961.

1. *Scale weights. The Jockey Club promulgates what is known as a scale of weights. This establishes the weight that must be carried for every distance run; for every age group; and for every month of the year—from January to December, inclusive. The inquiring mind may wonder why a weight penalty should be influenced by the month of the year. I previously told you to keep in mind the birthday of horses. A horse may be foaled in June contrasted to one foaled in January. For racing purposes they are both considered the *same* age. But in reality there is a spread of six months in age between them. Realizing this inequity an attempt is made to equalize it by increasing weight by months as horses get older and improve in their development. (Note: The scale of weights is frequently published in the *Telegraph* and the *Racing Form*.)

2. *$75,000 added. In addition to all fees paid by the owners of the horses nominated, the racing association where the race is scheduled throws added money into the pot, to increase its total purse value.

3. *Aug. 16, 1965. A fee of $10 must be paid when the horse is first nominated. The horse is nominated when its dam shows she is in foal. So keep in mind—for future reference, as I shall discuss it later—that the horse is entered for this future race even before it is born. The nominator has up to Aug. 16, 1965, to pay $30. If it is not paid by that date the nomination ceases to be eligible and the horse is dropped by the association.

4. *The Matron. The age of horses *both* for the Futurity and the Matron calls for 2-year-olds. However, in The Futurity it does not designate what sex is required. Therefore any sex can be entered. But the Matron is scheduled for fillies so no other sex is permissible. Consequently, an owner can race his horse in both these races provided he meets all conditions required.

5. *Purses are allotted to the nominators of the three horses that finish in the money in this stakes race. The nominator is naturally the owner of the mare in foal. By auction or private sale he may sell this mare before the foal is born. Or he may sell the foal any time before it races in the Futurity. In any event, he receives the purse allotted for this purpose and it does not go to the owner of the horse at the time of the race.

6. *Weight 122 lbs. If this race instead of being a straight stake race was a *handicap stake* the weight to be carried would be assigned by the track secretary to equalize the chances of all in the race. (More about this later when all classes of races will be reviewed.) But in straight stakes, the weight is determined by the scale of weights.

7. *Closed Aug. 16, 1965. On this date no further nominations to this race were accepted. Note this is *two years* before the race was actually run. Also note that continued payments had to be made, the last payment, of $200, due by Aug. 1, 1967—*seven weeks* before the race was scheduled to take place.

And you'll note that covering a period of three years, fees had to continue in order for the nominated horse to run in this race. Even so, a further fee of $1,500 had to be paid if the horse was to actually start.

This particular race was won by Captain's Gig at odds of $3.40 to $1.00 or a mutuel of $8.80. He won by three lengths and established a new track record of 1:15⅘. The former record was made in 1963 and was 1:16.

Reviewing the Futurity Stakes race rings an echo in my memory. In Chapter 3, I related that one of my greatest thrills in racing came from betting on the winner of a race that paid over 100 to 1. I now am inclined to think the *payoff* was over $100.00 and the odds were not over 100 to 1 but over 50 to 1. I mention this only because now I recall the name of the horse. It was Nellie Flag who won the Matron Stakes futurity in 1935.

The study and analysis of this Futurity Stakes and what transpired from the day a mare came into foal until the race was run is almost a complete education by itself in the art of picking winners.

The cost in fees for each horse that actually ran in this race was respectively $10, $30, $50, $200, and $1,500, for a total of $1,790. A horseman has a horse serviced in the stud and when he finds the mare in foal he figures the blood lines in the pedigree have potentialities of producing a very good horse. So he has nothing but a $10 bill to lose by immediately nominating the foal in the futurity race, which he proceeds to do. He has no way of knowing whether the expected foal will be male or female.

So he literally places two arrows in his bow and pays $10 to nominate the foal in each race, that is in the Futurity and in the Matron. If the mare miscarries, or if for any other reason a good foal is not produced he has risked only $20 which means little, in view of the possibilities present in the developing drama.

Within a few months, August 1, he is faced with the payment of the first eligible fee. By this time he has been able to assess the conformation of the foal. If it is lacking in any respect as to the specifications he requires, he does not pay the fee and just forgets what he had hoped for.

By November 1, 1966—more than a year later—he must make the decision whether or not to pay the $50 fee required by that date. Keep in mind that at this date the horse is a yearling and has never raced. So what the owner does must still be predicated upon his judgment of horse flesh.

Then comes August 1, 1967. Now the horse is a 2-year-old and has been to the races. On the basis of how this horse has performed up to about seven weeks before the race it has long been prepped for the owner makes his decision. He has seven weeks longer to decide if he will pay the final fee of $1,500 to start in the race.

At closing date of Aug. 1965, there were 1,037 possible starters.
By Nov. 1966 there were 493 possible starters.
By Aug. 1967 there were 111 possible starters.
By Sept. 1967 there were 6 possible starters.

Only 6 started out of 1,037 entered! What happened to the other 1,031 originally nominated? What a drama! What a story a good fiction writer could produce on these related facts.

1,037 Entered—6 Run

Out of the total horses nominated for this race only six actually participated in the race. What happened to the other 1,031?

Between the dates of August 1965 and August 1967 there were only 111 nominees left. One can only speculate as to what happened to the other 926. In the interim, between these two dates, some of them had become incapacitated for innumerable reasons. Most of them had shown to their connections—owner, trainer—that they were not of sufficient caliber to compete in the Futurity.

But right up until seven weeks before the race was to be run, 111 of the original nominees had proved the owners thought well enough of their chances to pay a further entry fee of $200 on them.

Now coming down to the wire only six owners thought their horses had a possible chance to win this race and were willing to gamble, by paying $1,500 to start, thought they had a good chance, if not to win, to be in the money.

We can relegate to the past and forget about all but the 111 horses. They had proved that the envisoned theoretical possibilities they represented were sound or the next to final fee of $200 would never have been paid on them.

Clear reasoning justifies the assumption that these 111 horses have real class of the type that wins the better races. The horse player should keep track of these for future play. This can easily be done because long before the Futurity is run the names of the 111 nominees will be published in newspapers and the racing papers. These horses reveal to the knowing player what the public does not know. It is not shown in the past performances and thus gives him an ace in the hole. Past performances will not indicate to the public the total fees paid. You know the horse has to have class. And as time passes, these horses will be entered in races where the competition is infinitely less keen.

But even more important is that especially the six horses that actually did compete in the race should be regarded as future playing prospects. Even though not all won or ran in the money, they represent horses with real class. And when they are entered thereafter in overnight handicaps or allowance races, they should be carefully considered.

I know many players do not like the idea of listing horses and watching for them to run in a future race. However, I doubt if there is a single successful player who does not follow this procedure to some extent. And let me assure you that some of the best bets of my career were made and won on this method of waiting.

It should be apparent from what has appeared in this chapter that one of the important necessities for success in picking winners is the reading of the "conditions" which appears at the head of the past performances of every race run. It is so important that a complete chapter will be devoted to the subject.

However, I feel many would be interested in the conditions of the most famous race in the world, the Kentucky Derby, followed by the second highest valued race run in 1937, the Garden State Stakes. Note: The richest race run in this country in 1967 was the Arlington-Washington Futurity with a value of $371,750; Garden State Stakes had a value of $314,535.

Conditions—Kentucky Derby 1967

7 C. D. May 6, 1967, 1-1/4 Miles. Ninety-third running Kentucky Derby. Scale weights, $125,000 added. 3-year-olds. By subscription of $100 each in cash which covers nomination for both the Kentucky Derby and Derby Trial. All nomination fees to Derby winner. $500 to pass entry box, $1,000 additional to start, $135,000 added of which $25,000 to second, $12,500 to

third, $5,000 to fourth, $100,000 guaranteed to winner (to be divided equally in event of a dead heat). Weight 126 lbs. The owner of the winner to receive a gold trophy. A nomination may be withdrawn before time of closing nominations. Closed Wednesday, Feb. 15, 1967, with 162 nominations. Value of Race $162,000. Value to winner $119,700; second $25,000; third $12,500; fourth $5,000.

This was the race in which Damascus, the favorite, ran third. The winner was Proud Clarion, paying $62.20 in the time of 2:00 $\frac{3}{5}$, $\frac{3}{5}$ths slower than the track record.

Conditions—Garden State Stakes 1967

8 G. S. November 18, 1967, 1-1/16 miles. Fifteenth running Garden State. Scale weights. $125,000 added. 2-year-olds. By subscription of $25 each if made on or before Aug. 15, 1966, or $40 each if made after Aug. 15, 1966, and on or before Dec. 15, 1966, fee to accompany the nomination or the entry shall be void. To remain eligible, the following cash payments must be made: March 15, 1967, $125 each; June 15, 1967, $250 each; $1,000 to pass the entry box and $1,000 to start.* The Garden State Racing Association to add $125,000. The added money together with all nomination fees, eligibility payments, entry and starting fees for the Garden State of 1967 to be divided 60 percent to first, 20 percent to second, 10 percent to third, 5 percent to fourth; with 5 percent for nominators' awards to be distributed as follows: 60 percent, 20 percent, 13 percent, and 7 percent to the nominator of the first, second, third, and fourth horses respectively. A supplementary made subsequent to an original that became ineligible, the nominators' award will be distributed to the original nominator.* Colts and geldings, 122 lbs.: fillies, 119 lbs. The first four finishers in the Garden State are automatically made eligible for the Jersey Derby of 1968 as to nominating fee. Closed Aug. 15, 1966, with 763 nominations at $25 each. Final closing Dec. 15, 1966, with 174 nominations at $40 each, of which 456 made the second payment of $125 each on March 15, 1967, and 238 made the final payment of $250 each on June 15, 1967. *Supplementary entries, made at the closing time of entries by the payment of a fee of $10,000 each, closed with two nominations.* Value of race $314,535. Value to winner $188,721; second, $62,907; third, $31,453.50; fourth, $15,726.75; nominators' awards, $15,726.25.

*$1,000 must be paid at the time the horse is actually entered in the race.
*A supplementary here means this: A horse that was originally nominated became ineligible because the continued payments were not made. This same horse may again be nominated by a different owner but the nominator's award will not be paid to him but to the owner at the time the horse was originally nominated.
*Two supplementary nominations were made at a fee of $10,000 each. This means for all practical purposes that at the time of the race the owners and trainers of these two horses wagered $10,000 their horses would win or place in the money.

A sum of this magnitude is not peanuts to anyone. Even should a supplementary entered horse not win or show in the money, invariably it will win later races, especially where less competition is encountered. But these horses may make a poor showing in this race. On this showing the public and selectors will assess their findings and because of this often these horses pay a big price far greater than their winning chances indicate.

If you keep track of these horses you have an edge on the public because it is one chance out of a million that they will stop to consider the owner and trainer thinks well enough of this horse to wager $10,000 on it. Let me put it this way. If you were alongside of Hirsch Jacobs, Max Hirsh, or any of the great trainers and saw one of them bet $10,000 on his own horse, what would you do? And if the horse lost would you not watch for it to again run and bet it? (Incidentally, Hirsch Jacobs was never a betting man. To the best of my knowledge, he never bet and if he did, it was a *very* small nominal bet made for sentimental reasons.)

The same recommendations I suggested for players, following an analysis of the Futurity Stakes, applies to both the Kentucky Derby and the Garden State Stakes as well as to all the top purse classic races. Practically every horse that runs in these races can be used as a future guide and key to winners.

I have spoken thus far about using these races for future purposes. However, after I have completed the spade work necessary to understand the fundamentals before proceeding to the actual making of winning selections, I will have a most important chapter on race conditions. In this current chapter conditions of a race that has already been run are discussed. For more practical purposes a prestudy of race conditions, before the race is run, will be analyzed. You'll learn that one single word or figure in the conditions can change the whole aspect of the real actual class of a horse that will compete.

From a perusal of the syntheses given in the three preceding stakes charts it will be apparent to all who read it that stakes rank highest in the order of importance. It is an anomaly and paradox that the purse value of a race does not inevitably signify the importance of a race. The quality of the class of a race depends upon the quality of the horses participating in it.

There are so many ramifications to all grades of races that at best their listing in order of importance can only be approximately and roughly arranged.

1. *Stakes.* These are run under scale weight rules. To distinguish a stakes look at top of conditions and it will say scale weights.

2. *Handicap.* This means the weights are assigned by the Track Secretary in an attempt to make the chances of all in the race equal. Example: Gazelle *handicap.*

3. *Allowances.* For all practical purposes allowances is synonymous with weights. The instrumentality of a certain prescribed amount of money won or number of races is applied and thus determines the weight to be carried. Example: Gotham *allowances.*

4. *Claiming Races.* These may be any claiming price from $1,200 to *any* amount and frequently are for $25,000; $40,000 and higher.

On the star tracks such as those in New York, in order to up-grade the quality of competition the minimum claiming race is for $3,000. The track association rule is: "Entries will not be accepted for any horse that has started for a claiming price of less than $3,000, unless winning for a claiming price of $3,500 or more, since starting for less than $3,000."

Thus a horse that had been running at one of the cheaper tracks for $1,500 or $2,500 or anything less than $3,000 would not be accepted on a New York track unless it had won at a claiming price of at least $3,500 since it had raced at less than $3,000.

The point is obvious here, but it needs meticulous thought to appreciate. A horse has been running in claimers and not winning is steadily dropped down the claiming scale. It may have started at $6,000 and gotten down to where it may or may not have won at a claiming price of less than $3,000. Whether it had won or lost is immaterial; it would not be accepted for entry at New York tracks.

Let us assume this horse had run for a claiming price as low as $2,000. Now it begins to improve and finally wins a race in a $3,500 or higher claiming race. If this win took place after it had raced for $3,000 or less it would be eligible for entry.

The minimum claiming price race is established by every racing association and is predicated upon the purse distribution at their respective tracks.

5. *Optional Claiming Race.* While this is a claiming race the difference is that in a straight claiming race every horse in that race is subject to being claimed, subject of course to claiming rules in force. However, in an optional claimer a horse may be entered in either category, that is, the owner can select to enter the horse to be claimed or not to be claimed. Hence it is optional.

You must distinguish in the past performances whether or not the horse can be claimed. Here is how you do it. If the horse can be claimed a small "o" follows the amount it can be claimed for: 6000°.

If the horse is not subject to be claimed, small "o" precedes its claiming price: °6000.

Let me set forth the actual conditions of an Optional Claimer 3rd race, Oaklawn Park, March 1968.

> 6 Furlongs. Optional claiming. Purse $3,800. 4-year-olds and upward entered to be claimed for $4,500 and those which have started for a claiming price of $4,500 or less and have not won a race for a claiming price over $4,500 than claiming since last starting for $4,500 or less. Weight, 122 lbs. Nonwinners of two races in 1969 allowed 4 lbs; a race, 7 lbs. *If entered to be claimed for $4,500, allowed 4 lbs.*

Observe that in addition to weight allowances given under the conditions that if the horse is entered to be claimed for $4,500 it can have an *additional* allowance of 4 lbs.

I cannot urge too strongly that each reader send to the *Morning Telegraph* or to the *Daily Racing Form* and ask for the free booklet on "How to Read Charts and Past Performances." But enclose 10¢ for mailing costs. Without an intimate knowledge of the past performances no man can succeed at playing the races any more than a builder could build a house without a foundation.

With your indulgence, I should like to recapitulate the main features of this chapter. Prior to the running of the classic races a list of horses to run in each such event is published on sports pages and in the racing papers. Note those horses that do not run. All the horses eligible for these events are of above average class. You should always give them a little edge in considering them relating to other horses in a race. I refer particularly when they are entered in allowance races.

11

Spot Plays— Winning Patterns

THERE ARE THREE most generally used ways of playing the races. The first way is to attempt to play every race on the card. Those who follow this practice defy the realities of making profits and failure is foreshadowed! The exigencies of every race are dissimilar. The conditions of the race, the price possibilities must be taken into consideration, and when not favorable the race passed.

The second method is to await a "spot." Only when clearly perceived possibilities such as a *good spot* is a play made. Players of this inclination are willing to pass up races and do not have to have action in every race.

The third method is to watch for "spotted" horses and play only these.

Spot horses and spot playing are not synonymous as I use the term. By spot horses I refer to a horse that after meticulously being observed in a certain race is watched for it to be *entered in the future* and then played provided it meets the requirements of the particular factor or factors applied to discover the play.

By spot playing I mean all races on the card are studied and only if a certain horse is well placed or over priced is it played.

The difference in use of spot playing and spot plays is that with the former daily observation is made for a play; and with the latter, play is spotted for future play.

There is only one justification for playing every or nearly every race on the card. This is when a strictly mechanical system is being used such as playing the favorite using the proper betting method. I am speaking of the serious player who wants to win at racing. What I've said does not apply to the occasional visitor to the track who bets small amounts and whose primary purpose is for enjoyment. There is little enjoyment watching a race without betting on one of the contenders.

The argument advanced by those who do not like to watch for a spot horse to be entered is mostly that there is not enough action. They do not seem to realize that this lack need not necessarily be true. Suppose you have more than one method of discovering a play. It is possible to have as many plays and as much action as desired once this method is properly grasped and directed.

I am sure that every reader has at some time played a horse and whether it won or lost made up his mind then and there to play this horse again some time in the future. There are a multitude of reasons why this decision developed. You liked the way the horse performed; thought it had a bad ride; felt with better racing luck it would have won the race, in the case of any that lost, and so on.

I am as sure as anything I believe in, in racing, that not a single professional play and not a successful player exists that does not make spot plays. The histories of all the great famous plungers is replete with incidents of their biggest winnings resulting from this type of play.

Perhaps the words of "Pittsburgh Phil" will best illustrate what I am trying to convey. Quote: "During the running of the race my glasses never leave the horses engaged. *I see every move they make.* I can see that this one is not in his stride, or is running unnaturally, or is being ridden poorly. I can see if a horse is sulking, what horse is fit, what horse is unfit." After the race is run, it is sometimes said a horse has had a bad ride, or that the trainer has has sent him to the post in unfit condition or anything and everything, except the truth.

"The race is run, let us say. The shouts of the winners and the groans of the losers die away. From the grandstand there comes a rush of men on their way to the betting ring. Some to cash their wagers and others to make wagers on the next race. The horses which have been the object of all their hopes a minute before are forgotten by the multitude. They are pulled up on the back stretch, turn and canter back to the stewards, the jockeys dismount, by permission, and the animals are turned over to their handlers with no more than a little perfunctory applause from the grandstand. I say the multitude has forgotten, the multitude generally, but there are some men at the track to whom this period is of the utmost importance. You will see these men along the rail close to the judge's stand, or up in the big stand with their eyes glued to their field glasses. (Note: The procedure "Phil" relates here would be confined to the area where the returning horses are unsaddled. In these times the judges' stand is located on top of the grandstand at the finish line.) I have heard the uninformed say, when observing this: 'That man is still running the race.' It is not necessary to reply to such remarks. I want to know how a horse pulls up after a race, how the effort has affected him, whether he has won easily without calling upon his reserve power or whether he was distressed and all in. Many a time one horse has beaten another by a length or two, but with an expenditure of effort that told, while the beaten horse was not palpably distressed. It will take considerable time for the winner to recover from his effort. The second horse will be improved by the race. The physical makeup of horses has much to do with this. There are some light-barreled horses, mares particularly, who feel the effects of a race more than others. Suppose such a mare was entered in a race two or three days later, against practically the same field, being convinced that the strain had taken its toll I might bet, other conditions being favorable, on the horse that ran second, or even third."

Winning Patterns

The dictionary definition for "Pattern" is: "a good example—a model from which to copy." And let me tell you if the models I am about to discuss are followed there is no better way to get winners. Invariably, these winners are overpriced since the related facts are completely unknown to the public. I might say also unknown to public selectors, otherwise they would not go off at such overlay payoffs.

In disclosing these patterns herein, I will give examples of horses that I have wagered on and have records of. This means the races were run in the past. However, any one who has read thus far knows by now that the element of time is immaterial, because *if a premise is sound it will function equally well now and in the future as it did in the past.*

Claim Pattern

First let's discuss the horse First Lead, the past performances which follow:

First Lead

Date	Claiming Price	Finish	Beaten Lengths
28 Jun 60—2 Bel	5500	1 WON paid $37.40	
23 Jun 60—8 Bel	c4200	4	3¼
13 Jun 60—2 Bel	4000	8	8½
23 May 60—9 Aqu	4500	5	7¾
17 May 60—8 Bel	4600	3	1¾
7 May 60—1 Aqu	4611	1	
22 Apr 60—3 Aqu	c3500	1	
19 Feb 60—2 Hia	7500	5	6¾
21 Jan 60—4 Hia	7500	5	8¾
6 Jan 60—6 TrP	6500	2	nk
1 Jan 60—6 TrP	6250	3	¾

On June 28, it ran in 2nd race at Belmont for $5,500 and won paying $37.40.

Note by the small *c* before claiming price that this horse was claimed twice. The secret of this pattern is not that the horse was claimed but *why* it was claimed. Starting early in January, First Lead ran well for $6,200 and $6,500 but when raised to $7,500 ran miserably. On April 22 it was entered for $3,500 —a big drop from $7,500. It won this race by 1½ lengths and was claimed.

It is normal for a claim to occur only when a horse has been dropped considerably in claiming price. Nothing to be concerned about here.

It then ran well for two races at $4,600, first winning and then running third, beaten only 1¾ lengths. Then on May 23 it ran 5th, beaten 7¾ lengths, followed by running 8th, beaten ½ length on June 13. Thus we have two very miserable races and the *last even worse than the first*. Note that after the June 13 race despite its miserable race it was raised in claiming price on June 23 and claimed. This claim exposes the secret and gives you the key with which to unlock the treasure chest.

Keep in mind that the claimer of the horse for $4,200 *did not know* where the horse would finish in this race. The claim had to be put into the secretary's office with the $4,200 at least fifteen minutes before post time for that race.

Now, for a horseman to see a horse perform miserably, each time at a reduced claiming price, then see it raised in price and invest $4,200 in buying it, he had to have a lot of confidence. Under normal circumstances of claiming this would not be considered a good claim. This trainer had to base his judgment on insider information, such as a stable leak, or on observing the horse in action and feeling he could improve on its running.

This offers a definite pattern which you should be on the lookout for at all times. The important thing to remember is a horse well beaten for $4,500, then worse beaten for $4,000, then running its next race at a higher claiming price and claimed for this higher price. Seldom will you lose betting this horse after the claim.

Jet Joy

31 Aug 60—5 AP	6000	1	$21.40
4 Aug 60—6 AP	6500	8	13
25 Jly 60—5 AP	7500	4	3
18 Jly 60—3 AP	7500	4	7½
6 Jly 60—6 AP	7500	4	1¼
29 Jun 60—6 Was	c6000	5	3
22 Jun 60—3 Was	6000	5	8
9 Jun 60—4 Was	c4500	1	
26 May 60—9 Was	5000	5	5¾
19 May 60—2 Was	4000	2	9
6 May 60—6 CD	5000	5	8¼

Jet Joy was claimed on June 29 after a raise in price of $1,500 since its last winning race and, what is really important, immediately after running 5th beaten 8 lengths on June 22 for the same price as it is being claimed. You recognize the pattern, I'm sure.

On August 31, it ran in 5th race at AP for $6,000 and won, paying $21.40.

Observe that both of these horses were each claimed twice. Irrespective of raise or drop in placing two horsemen thought enough of the potentialities of them to invest several thousands of dollars. Therefore, if you spot these horses your judgment is fortified by the confirmation of two horsemen who have come by their expertise by making their living relative to the subject.

Note in the case of First Lead that it won the next race on May 7 after being claimed, even though it went up in claiming price.

However, Jet Joy required four unproductive tries before it won. Don't let this discourage you. Suppose you had wagered on these four misses. Wasn't it well worth the try when you won $21.40 or $13.40 net profit? I'll bet you have lost four races in a row and that if you did win on the fifth try you did not make as good a net profit.

There is still another guide and key:

Whenever such horses, after being claimed, fail to win but eventually are dropped down around their claimed price, and especially below it, they are most frequently sure winners.

The elucidation of all puzzled by the task of recognizing the distinct difference between this patterned claim and the normal claim requires a comparison of the normal claim. So let's survey the record of the following:

Everetts Pride

			Finish	
25 Jly 60—5 AP	c7500	1		
2 Jly 60—6 Was	10000	8	8	
25 Jun 60—6 Was	9000	6	6	
16 Jun 60—6 Was	c7000	1		
18 May 60—7 Was	10500	5	6	
1 May 60—6 CD	7500	1		
26 Apr 60—5 Kee	c5500	5	3½	
23 Apr 60—7 Kee	7000	5	4	
19 Apr 60—5 Kee	9000	6	10	
13 Apr 60—5 Kee	10000	8	14	
15 Mar 60—6 OP	Allowance	7	11	

Everetts Pride is the usual type of claim. Starting in an allowance race it continually dropped down in class. Contrasted to the other two examples I have shown, although it was claimed three times, each time it was at a lower price than since its previous win, thus meeting less competition. The other two were claimed at a higher claiming price, where the competition is keener after their previous wins.

The fact that Everetts Pride was claimed three times indicated three knowledgeable horsemen were high on it and this should be considered. My policy with this horse would be when going over daily entries to watch for it and any time it was entered for less than $10,000 I would consider it a probable winner if placed right and would give it meticulous thought—provided the price was right.

Age Pattern

The birthday of *all* horses is January 1, of each year. This is an arbitrary date, applied because it would be impractical to figure the individual birthday of thousands in training. Horses are born (foaled) over a period of *many* months. Thus a horse foaled in January is properly one year old the following January. But what of horses foaled in May, June, July—sometimes even later? Instead of their being 12 months, or one year, old the following January, they may be only 6 months old.

In the case of humans this may have little bearing since their average life span is about 62 years or 744 months. However, the average *racing span of life* for a race horse is about 6 years or 72 months, so that even six months is *nearly* 10 percent of a horse's useful racing career. This should indicate the *importance of age under certain conditions.*

A horse does not reach maturity of age until it is 4 years old. The prime of a horse's life, referring to race horses only, is at the 4- and 5-year-old state. Now, you do not send a boy to do a man's work; nor can you expect an immature horse to compete with older horses. This fact is so well recognized that races are carded for 2-year-olds exclusively, 3-year-olds exclusively, and then for 4-year-olds and upward.

A 3-year-old must be exceptionally good to compete with older horses, therefore early in the racing season you find races for 3-year-olds exclusively. However, as the season progresses into fall and winter you find mostly races for 3-year-olds and upward. The theory is that a 3-year-old approaching his 4-year-old birthday can now handle older horses.

Now, if all horses were foaled on the same date this theory would work out better than it actually does. But since there may be such a wide variation between horses in the same age group, it is apparent that this theory has many advantages. The false conclusion has been drawn that whereas it is not wise to play a 3-year-old against older horses up to certain months, it is all right later in the season.

In the past, I have disagreed with accepted theories in racing that have existed for hundreds of years. Readers of my writings will know whether or not I have been correct in my personal conclusions. The fact that my writings are so well recommended and are in constant demand, even many years after their publication, would seem to indicate my own conclusions have been proved correct. *Once again, I now disagree* with the idea that it is good judgment to play a 3-year-old against older horses later in the racing season.

Race Chart of Cosmic Boy, 2nd Race A.P., September 3, 1960

Horse	Age	Finish	Lengths
Kope's Hope	8	1	neck
Noble Greer	5	2	1
Cosmic Boy	3	3	
Rac'g W'ch Dog	4	4	
Rimente	4	5	
Miss Wooddch'k	4	6	
Mackey Boy	7	7	
Beau Tacer	4	8	
Little Dip	4	9	

Cosmic Boy ran 3rd, beaten only by a neck and 1 length by a 5- and an 8-year-old horse. Here are the chart caller's comments in this race. "Noble Greer survived a claim of four lodged by rider of Cosmic Boy for *alleged interference through stretch run when it was ascertained that the latter raced into closer quarters through the closing strides.*"

Past Performance Chart of Cosmic Boy

3 Oct 60—5 Haw	5000	1	$19.40
15 Sep 60—3 Haw	c3500	2	nk
3 Sep 60—2 AP	3500	3	1
25 Aug 60—2 AP	3000	1	
12 Aug 60—2 AP	3500	2	3¼
2 Aug 60—1 AP	3250	2	2¼
26 Jly 60—5 AP	5000	9	24
18 Jly 60—1 AP	4000	1	
7 Jly 60—1 AP	6500	2	nose
1 Jly 60—1 Was	4000	2	head
24 Jun 60—9 Was	4000	8	13

Cosmic Boy was claimed out of its race on September 15 for $3,500, in which it was beaten only by a neck at odds of 3 to 1. It was raised to $5,000 in its next race, 5th race at Haw on October 3. *It won, paying $19.40.*

To keep your memory refreshed, jot a note in the back of this book because what I tell you here is *most important* for getting winners. In its race of September 3, here is the running positions of Cosmic Boy:

Str	¼	½	¾	St	Fin
4	5	4	6	5	3

The horse had *gained* 1 position from the start to the ½ mile post and then *lost* 2 positions by the time it reached the ¾ mile post. From the ¾ stretch it gained one position and from the stretch to the finish gained 2 positions. This I have named "the irregular race factor." Remember this term. At its proper place you'll learn all about it. Suffice it to say, this single factor is one of the most prolific of all factors in getting a multitude of winners at the highest possible prices. Again, I strongly urge that you remember the term for future reference.

I made a wager on this horse and here is the detective work I did.

I spotted the horse for play out of its race of September 3 when it ran an *irregular* race. This gave me *one* arrow to shoot at the bull's eye. The fact is that it ran such a good race against *older horses*, and undoubtedly would have won except for poor racing luck in this race. This gave me a *second* arrow to my bow. Then it was claimed out of its race on September 15. I now had a *third* arrow to my bow.

This claim by itself would have meant little ordinarily, as it is not to be considered in the same light or having the same value as if the claim had been a claim pattern, as discussed previously. But supported by the age and irregular factors it became most serious in this particular instance.

As stated, when I spotted this horse out of its race of September 3, I put its name on a card and watched for its next races. I had three strong reasons for forming the valid conclusion that this horse was as sure a probable winner as is possible to ascertain.

When I was racing my own stable it was customary to card many races for 3-year-olds and upward all through the racing season. I never worried about any race in which I had figured Jim's Niece would and could give her usual honest race except when as a 3-year-old she was entered with older horses. When she arrived at 4 years of age this question never bothered me.

Most fortunately for me was the fact that before I could race my horses, my writings on handicapping and picking winners had to be approved by the racing officials. This gave me a relationship with them that never could have happened otherwise. They were most friendly and I could discuss matters that under ordinary circumstances would be impossible.

Francis Dunn was the racing secretary at the time and I spoke to him about carding races for 3-year-olds exclusively. He is one of the most kindly and gracious persons in the racing picture. He listened to me and did card more races for 3-year-olds exclusively. New York is the racing center in this country and its practices are many times adopted by other racing centers. I note that now more races for 3-year-olds are carded, even earlier in the season than used to be the custom.

In conclusion, just one admonition about this age pattern. Do *not* play 3-year-olds against older horses, *except* those that qualify as *age pattern* horses. This does not mean however, that you should not play a 4- or 5- or 6-year-old against older horses. This rule applied to 3-year-olds only. A repeated survey over many years has convinced me that it is not profitable to play any horse seven or more years of age.

Comparison Pattern

PAST PERFORMANCE CHART OF BRONZERULLAH

	Class	Finish		Winner	Comments
17 Aug 60—7 Sar	Stakes	1		$83.20	
6 Aug 60—7 Mth	Stakes	14	12	Hail to Reason	Far back
20 Jly 60—7 Aqu	Stakes	2	2	Hail to Reason	Gamely
6 Jly 60—7 Aqu	Stakes	2	2	Hail to Reason	Rallied
11 May 60—7 Aqu	Stakes	7	8¼	Hail toReason	Made slow start

In its last four races Bronzerullah was defeated by Hail to Reason. At the time, these two horses met in competition August 17, 1960, Hail to Reason had already won $117,040 against Bronzerullah's $19,385 and was an outstanding stake horse. It ended up "horse of the year" with winnings of $328,434. Both horses, of course, were 2-year-olds.

It is reasonable to assume that practically everyone would consider it the height of idiocy to play Bronzerullah against Hail to Reason the next time they competed under the same conditions. But is it? Let's reason it out.

The comments on their August 6 race show Bronzerullah so far back that this race can be completely disregarded as if it did not run as can also the race of May 11. In the July 6 race, Bronzerullah finished 2nd after rallying in the stretch. Then on July 20, it again ran second and ran gamely. Each time it finished 2nd to Hail to Reason the latter had to be *driving* to win.

One has to confine his final analysis of the races to these two horses where they ran one-two. The other races can safely be consigned to obscurity. There is nothing sure in horse racing. Any horse can lose as well as win. So many unforseeable things can take place that frequently the best horse does not win the race. Since Hail to Reason had to go all out to win, it is within the realm of logic to reason that with the slightest hindrance to the one and with the slightest break in its favor to the other, the tables were reasonably certain to be turned.

I had reasoned thusly and wagered on Bronzerullah. Imagine the thrill when I witnessed the race over live TV—7th Race, Saratoga, August 17, 1960, *Bronzerullah* won by 4 lengths.

Hail to Reason, after being in good position within striking range at all times, ran 6th, beaten 8 lengths. What had happened? It's not inexplicable if you apply the reasoning I applied. Remember I stated that it had to go all out and driving to beat Bronzerullah. On August 6, it won by only 1 length and *driving*. Then only 11 days later, on August 17, it was beaten 8 lengths. The driving it had to do to win took enough stamina out of it to cause this defeat.

It went off at odds of $1.10 to $1.00 and had it won would have paid but $4.30. This is contrasted to Bronzerullah's odds of $40.60 to $1.00 or the payoff of $83.20.

Let me assure you that had the latter been at odds of less than 15 to 1, I never would have played it despite my reasoning. But if it was entered in a race where Hail to Reason was absent, I'd most likely have played it even if the odds were shorter than 15 to 1. *Any horse that can run 2nd even once to the outstanding horse of the period is always worth a gambling chance!*

Irregular Race Pattern

I will try to illustrate by graphs just what I mean by an irregular race. Horse positions are indicated by dots. The left hand figure represents the position of the horse in the running of the race. The call positions are self-explanatory. I am not showing the start or the post position since this tends to confuse the issue. The horse's running should be judged on its performance after it has reached the 1/4 mile post.

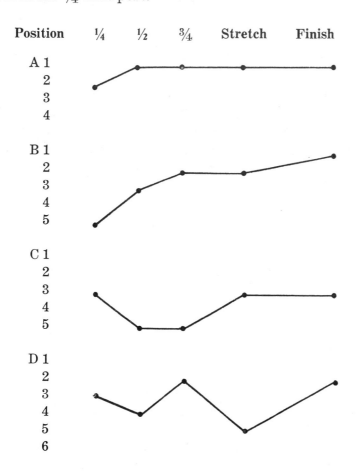

A horse in graph A was 2nd at the 1/4 pole, 1st at the 1/2 and thereafter. There is no significance in this race so this type is ignored.

B horse was 4th at the 1/4 and coming from behind continued to gain position right up to the finish. There is no meaning to this type of race. Many races are run where a horse comes from behind steadily gaining to the end but loses. The uninitiated frequently play this horse in its next race on the theory that had it gotten off quicker it would have won. This is not true. This horse most likely ran as good a race as was within its power.

C horse is what we are looking for. In 3rd running position at the ¼ it drops *back* to 5th at the ½ and continues to run 5th to the ¾, then puts on a burst of speed to gain 3rd at the stretch and continues 3rd to the finish. This is an *irregular* race pattern.

D horse 3rd at the ¼, drops *back* to 4th at the ½, gains 2 lengths at the ¾ to be 2nd. Thus far this horse has dropped *back* then *gained*, making it an irregular race to the ¾. From the ¾ to the stretch it drops *back* to 5th at the stretch and in the stretch comes on again, making another irregular pattern in the same race. In other words, this horse has run a *double irregular*.

The only qualification for an irregular pattern is that the horse at some time in the running dropped back and then gained (or came on) after being back and thus gained at some point. It makes no difference about the start or the finish.

If anyone has difficulty visualizing this movement in the running of a race, I suggest you get race charts out of the *Form* or *Telegraph* and plot races the same as I have. A first glance at a chart may not make it immediately apparent when an irregular type is present. But after a little practice, a glance at the chart makes it stand out like a beacon light.

For the purpose of illustration, the previous graphs represent hypothetical races. Here is the graph of an actual race of Sue Harpen qualified by me as an irregular pattern. The qualifying was done from the following race:

8th Race Suffolk Downs, June 6, 1940. 1 Mile 70 Yards

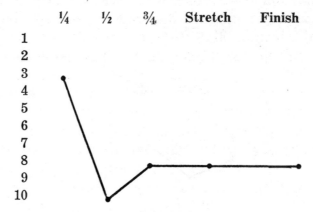

This is an irregular race—drop back and gain, no matter where in race, or where finished—but a trifle more difficult to recognize until one becomes more familiar with the pattern.

After qualifying the horse and making a card on it to play in the next race, I watched for it and it was again entered on June 14, only 8 days after this irregular race. It was entered again as follows:

8th race, Suffolk Downs, June 14, 1940. 1⅛ miles.
Sue Harpen won, paying $445.20 $146.40 $61.00.
No! I did not play it!

After I qualify irregular pattern horses I list them on 3 x 5 cards and file them alphabetically to watch for their future races. On some patterns you can play them blindly. But on this particular pattern you must consider the race it is entered in and discard it if it does not meet requirements. This will be discussed in its proper space. I can't recall now why I passed up this horse.

But in reviewing it here in view of four factors that favor it I should have played it. These four indicators are:

1. Note that in the original qualifying race the distance was 1 mile 70 yards and that in the winning race it was 1⅛ miles. The manner in which the horse performed in the shorter race indicated the added distance would be much in its favor and proved it was.

2. It qualified as an irregular pattern.

3. In its favor was the fact that showing it was at the peak of its form (in qualifying race even though it finished 8th) it was racing within 8 days of its last race.

4. Its price was an inducement. Had it been under 15 to 1 this in itself would have kept me from betting.

This horse sticks in my memory because, as far as I can remember, it was the biggest price horse I was ever personally interested in, even though I did not play it.

Naturally, having discovered this irregular race principle over thirty years ago and having won innumerable wages by using it, I have it at my finger tips and can spot it in the blink of an eyelash. It may be a trifle difficult for some readers to understand it thoroughly. Perhaps I can elucidate better by this illustration.

You and a companion decide to make a bet as to who can run four blocks the fastest. You both go into stride on equal terms for a half a block. At this point your opponent's shoe laces become untied and he has to stop, bend down and tie them securely, or some small child runs out of an alley and trips him.

Supposing you win but only by a relatively short margin. Wouldn't you agree that it is most likely except for the interference he would have won and not you?

Or supposing by reason of his delayed running you beat him by a large margin. Wouldn't you agree that it is unlikely you could determine his ability against you with reasonable certainty?

Suppose again that he had to stop twice instead of once, first to tie his shoe laces, next to pick himself up after being tripped. Wouldn't you be afraid to bet him $1,000 on a future try?

This is akin to what happens when a horse runs irregularly. The irregular race proves the horse is more fit, has more stamina, and is better than its race evidences.

Those readers who have watched a skating speed race probably can best assess this principle. The speed is terrific and the turns hazardous. I would suspect that there are spills in probably two out of every five races. I have seen spills where the fallen contestant has been lapped and gotten up to run second or third and even win. In every such instance that I can recall the fallen skater would have undoubtedly been the winner *had he not fallen.* This perhaps may be due to the fact that the speedier the skater the more apt he is to slip.

I hope these illustrations better clarify the picture for you. If not, just practice charting races that you think show an irregular pattern and it is certain to eventually become as plain as the nose on your face.

Time Between Races Pattern

The time elapse between a horse's last race and his today race is a contributory factor in whether or not it is worth a wager. I never ask a conclusion of mine to be accepted on its face value. Inevitably the shorter the time between two races, the more advantage it gives the horse. Here are my reasons:

1. No matter how poorly a horse finished in its prior race if the trainer enters it soon thereafter he must think the horse has a good chance. If it ran an unimpressive race the chances are in favor of improving its fitness.

2. The trainer could have purposely entered his charge where it had no chance of winning in this prior to winning race.

3. The trainer could have used this next-to-last race in place of a workout knowing it would bring the horse closer to its peak condition.

4. If it ran a good last race this proves it is in fit condition and the sooner it runs again it is less apt to go off the peak of its form.

I have never conducted a research on this matter myself, but I have read the result of some research on the number of days between horses' *last race.*

> 63% of all winners raced within past 7 days
> 21% of all winners raced within past 8 to 14 days
> 11% of all winners raced within past 15 days

These figures are illuminating and should be given thought.

I just this moment haphazardly picked up a *Morning Telegraph* and opened it in the middle. I looked to see the days between horses winning race and its prior race.

Here is what I found on only two pages of past performances for March 31, 1969:

Horse	Date of Winning Race	Prior Race	Days Between
Hail's Image	3 Bow Feb 24	Feb 13	11
Travel Agent	9 Aqu Mar 17	Mar 11	6
Amstel	10 Hia Mar 4	Mar 1	3
Sky Augie	5 Aqu Mar 14	Mar 1	13
Sky Augie	5 Aqu Mar 21	Mar 17	4
Judge Honor	4 Bow Feb 21	Feb 14	7
Tully, Jr	1 Pim Mar 8	Mar 5	3
Noble Destroyer	8 CT Mar 17	Mar 8	9
Legal Measure	3 Lrl Dec 13	Dec 6	7
Al G Specialist	5 Pim Mar 15	Mar 8	7
Mystic Mass	9 Bow Feb 25	Feb 17	6
Multi Play	5 Bow Feb 28	Feb 21	7

The amazing thing I observed was that in the prior to winning race the horse could be last beaten as many as 22, 30 lengths, or more. But this made no difference except that the payoff in many instances is astronomical. It is apparent from this and from my back memory that how the horse finished in its next to last race is immaterial. Twelve races are shown above. Nine or 75 percent were run within seven days of last race.

If the reader hopes to make the most success out of playing the races as is possible for himself he must learn to do as I have always done. He should research every angle that comes to his notice or pay someone to do it for him. Only thus is it possible to achieve the pinnacle of success.

I could go on indefinitely giving you examples of this factor but it will serve no purpose; the reader should do it for himself. True, this limited research is of little value by itself. But when fortified by my over thirty years of observation it assumes importance.

Here Are Seven Guide Posts To Profits

1. First time starter pattern

2. Imported horse factor

3. Claim pattern

4. Age pattern

5. Comparison pattern

6. Irregular race pattern

7. Time between races pattern

Daily observation should be made of both the race run charts and the past performances. When your search locates one of these patterns the horses' names should be listed on a card or otherwise. Consult each day's entries to spot when one of these listed horses is running.

When any are entered, there are many ways to utilize to best advantage the "know-how" these patterns give in locating winners. No one way of application is best. All of them, properly used will produce the most probable winners possible to attain. Which is best for one person contrasted to another depends upon the effort put forth, the intelligence, and general basic racing "know-how" of the individual.

No. 6, irregular race pattern, occurs more frequently than the others. These can be played separately and blindly with great potentialities for profit because most pay off in telephone numbers. However, a judicious study of the conditions of the race and the competition will permit the sensible player passing up of many poorly placed contenders, thus enhancing possible profits. For those reluctant to use spot playing because they imagine they will not get enough action it should be evident that with seven patterns going for them, the action can be as lively as desired.

No. 6 and No. 7 will be observed almost daily and you'll get so many as to be impracticable. This can be overcome by requiring that more than one pattern be present in a horse's record.

You will learn more about this later when I describe how I go about a day's work in planning the wagers I am to make. This I will leave to my last chapter.

What I have tried to bring out in this chapter is that the player must be a constant and avid reader of the race run charts. Only thus can he discover patterns that may well reward him. And keep in mind that the past performances do not expose some of these patterns. These different pattern plays, since they may not turn up too frequently, lend themselves ideally for play with favorites.

12

Races Won, Purse Earnings and Consistency of Workouts

THERE SEEMS TO BE reasonable validity to the process of assigning great value to the total number of races won by a horse and to the total of money won. Many systems have been offered to the public based upon each of these factors and/or by combining them both. But, despite its seeming value, there are many pitfalls in this hypothesis.

True, this data has a value, but not to the degree that appears upon the surface. An assessment must be made of what class of races were won. A win by Damascus has higher value than fifty races won by some horse in most handicaps and allowances. The degree of worth placed upon the purse winnings of a horse must be reasoned with respect as to how much of the total winnings is represented for finishing in second, third, and fourth positions. This computation is not revealed in the past performances.

Low wages are paid to inferior workers, and high wages are paid the best, most skilled, and intelligent workers—the same is true in horse racing. A trainer who has a horse capable of winning $5,000 purses is not going to run it in races which offer a purse of $2,000 or $3,000 or $4,000, unless in the event there is no $5,000 race available currently or in the near future. So long as his horse is capable of taking down these $5,000 races, the trainer is going to keep shooting for them. The ownership of a horse is an investment and it has to earn its way.

The situation of stake horses is a trifle different. With races offering $50,000 to much over $100,000 the trainer is not going to waste time and effort in races offering $5,000, $10,000, or $15,000. He can afford to wait, even though there might not be a spot for his charge within the immediate future. However, in order to keep it in as near a peak of condition as possible he will enter it in small purse races. The purse here is not of primary interest to him.

91

The race takes the place of a workout. And a horse, unless on the downgrade, will be infinitely more benefited by a race within its powers than it will from a workout. This is true, of course, of all classifications.

Let me give you some examples:

Example No. 1

	1st	2nd	3rd	4th	Earnings
Horse A	1	0	0	0	$2,000
Horse B	1	0	0	0	$3,500

If these two horses were entered in the same race, the quality of the class between them is readily established and horse B the selection, other considerations being equal of course.

Example No. 2

	1st	2nd	3rd	4th	Earnings
Horse C	2	0	1	5	$16,000
Horse D	4	3	0	1	$16,000

Many evaluate on the earnings per race won, rather than on the total earned. Horse C won two races, so it figures $8,000 per race. Horse D won four races averaging $4,000 per race. Both horses show eight races run. Both win the same amount of purse money. D wins four races to C's two.

Many evaluate this factor by dividing the races won into the money earned to get a per race figure.

Example No. 3

	1st	2nd	3rd	4th	Earnings
Horse C	2	0	0	0	$16,000
Horse D	4	0	0	0	$16,000

Horse C averages $8,000 per race won; horse D $4,000 per race. Ergo, Horse C should be the selection. The conclusion presupposes that if a horse wins $8,000 per race contrasted to another winning $4,000 the former horse raced in high class races with keener competition and therefore is the better horse. This is a meritorious decision!

Example No. 4

	1st	2nd	3rd	4th	Earnings
Horse C	2	1	1	2	$16,000
Horse D	4	1	1	2	$16,000

The past performances give the total earnings of a horse. But there is no way for you to know, or to find out, what the average earnings per winning race actually are. The earnings gleaned from running second, third and fourth can be disregarded. Only those earnings accumulated from *winning races* have any value in determining the class factor.

The distribution of purse money is divided between the first, second, third, and fourth horse finishing in a race. This division is not equal, but is made percentagewise; the winner getting the most, second horse less, and so on.

Purse money at New York tracks is distributed 65 percent, 20 percent, 10 percent, and 5 percent to the first four horses finishing in any race. The distribution of the purse money percentagewise is entirely at the discretion of the track on which the race is held. To my knowledge it varies from as low as 50 percent to the winner to the 65 percent offered at New York tracks.

There are a few stakes events under which the conditions of the race call for a guaranteed monetary distribution which is different from the 65 percent down to the 5 percent offered at New York.

Horse D could have earned $6,500 in one of his winning races and $7,500 in another. While a purse of $5,000 compared to one of $10,000 would indicate a tremendous differential if you figure them as claiming prices. However, this same spread does not denote the same when it comes to purses. In other words, horses competing in $5,000 to $10,000 races may be in about the same approximate class bracket.

In actual practice you may not always see such a wide variance in the figures, which I have adopted to make the point more easily discernible. But, the fact remains that unless the earnings for each winning race is known exactly, little dependence can be placed upon using the figures as they now appear in past performances.

Undoubtedly you have observed and most likely played a horse coming from a track outside the state you are operating in. This horse shows what appears to be an impressive record both as to races won and/or money won. Should this out-of-state track be even slightly inferior in its class of horses, the horse coming from that track will lose in a very high percentage of the times.

Before I leave this question of money earned, I'd like to comment on the first horse I raced. This was Dohoev. This horse won only one of its races for me. Aside from this winning race it *never* ran worse than third. It never failed to more than pay its way.

If this horse was figured on her earnings it had to be picked to win over horses it never would have beaten. It always came from far back to finish no worse than third. It always worked well, and on timing in its workouts should have won more than that single race. I sold it to a trainer going to Havana and later saw her past performances for races run in Havana and it won eight or nine out of ten races taking the lead from the start and never being headed. This change in its races can be attributed to less keen competition, of course.

I only mention it to illustrate that fast workouts and money earned is not necessarily conducive to pointing out a winner.

Consistency

Cynical players proclaim that consistency has no value in an attempt to predict a winner. But one must not lose sight of just what consistency denotes. It should not be considered in the light of ability. A horse is or is not consistent relative to its temperament. Some horses always race consistently and are in the money, and yet show few wins. This proves that the horse is willing at all times to give its best every time it runs, unless bothered by some physical ailment. It is an honest horse, but simply is running over its head, or is just unlucky, and take it from me there are horses who get most of the breaks while others always seem to get the bad breaks.

In considering a horse for play, you should allot some value to its consistency for these reasons. Innumerable things can happen, and do happen in the running of a race. Just take for an example what I have seen many times and I am sure every reader has if he visits race tracks. Coming around the turn the whole field often goes wide. This can be caused by a number of reasons. Be that as it may, it frequently allows a horse to come through on the rail and win a race that it never would have won, except for this break.

Another example is when one of two horses takes the lead from the start and gets far out in front, and then begins to tire and fade away.

These are but two ways in which a consistent horse may be benefited. Always consistently running up near the leaders to be in the money, such a horse is in an enviable position to take advantage of the opportunity presented to it. A player has no clairvoyance and can't foretell what will happen in any race. Supposing three contenders are selected in a race. The player is presented with the decision as to which one of the three should be the final selection. This is a spot where consistency should be used. All things being equal, and if there are three contenders they must be equal, giving the consistent horse the nod will often tip the scale to a win.

Workouts

My only use of workouts is to see if a horse entered today has been worked, and how recently and how many times since its last race. I *never* look at the time in which the workout was run. It has absolutely no meaning to me.

There are certain horses who will work out in what is sensational time, and that same horse will *never* come near its workout speed when it actually races. In contrast to this are horses that never run fast-time workouts, and yet when in an actual race are much superior to their workout performance.

It puzzled me why this was so. I had never known of any one to give a sensible explanation for it. Even the smartest horsemen reason some are work horses, others are not and let it go at that. But my curious mind sought an answer. I have formed this opinion. I do not know how much validity there is to it, but I can say it has paid me off well to ignore the actual time figures in any workout.

I recall the days before the automobile when all milk delivery was made by horse and wagon. Often, in the early hours of the day I have seen one of these delivery horses prance around like a young colt. The nature of a work horse is to be docile—not fooling around—whereas a thoroughbred race horse is apt to be and is frisky at all times. I noticed that early in the morning the same was true of cavalry horses and artillery horses. These horses are inclined to be most tractable by reason of the fact that they have humans around them twenty-four hours of the day. Even when all other horses are at rest during the night these army horses have close contact with humans since even guards are around them all night long.

At first, I concluded that since a race horse was worked early in the morning, it was rested and felt fresh. But this did not stand close scrutiny, for if it was so, then when it raced in the afternoon it had a longer rest, and therefore should be even more invigorated. Hence, it should run even faster than it would in its workouts.

I finally came to the conviction that has stayed with me ever since, that this question could only be resolved by considering the temperament of both breeds of horses. The work and the army horse would expend its spirits early in the morning because of the invigoration it received from the brisk air. As the day passed along they settled down into a daily routine and went along evenly discharging their duties without fuss or fanfare.

But the race horse is different. It is always inclined to be active and frisky. It cannot be depended upon to go along on even keel and is apt to break into activity at the slightest provocation and even without any.

The great difference between the two breeds is the evenness and docility of the work horse and the excitement and friskiness of the race horse.

When the race horse leaves its barn for a workout, it is saddled in the quiet of its stall, its home, its castle. More than any animal I know of, the horse loves its home. Probably every reader knows that when a stable catches fire, if handlers are able to get a horse out of the barn, it will often break away and rush back through the flames to its stall and destruction. In practically every race track blaze this happens. It is also a recognized fact that horses running in open pastures on a ranch, if taken miles away from that area will travel hundreds of miles and return to their original home.

The horse is prepared for its work in the familiar surroundings of its home. It calmly is led or ridden to the track. On its way and on the track it sees individual horses slowly walking, trotting, cantering, and even galloping fast in their own workouts. No excitement, everything normal. A horse likes to run. It is born to run. When asked it will run and give its best and is happy to do so.

Now, let's follow this same horse when it goes to the paddock for an actual race. Even as it enters the racing strip on its way to the saddling paddock, it is excited by the mass of the crowds and the noise. You'll see many such horses strain on their lead strap, and try to pull back to get free. Then it arrives in the saddling paddock and has to stand there waiting until the order to saddle is given by the paddock judge. This wait and all this confusion causes it to fret and sweat and to get more and more nervous. Note how many horses are covered with sweat in the paddock. Even when the weather is cool, you'll observe this. Most times this is a nervous sweat and all this has taken its toll of the horse, and by the time it reaches the starting gate some of its stamina has diminished.

This is the only reason I can figure for a horse to fail to measure up to a good workout time.

Now let us consider horses of a different temperament. They are of two types. One will give an impressive workout and in the actual race it was worked for will perform as its workout indicates it should. The other type simply will not do its best in a workout, but when entered in keen competition will give its best in the excitement of the race. Jim's Niece is a horse I can't place specifically. She worked willingly and always ran to her race. But I never asked her to work out at the utmost of her speed.

Many competitors in all sports, especially golf, are of these two types. With one type, if the competition is keen it will fall far behind its normal performance. With the other type, the better the opponent at the sport, the better its performance. Many golf players with a low handicap when they enter a tournament fall far below their usual mark. On the other hand tough competition in a tournament results in a score far above the usual.

"Pittsburgh Phil" on the subject had this to say: "I have seen horses work for a race and the work has been so impressive to my mind that I have made very large wagers on them; yet two days later in the actual race, when they should have run up to their work, they have fallen far behind."

Make no mistake about it, Phil in my opinion never wagered on a horse simply on the basis of an impressive workout, as it may appear from what he said that he did. You can bet that the work only fortified his other reasons for liking the prospect. Even as you and I lose, Phil had his share of losers. He said that he lost more than twenty-seven wagers in a row at one time.

What a workout really discloses, and the way I personally make use of it, is this: During the morning when horses are worked there may be five or ten horses working. Who can follow them all? It is impossible to know whether the rider is trying to make the horse go faster or not. Except in preparation for a big moneyed race the rider of the horse is just a stable boy, unlikely to get as much out of his charge as a capable experienced jockey.

Incidentally, a real workout is never given a horse the day before it is to engage in an actual race. The day or two before a horse is given what is termed a "blowout." This is to keep the horse loosened up and has no meaning as to what speed it will produce in the race.

I glance at the workouts shown below each horse's past performances. I do *not* observe the speed of the workout. This has no useful meaning to me. The only thing a workout reveals to me and to a horse's trainer is whether or not the horse is in condition. If it has three or four workouts showing, you know the horse is physically fit, otherwise it would not be called upon to work, but would be laid off for a time.

There is an incalculable amount of money lost on playing horses that show impressive workouts simply on this premise. Public selectors seem to have a liking for this factor, as evidenced by their comments when a horse works fast. I can understand this and I'll explain it in the next chapter about public handicappers.

13

Public Handicappers and Selectors

HAIL TO THE public selectors!

I tip my hat to the selectors whose picks appear in the experts selections page of the *Racing Form* and *Morning Telegraph*. The experts employed by these racing papers are *Hermis, Sharpshooter, Reigh Count, Sweep*, Analyst, and Trackman—six in all, for the *Morning Telegraph*; and Trackman, Clocker, Analyst, *Hermis*, and *Sweep*—five in all, for the *Racing Form*. The names in italics are those taken from famous race horses. These are legally registered names owned by the publishers of the papers.

When the paper employs a new handicapper one of these names is assigned to him, and kept as long as he remains employed and of course can be used by him only when thus employed. Notice that the *Form* uses five, the *Telegraph* six. This difference is because the format of the former has space only for five.

Both the *Racing Form* and *Morning Telegraph* are owned by the Triangle Publishing Co., Inc. Different editions are published. One in New York covering the East; one in Chicago covering the Central states; one in Los Angeles covering the Far West, and one in Canada. Each edition uses the same registered names as the others. "Sweep" in each edition is not the same but a different person. This is true also of the other names such as Trackman.

It is impossible even remotely to guess what immeasurable influence these six men have on racing. I am certain that every horse player has referred to the work of these experts. Unquestionably, it is their opinion that creates the three choices in a race. If all race players had nothing else available aside from the past performances the complete playing of races would assume an entirely different aspect.

These men are expert, make no mistake about it. And still it is *impossible* to win by playing their selections. But this does not detract from their value to the player, as you'll see. Everything I say concerning these experts relates also to the expert selectors in the newspapers across the country and scratch sheets.

These experts, under the byline heading *graded handicaps*, give the approximate odds the horse should pay in their opinion. Each selector handles a separate track. Along with the odds appear comments on each horse. Seldom are these of any worth, as you'll see by the following listing of such comments for a nine horse race at Aqueduct.

Horse
1 Be along in time
2 Keen contender
3 Can prove troublesome
4 Possibility on best
5 Hard to gauge
6 Merits consideration
7 Not off last
8 May better rating
9 Chance to upset

If anyone of these nine horses won the race the selector is protected by his remarks. You'll note the reader has no real lead as to which horse the expert is more sure of than another. On his remarks any one could win and the selector is covered.

Occasionally he will comment, "Does not figure" or "Will have to improve" or "Needs more racing," and the like. But on the whole his remarks cover every possible chance of any horse in the race winning.

Considering the time element and the conditions under which these experts perform their work makes one wonder. Entries for tomorrow's race are made early *today*. The entries for each race are released around noon time at the track. This data is rushed to the selector's desk. From then on he has to consider from eighty to one hundred horses for the following day's races. After receiving the entries he has to get out their past performances and their workout data. By now the time is two o'clock. He must have his work completed by four o'clock, the deadline for the printer. Thus, he has only two hours to handle maybe one hundred horses. Contrast this to a horse player who may spend almost this much time on one race with possibly five to twelve entries.

The employment of these men is not predicated upon how much profits their readers can make playing the races. The publishers have no interest, naturally, in this aspect. His continued engagement depends upon a reasonable percentage of winners he must maintain to keep his position.

It is inevitable that when the entries come into the hands of the expert that he likes one race better than another because of his familiarity with some or one of the horses in it. This is his chance to select a winner, which is his sole purpose. He therefore is apt to give more attention to this race. He consciously or unconsciously eventually does better predicting certain races than he does others.

You should do spadework and seek to learn to distinguish the type of races each selector excels at. It may be the class of race such as claiming, allowance, handicap, or stake races. Or it may be that he is better at picking at certain distances. Once you are able to detect a definite pattern of this nature you have an invaluable guidepost to more winners.

The selector called Trackman works differently from the others. His time is spent at the track. He is in close contact with jockeys, trainers, owners, exercise boys. He gets the entries much sooner and has more hours in which to scout around and get a line on the entries before he calls in his selections.

In the New York edition *Hermis'* price line and comments appear for one or more tracks and some other selector for other tracks. I make use of these selectors who make comments along with the price to be able to detect a possible sleeper. For example, I look to see if he has a selection no other selector mentions.

I reason that if he even considers a horse no one else has it is because he has observed it in a race or has received some information about it not revealed by its past performances. I take this particular horse and give it extra time to see if I can place it in my playing plan for the day.

My experience over a period of many years has been that there are certain comments in the graded handicaps that apparently mean more than appear on the surface and get winners. These comments are, not necessarily in order of their relative importance, "merits consideration," "possibility on best," "chance to upset," "can't be eliminated."

So many horses win when these comments appear, I feel they have some significance. As the selector performs his task he subconsciously may feel that certain horses he can't pick to win may upset the apple cart, covers the situation by certain pet comments. What I mean here is that while he uses some comment to fortify against a losing pick he uses these specifically mentioned phrases when in the depth of his mind he has reason to feel a horse might well win even though the possibilities do not appear on the surface.

Scratch Sheets

The *National Armstrong Daily Scratch Sheet* lists four selectors, viz: Green Sheet, The Turf, Keen Observer, Trackman and, of course, a point consensus column. Listing the top three selections for these five columns means there are fifteen possible selections. What I have said about when "One Selector" mentions a horse that no other selector lists, namely, that it should be sorted out and given the utmost possible scrutiny and analysis, also applies here. Mind you, I do not recommend that just because it is thus brought to your attention it should be wagered on. But study it in connection with other determining factors favorable to its possible chance of winning.

Standing of Leading Selectors

Turf and Sport Digest magazine has given me permission to print the following cumulative record of selectors in the *Racing Form, Morning Telegraph* and *Armstrong National Scratch Sheet.* Following the name of each selector is his highest number of consecutive losers (in brackets), total selections after scratches, numbers of winners, seconds and thirds, number unplaced, percentage of winners selected, and the profit or loss on a two dollar flat bet to win. In the grand summary, which is the only part I am printing, the profit or loss is the actual figure for each unit of two dollars wagered.

The upper column shows *entire card selections* and the lower column shows *best bets.*

Grand Summary (All Tracks) March 11 to July 15, 1968, incl.

Handicapper	Sel.	1st	2nd	3rd	Unpl.	P.C.	Profit	Loss (per $2 wager)
Post Favorites (16)	4269	1410	865	601	1393	33.0		$0.23
Handicap (29)*	2764	684	491	382	1207	25.0		0.23
Morn. Tel. Cons. (18)	2887	842	558	405	1082	29.0		0.29
Armstrong (18)	2630	731	520	378	1001	28.0		0.29
Analyst (20)	4262	1141	800	577	1744	27.0		0.32
Hermis (28)	4253	1115	801	581	1756	26.0		0.32
Rac. Form Cons. (22)	2768	782	549	403	1034	28.5		0.33
Sharpshooter (26)	2884	755	520	428	1181	26.0		0.33
Sweep (25)	4264	1133	812	588	1731	26.5		0.35
Trackman (24)	4266	992	775	694	1895	23.0		0.35
Reigh Count (33)	2887	569	449	380	1489	20.0		0.36

26.4% average

Handicapper	Sel.	1st	2nd	3rd	Unpl.	P.C.	Profit	Loss (per $2 wager)
Handicap (12)*	274	112	38	31	93	41.0	$0.12	
Armstrong (9)	285	123	55	36	71	43.0	0.06	
Reigh Count (11)	284	75	47	39	123	26.5		$0.08
Analyst (9)	426	159	82	54	131	37.0		0.19
Sweep (12)	421	157	81	58	125	37.5		0.20
Trackman (15)	431	133	97	67	134	31.0		0.34
Sharpshooter (15)	279	92	53	41	93	33.0		0.38
Rac. Form Cons. (11)	283	110	53	42	78	39.0		0.42
Morn. Tel. Cons. (7)	287	114	62	47	64	40.0		0.44
Hermis (10)	427	131	86	79	131	30.5		0.54

37.6% average

* Includes Clocker

Despite their showing these selectors can be most useful when used as guideposts in your work.

To reiterate my thesis or central point pertaining to this chapter, *Scratch Sheets*, the *Morning Telegraph* and the *Daily Racing Form* employ handicappers to predict winners for the public. These men are real experts despite the fact that you cannot win on a flat bet by playing their picks. But they should be used as a crutch or guide when figuring a race. Their opinion, if followed, will often turn the tide in your favor when you are indecisive.

14

Playing Claimed Horses

A SOUND METHOD of playing claimed horses exclusively can be one of the most profitable ways of horse playing. There are many advantages to this method over all others. It deals with a single factor and thus permits the player to concentrate all his efforts thereto.

The late Hirsch Jacobs was one of the most famous of trainers of all time, and was one of the nicest persons I have ever known. Many times he was the year's winning trainer for the honors of the number of races and by purse earnings won by horses he trained.

He started off as a pigeon fancier in Brooklyn with racing pigeons and graduated into horse racing. He was the most prolific claimer of horses and the most successful of all time. After Stymie was claimed by him for $1,500 it went on to win $918,485. I am sure it was the first horse to come close to winning the first million dollars in turf history.

There have been successful systems sold based entirely on playing only claimed horses.

Claiming races dominate the racing picture. Without them racing as now conducted could not exist. For every horse of even minor class and quality there are thousands of inferior quality. Unless races are provided for them they would have no place to go. It would not take long before the breeding of race horses would become extinct. For every single Damascus or Man O' War there are literally thousands of horses bred that are worth little more than a couple of thousand dollars on the auction block.

Every race association would prefer not to attract claiming horses and not to condition races for them. But they have no alternative. If they eliminate claiming races the gates would have to be closed. From this one can fully realize that the claiming horse is the backbone of all racing.

There are few stables, even among the leading ones, that do not race in claimers. But other than these millionaire stables, few stables could stay in existence unless they possessed a majority of claiming horses.

How horses are claimed must be common knowledge to all players who are serious about making profits. In order to be eligible to claim a horse, these qualifying rules must be observed. From the race in which an owner has first entered a horse he can claim any horse at its entered claiming price until the completion of that particular meeting. He cannot claim his own horse nor can he claim more than one horse out of the same race. He cannot claim any horse prior to the race in which he has first entered a horse. But he can claim a horse out of the first race he enters.

Here is the process in making a claim. The owner at least fifteen minutes before post time must in writing sealed deposit the claim in a locked box provided for this purpose by the clerk of the course. No money shall accompany the claim. Each person desiring to make a claim, unless he shall have such amount to his credit with the Association, must first deposit with the Association the whole amount of the claim in cash, for which a receipt will be given. (It is customary as soon as a new meeting opens for stables to deposit with the Association a sufficient amount of cash or check to cover incidental expenses such as stall rent, rider's fees, entry fees, and the like. If he wins any purse money this is added to his credit. At the close of the meeting the Association gives a check to the stable for any credit available at the time.)

When a claim has been lodged with the clerk it is irrevocable, and at the risk of the claimant. This is to say as soon as the start is effected whether the claimed horse be alive or dead, sound or unsound, or injured before or during the race, or after, it is the claimant's risk and he is the actual new owner. He must even pay the costs of disposing of the carcass should the horse be killed.

It is not unusual for several owners to place a claim for the same horse. In this event the stewards decide who is to get the horse by lot. The original owner of the horse cannot be informed that a claim has been made until after the race has been run. Any horse so claimed when it comes back to the unsaddling paddock is delivered to the claimant.

If a horse is claimed it cannot start in a claiming race for a period of 30 days for less than 25 percent more than the amount for which it is claimed. This ruling is for the purpose of protecting the original owner. A possible claimant will hesitate to make a claim realizing he can't run the horse for the same price, but must raise it where theoretically it has less chance of winning than it has if entered at the same claimed price. Of course, a claimed horse can run in the new owner's registry in allowance, handicap, or any other type of nonclaiming race from the day it was claimed.

As a further protection to the original entrant, a claimed horse cannot be sold or transferred to anyone wholly or in part, except in a claiming race, for a period of 30 days from date of claim, nor shall it, unless reclaimed, remain in the same stable or under the control or management of its former owner or trainer for a like period (30 days), nor shall it race *elsewhere* until after the close of the meeting at which it was claimed.

Again this last ruling is for the protection of the original owner. This is what it means. An owner can come from one state into another with the sole purpose of claiming a horse or horses to take back to the first state to race. Let's say he comes from New Jersey or from Massachusetts. The moment one of his own horses races he is eligible to make a claim or claims. He could then leave the area and return to another state taking with him as many horses as he had claimed. This would be most unfair to those horsemen who race their horses year after year at the same track. Let us further examine this deterrent to such practices. The Aqueduct 1969 meeting is of 72 days' duration. It starts March 10 and runs to May 31. A claim made in the early days or in the middle of the meet would disqualify the horse from racing on any other track except Aqueduct for a long time. And few claims made are good enough to be worth this unprofitable waste of time.

The impression may be conveyed that a claim can only be made by an owner who has previous—to the day claimed—raced a horse in a claiming race. This is not a fact! Eligibility to make a claim depends wholly upon the fact that a claimant must first have raced a horse at the track. It can be in any type of race—allowance, handicap, stake, or claiming makes no difference.

Perhaps some may ponder as to what happens if the claimed horse runs from first to fourth thus winning purse money in the race claimed out of. Any such purse money goes to the original owner.

It is of utmost importance that the player thoroughly understand every facet of a horse being claimed. If it is as familiar to him as 2 plus 2 equals 4 then he will realize he can become a specialist in this field and utilize his knowledge in wagering on many a winner, and most often at the biggest imaginable payoffs. If I may, I suggest you read over the requirements more than once to impress the facts upon your mind.

The data incident to the claiming of a horse will, I am positive, convince the reader that the claiming horse is the real backbone of racing, as I have previously stated. It should be evident, therefore, that the reader should absorb every detail involved.

Why Horses are Claimed

Infrequently, a horse is claimed, mostly females, because the claimant feels its blood lines fit into his pattern of horse breeding. This happens so seldom it is not worth thinking about.

Claiming a *police horse*. A man does not own a horse but wants to get into the racing game. He can acquire a horse through private purchase. Or, he can use a police horse for this purpose. This is how it works. He approaches an owner and has him claim a horse which is run under the claimant's colors for the required time and then openly sold to the new owner. This is contrary to racing rules but it is practically impossible to detect that the claim was made for another person. Now the new owner is in business and on his own. Any other horses he desires can now be claimed by him after his newly acquired horse races.

There is another connotation to the words *police horse* and more commonly applied than in the specific instance just stated. You've probably seen dozens of horses that run a multitude of races and have never won. In its two-year races run record it won't show one win although it may have run 20, 30, 40, or even more times. It costs a rider's fee every time he rides. It costs a minimum of $10 on tracks where the purse value is $400 up to a maximum of $25 where the purse value is $2,000 or more. Therefore, on most tracks the minimum fee is $25, for a losing mount and proportionally higher if the horse runs in the money.

When I was racing my stable a horse's maintenance cost about $9.00 a day. Today it is probably $15.00 to $20.00 a day.

Reaching over I haphazardly picked up a *Morning Telegraph* dated March 31, 1969, and running through it gleaned these facts. I'll give the cost of keeping a horse in racing and its earnings. I will use the minimum of $12.00 as daily maintenance. I will give the jockey fee paid for the purse value of the race.

Seat of Learning	1969	5	1	0	0	$1,050
4-year-old	1968	23	1	3	0	1,839
		28				$2,889

Maintenance cost

455 days @ $12 per day	$5,560
28 Jockey fees @ $19	532
	$6,092
Money won	2,889
Net loss	$3,203

Next I reached for a *Racing Form* dated August 2, 1967, and found the following data, on a horse racing at Bay Meadows.

Hunker Down	1967	17	1	2	1	$1,325
4-year-old	1966	40	3	4	2	3,511
		57				$4,836

Maintenance cost

495 days @ $12 per day	$5,930
57 Jockey fees @ $17	969
	$6,899
Money won	4,836
Maintenance cost	$2,063

These are both 4-year-old horses. Had they been 2-year-olds their owners may have hoped for better return on his investment as they matured. The picture is worse than it appears because I only charged $12 a day maintenance whereas $15 would probably have been closer. Also, I charged the minimum jockey fees, whereas the fee for a *winning* race of this last horse is not $17 as I charged but $39.00. However, it means little in the overall picture.

I could pick innumerable examples in which the loss was greater. Keep in mind that it is a very poor stable that will race such low-caliber horses. How can they stand the loss? There are several reasonable answers to this question. The majority of small trainers train for a number of different owners. They keep telling each owner the horse is going to win and some owners can take a lot of punishment. There are a multitude of people owning horses with no hope or intention of making a horse pay its way. They are given owners' privileges and prestige which means a lot to them. They get in and keep in the racing picture at a minimum cost of owning some crippled old plugs. Many horses run that have not won a race in several years.

However, hidden among these plugs is one that is used as a police horse. It matters not how often it runs which might ruin a fairly good horse. It is entered solely for the purpose of the owner becoming eligible to make a claim as early as possible in every new meet. So the plug as a police horse has its use.

The main, and the only important to you, reason 99 percent of claims are made is for investment purposes. Naturally, the aim of every stable owner is to get the best horses possible. But best does not mean the most expensive. It means one that returns the most profits based upon the price paid for it. Horses can be bred by an owner, bought at private dispersal sales or at public auction. The only other way is to claim a horse, which in reality is merely a different way of buying a horse. If a horse costs $3,000 and wins purses that pay its keep *plus a net profit* it is a good investment. If a horse costs $10,000 and can't make a profit it is a worthless investment.

There are more poor horses than good ones. It is practically impossible to buy a good recognized horse. Why should any owner sell a good horse unless he is retiring from racing? Thus it is apparent that the claiming of horses is of the most importance insofar as racing a stable is concerned. It is for sure that *without claiming races 75 percent of the stables would not exist.*

Since the majority of races are for the claiming class, success of a stable is dependent upon making good claims. This does not apply to the few stables who do not race claimers and who breed their own stock or buy yearlings at auctions. When a stable of this type wants to get rid of stock they drop it way down in a claiming race—that is why one should be suspicious of a big drop. This type of stable never makes any claim of its own. For every such stable there are many whose sole dependence is in the claiming horse field.

What Goes On in the Mind of a Trainer Before He Claims a Horse?

A trainer will not get very far if he claims horses just to add to the string he handles. He must claim horses that will win for him. (Some owners train their own horses and are known as *owner-trainers*. Others do not own but train for owner-stables.) Trainers like Jacobs and Bishop—and others you'll come to recognize—possess uncanny ability to size up a horse and evaluate its present future potentialities. They watch a horse in its workouts. They observe it when it races. They look it over in the paddock and consider any possible deformities. They may be told something about a horse by a jockey who has ridden it.

Probably every trainer feels he can handle a horse better than the next one. So he spots a horse and figures he will change this or that accordingly. Often the slightest change will make for amazing improvement in a horse's performance. A change of shoeing—and by this I do not mean the type of shoes—will make a big change. Cutting more or less shell off the toes or heels or sides will completely change a horse's going. The trainer may think a prospective claim will do better with more or less weight on its frame. Taking blinkers on or off may be the answer to better performance, he thinks. Or a change in the type of blinkers, such as open blinkers compared to those that have eye cups which prevent a horse from seeing to the side or back and only straight ahead. Often blinkers have a cup over only one eye, this to prevent a horse from the habit of swerving to one side or another. When charts show blinkers have been added or taken off a horse they do not tell you these things I have mentioned.

There are innumerable little things like this that can cause a horse who has been performing miserably to suddenly go far up in class and run away from its higher competition. So when you see upsets, don't think it is crooked racing.

These things I have been mentioning are the thoughts that go along in the mind of a trainer before he makes a claim. Obviously, he can't be right all the time. But this does not prevent you from making real profits once you become a claimed horse specialist, and this treatise will start you on the road to achieve that purpose.

Becoming a Specialist

Unfortunately, there can be no magic formula provided that will enable a player to become a specialist without an effort being put forth on the part of the reader. Following are examples of claims for your study. You must analyze what is given herein and then apply your own technique based upon the knowledge of the factors discussed herein.

It is axiomatic that when a horse drops down in claiming price, its winning chance is thereby increased. Even public selectors ridiculously lean heavily to this opinion. So let's first consider horses that are dropped down in claiming prices and claimed in the race in which this drop takes place.

I. J. Mito running for $15,000 on March 18 loses badly and then only 8 days later is dropped down to $7,500, again losing. The horse was top consensus choice and went off as post favorite. A specialist would be suspicious of such a large drop, and it is again beaten this time by 13 lengths. Yet it was claimed. Watch trainers with such poor judgment and be wary of *any* claims they make.

No horse with any potentialities is dropped 50 percent. It is obvious that the first owner knew something was wrong with the horse or that something was *developing* that was harmful so he wanted to be sure and get rid of it through its being claimed. So he baited the hook by a real big drop. The horse stopped because something was hurting and as it heated up it pulled itself up. This was a bad claim, showing very poor judgment.

Fleet Pam was claimed for $2,500, November 25, at CT and then won at ShD three races in a row. This might look like a good claim, *except* that these two tracks are of the very cheapest where horses race. If it stayed on these tracks, it might have been a good claim. A win by 10 lengths at Pim, a better track, and at $3,000 claiming price looks good to the average player. But it was on a muddy track. A crippled horse may run better on a soft track because it will not hurt it as will a hard-surfaced fast track. It was claimed for $4,000 on February 15 but did not run for nearly a month when it ran for $5,000 (highest price it ever raced at) and was beaten only a neck. About 21 days later it was entered for $3,000. You have to ask yourself why should anyone drop a horse down $2,000 after beaten only a neck for $5,000? When it was claimed for $4,000 February 15 after its 10-length win, it was a very bad claim and even a worse claim out of its last race for $3,000. When a horse does not race back very soon (a couple of weeks) most probably it is ailing and needs time to be doctored up.

What you must learn to do is to analyze these claims as I am doing and get to know and avoid trainers who prove they have no ability by claiming a horse because it is dropped down in claiming prices. In time you'll learn to know *those trainers* who claim horses *based upon their sound judgment* and *these are the ones that claim future winners.*

Top Kick. This horse was dropped from $11,000 to $7,000 (a $4,000 drop) after three very bad races and foolishly claimed for $7,000. The "suckers" made it post favorite at 2.20 to 1. Although it got a good start, it was beaten by 10 lengths. This is a bad claim.

Greek Music. This horse was claimed after a $2,500 drop following four bad races, on July 10. It was next entered March 15, which was eight months later, with another drop of $1,500. A claim is made to get a coming winner and make money. Why do you suppose it took eight months to get the horse back to racing? Of course, the reason is the horse had to be doctored. The sucker public made it second choice in the betting. When the trainer made this claim he figured its drop was what the horse needed to win. He was not capable of sizing up the horse and knowing it was a crippled animal. *This is a poor claim.*

Kummel. Here we have a drop of $6,500 and it won and was claimed out of this winning race. It was next run in an allowance race and beaten by

13 lengths. This horse was then dropped from an allowance to a $30,000 claimer; runs bad. Then runs for $19,000, a drop of $11,000, and beaten 9 lengths. It then was entered for $12,500. Sure, any horse might win if it were continued to be dropped, but imagine paying $12,500 for this horse! Many but *specialists would think* at $12,500 it was a good claim *because* it won. But its winning does not necessarily make it a good claim. Note, it won $29,640 the previous year and was an excellent investment for its owner at the time. But for a horse to be dropped $17,500 (from $30,000 to $12,500) *within 19 days* is certainly a good enough sign to stay away from it. Smart trainers are able to detect when a horse is becoming a cripple before its ailment actually starts to slow it up. The trainer who dropped this horse knew what he was doing.

Birlon. Here is a situation similar to that of Kummel. Birlon won $30,000 last year and yet it was dropped by $5,000. I considered it a bad claim when made and from its race after being claimed assume I was right. It surprised me that Winick made this claim as he is one of the smart claimers I follow to advantage. You'll come to know that when he makes a claim it is seldom he does not win with it.

More of Mort. Won $32,000 last year. About the same reasoning applies here as for the two previous claims of Kummel and Birlon. Only beaten 1 length on March 9. Then dropped $5,000 in less than a month from that race. *Invariably a horse is raised in claiming price after a good race if the owner does not want to lose it.* Note horse was first claimed for $12,500 on December 6. In little over a month was dropped to $6,250. Then on March 9 beaten only a length for $10,000, and in less than a month dropped to $5,000 on April 3. Trainer Threewith knew he made a bad claim and was glad to get rid of it. Incidentally, Threewith is another clever claimer and seldom misses winning with a newly claimed horse. Jordan, who last claimed the horse, did so on the basis of its being beaten only 1 length for $10,000 so it looked like a good claim for $5,000. It is a bad claim.

I want to make an observation here before I forget it. Cross Road was in the same race with More of Mort. Originally claimed for $12,500, then for $6,250, then out in its last race for $5,000. In both instances the horses continue to descend in claiming price. Now remember this: When a horse continues to go down in claiming price—no matter if it won in between or how good its races may have been—be suspicious of it!

Horsemen must have great patience and can't give up on a horse too easily. So when you see a horse going lower and lower assume it is a worthless betting proposition. I could continue to give more examples of poor claims. It would serve no purpose. Enough are given so watch for and learn the pattern involved. Let us now look at those that constitute good claims of the type watched for by the specialist who profits from them.

Prisoner's Base. After being claimed for $8,000 it was badly beaten in its next race for $10,000. Chart comment says "no threat." Then in its next race it ran for $10,000 and won and was claimed at this higher claiming after being beaten for $8,000 and then for $10,000. Try to place yourself in last claiming trainer's place. It took nerve to make this claim, really not nerve but confidence in his ability. He had to figure he had to race the horse in higher class and he must have reasoned some way to cause the horse to improve. We don't know what he had in mind of the dozens of possibilities. But he knew what he was doing running the horse for $3,000 higher; he won with it on his second try. The first time chart says "rallied," which was encouraging. It paid $46.40 when it won and you'll appreciate why it pays to watch for such spots. And keep in mind that horses going down are invariably short-priced, almost always getting the worst of the odds. The claim of this horse on February 24 fulfills a specialist's dream. Everything seems against its being a good claim, yet by reasoning applied herein by the specialist it proves to the contrary that it is an extra good claim.

After the claim for $10,000 the specialist would have played this horse in its next race and lost his bet. But on the basis of what we have been discussing and this losing race, showing that the horse rallied, would have made a good-sized bet when it won paying $46.80. There was enough confirmation that the claim was a good one.

Red Redeemer. Now to prove Prisoner's Base is not an unusual example, let me give you another example—and also to prove conclusively that I do not reason from hindsight, that is, after a result is accomplished. Red Redeemer dropped from $10,000 to $6,500. One should be suspicious of such a drop and not consider this for a play. It ran a miserable race. Then it was raised $1,000 to $7,500 and *is claimed again at the higher price after a bad race at a lower figure*. The same reasoning applied to Prisoner's Base is used by the trainer here.

You now have knowledge that *two different trainers* think well of Red Redeemer, and the last one showing great confidence in his judgment since he claimed it after it raced so poorly at a lower figure. And there is still another most important secret about the possibilities of this horse as shown the first time it ran for the new trainer on April 4, when it ran second.

Joe the Barber. Analyzing this claim as a specialist, it is almost a sure winner for its latest trainer. Dropped down to $5,000, it runs a poor race. Entered next at an advance of $1,250 it wins by 5 lengths on a sloppy track. Had it won on a muddy track, you might figure it had bad legs. But a sloppy track is the same as a fast track where horses' legs are concerned. Also consider, it won for $7,000 on January 18. However, the specialist would not have played this horse. But, when it was again claimed out of its last race for $7,500 you *now* have a tip-off from two different trainers that this horse should win. Isn't their opinion worth more than public selectors or lengthy handicapping? Do not ever let horses pass you that conform to this pattern.

Mr. San-Jo. The specialist would have had this winner at $46.00. Here again you have three tip-offs that it would win. Two from different trainers and the third the secret, an irregular race.

The horse ran well in both its last two races. When entered for $10,000 it surely should have been played, especially in view of the fine price paid.

W. Co. Look at record of this horse for as probable a winner as it is possible to find.

14 Nov 67—4 GS	3500	1 by 5 lengths
29 Nov 67—2 Aqu	c3500	2 by 1¼ lengths
3 Jan 68—2 TrP	c3500	6 by 10 lengths
6 Mar 68—1 GP	3500	1 by ½ length
16 Mar 68—5 GP	c5000	1 by 4½ lengths

entered for $7,000

The next race of this horse was March 25, 1968, in 6th at G.P., which it won, paying $8.20. This is not a big price, which is irrelevant here, since we are studying the principles of the pattern. This horse was a 4-year-old in 1967 and a 5-year-old in 1968, at the prime age for a horse. It is difficult to know why the original owner kept racing it for $3,500 and also why subsequent claimants did likewise. From June 21, 1967, until it ran for $5,000 on March 16, 1968, it had raced ten times. This was the only past performances shown for it. $5,000, next $4,000, were the highest it was entered at. Eight times it ran for $3,500 and with the exception of three bad races its performances were good and consistent. The point concerning it is that three different trainers thought enough of it to claim it an even thought it was not claimed when raised, except on March 16 players should have been alerted that it was a good horse to keep track of and consider in any race within a reasonable price raise.

I feel that these are enough examples to impress upon the reader the wonderful opportunities offered in claimed horses and it may well repay him to become a specialist in this field. Any time you can include in your calculations a horse that shows one or more claims it should be given extra attention. Become a claimed horse specialist!

In a book written by two professors on betting horses, a research by them of claimed horses at Aqueduct, Santa Anita, and Hollywood, showed that all tracks show a flat bet profit. The claimed horse was wagered on its first runback after being claimed. If the horse won the first out, it was dropped and not played again, but if lost first time it was bet on its second try.

I attach little importance to this research because only fifty horses were selected at random for this purpose. But it has validity, because it substantiates my own analysis of betting claimed horses. My own research has covered every major and semi-major, even some minor tracks, and not fifty but thousands of horses.

I know of a mechanical system for at least twenty years under my observation, and my playing of it produces a flat bet profit. It is very simple, the rule being: Play all 4-year-old colts and geldings that are claimed out of their last or next to last race.

There are no rules as to playing these horses more than the one time if they failed to win their first start after being claimed. I played them according to the rule above given. But when they did not win I listed them to watch and continued to use them if they showed up in my daily task of picking winners. When I say use them, I do not mean mechanically, I mean this: Suppose in making selections one of these claimed horses who did not win as per above system was in a race that I was figuring, if it entered into my calculations I gave it a little edge because of its claimed background. Naturally, whether I picked it to win would depend upon how it had performed after being claimed. What I have tried to bring out here is that you must be ever alert to figure when a claimed horse is a good or a poor claim. Your correct assessment of this will in most instances result in a high mutuel payoff, if you wager on the horse so claimed.

15

Tips and Inside Information

QUOTING "PITTSBURGH PHIL" on the subject of information offers the best possible introductory opening to this chapter. "A man who has not an opinion of his own and the ability to stick to it in the face of all kinds of arguments—and arguments includes betting odds in a race—has not one chance in a million to beat the races for any length of time. One who is susceptible to 'tips,' or what is known as paddock information, may get along very well for awhile, but I have yet to find one who has stuck to this line who could show a bankroll of any dimension. Men like Charles Heaney, and others of their class, all exceedingly successful handicappers, never think of seeking information as a basis for their betting. They rely upon their own judgment entirely and never form that judgment until after the most careful consideration. To them paddock and stable information is only an incident to confirm their previous judgment. Frequently, I have met half a dozen owners and trainers of horses that have been entered in the same race and each has told me that his horse could not lose. I therefore had a half dozen 'tips' on the same race, and it was there that my judgment stood me in good stead. If he [meaning a player] is losing he becomes the prey of every type of information and influence. I have known men who bet thousands of dollars on a race when in that state of mind, to play a 'tip' given to them by a boy who sells chewing gum, a cast-off stable boy, or a bartender."

It has always been beyond my comprehension why otherwise intelligent persons will fall into the pitfall of being "touted" on horses. Let's review the practices of the "touts" that prey on the unwary horse player.

I. M. Tout gets a mailing list of horse players and writes a circular to mail out to them. The pattern of all these letters runs along the same general line. Mr. Tout has stable connections to which he has paid a fabulous sum for a sure-thing winner. Invariably a four-figure payoff is guaranteed. Seldom does such a letter state the sure winner will pay under 20 to 1. The letter continues to relate how the horse has been specifically "prepped" for this race.

Pay him $5.00 to $50.00 and he will reveal the name of this horse and the race it will run in.

The fairy stories related in these letters would stretch the imagination of Hans Christian Andersen and such fairy-tale writers.

There was a common practice in my days that was carried on outside every race track I ever attended. As you went through the gates leaving the race track, whether you were walking or in an automobile, a number of men would hand out to all a passout circular letter size (8½ x 11 inches). This sheet listed the advertiser's handicapping selections for that day's races. They would show that he had picked winners of the first five or six races and the last races showed losers or if the tout was lucky maybe a horse in the money. This happened daily and the unwary, observing that every day the tout had won five or six races, became interested. There was no nourishment for the tout in just having these passouts made. The payoff came from a notice on the circular that the advertiser had a sure winner going the following day, and it would be released *only* to those visiting his office. The gullible flocked to his office and paid from $5.00 to $100.00 to get the name of the sure-thing winner. Of course, the suckers were given a loser. If the tout had a sure winner he'd only have to play it himself and not pay the expenses involved in attracting the gullible to his net.

How was the tout able to show five to six actual winners each day? It was very simple. He had a hand-turned multigraph printing machine in a truck parked some place adjacent to the track. After the first three or four races were over one of his henchmen rushed to him with the results. It takes but a matter of seconds to set up a winner's name and price on a multigraph drum. The same thing happened with the next two or three races. For the last race or two the tout would make a stab and put in his own selections. Seldom did he get a winner, but if lucky might get a second or third run in. As the sheets were printed, they were rushed to the gates and passed out. Simple once you know the chicanery used.

I said the suckers calling at the tout's office the next day would pay whatever he could get from them, from $5.00 to $100.00. Should anyone doubt that statement let me relate this factual incident.

I made friends with a man in California who had read my handicapping lessons. He was a clever, successful businessman of some standing in his community. He telephoned me one day and said he was coming to New York to go to the track. He arrived and came to my office and made strenuous attempts to get me to go to the track with him. It was not unusual for this to happen. I had players visit me from every state in the Union for this purpose. I recall one who was a retired army officer from the State of Washington who came on. He owned race horses himself that ran in the Northwestern states.

I never succumbed to the frequent alluring offers made to me to go to the track with some student or friend. This was the time when bookies were in their heyday. When I turned down one of these offers to go to the track, although it was my custom to go every day, I would stay in my office and place my day's bets with my bookie, getting the results over the wire. This was possible at the time. I could even call the bookie and stay on the line while the actual calling of the race was given over the telephone.

I had good reasons for being reluctant to go to the track with another player. Again the words of "Pittsburgh Phil" will best illustrate.

I knew of "Pittsburgh Phil" from the time I first started playing the races. But it was long after I had written my first handicapping lessons and had met a good measure of success as a horse player before I came into possession of his secrets as told in the book written by Mr. Cole. I was thoroughly amazed to discover that I had on my own observation and reasoning been using many of his practices—particularly in my watching and analyzing the effort of every horse made in a race.

Now to quote "Phil": "One of the important rules of the men who win at the race track is that they must have absolute freedom from *distraction and interference* of all kinds. The successful race player knows there is a bar and a cafe at the track, and that there are some very interesting conversationalists to be met with every few steps, but he has no time for either the bar or the funny storytellers. I may appear to be exceedingly cold-blooded, but for the benefit of my friends I must say that a man who wishes to be successful cannot divide his attention between horses and women. A man who accepts the responsibility of escorting a woman to the race track, and of seeing that she is comfortably placed and agreeably entertained, cannot keep his mind on his work before him. Between races, a man has enough to do without replying to the questions asked by her. This is of so much importance in my opinion that it has been only upon rare occasions, and then in Saratoga, that I have asked even my mother to accompany me. Upon such days the card showed to me that there was little chance for speculation and I would, therefore, be free to devote my time otherwise."

He refers to women being a distraction. Without his mentioning it, this equally applied to men. And in my case it was men that I wanted to keep away from at the track.

Now to get back to my California friend, Joe . . . !

When Joe left me to go to the track he naturally carried with him a list of my selections for the day. I recall that I was playing only three races that day. A few days later he returned to my office to tell me to my amazement he was broke and going back home. I asked him how that could be if he had played my selections and then the story came out.

He had become involved in great financial difficulties in his business. He said, and his almost exact words are still impressed on my mind: "Al, I looked upon you as a God and came on East with the last money I had and thought I could recoup enough to straighten out my business."

I said, "Joe, how could you lose? Didn't you play the horses I gave you?"

He said he did but tried to make his own selections also, and played other horses in the same race with those I had given him. And he told me he had been handed one of the tout throw-away circulars and had gone to the tout's office and paid him $100.00 for a tip that lost. Joe was a big bettor, so paying $100.00 for a tip meant nothing to him.

He left to go back to California and shortly thereafter his wife, whom my wife and I knew well, as she had come East with Joe upon previous occasions, sent us a newspaper clipping about how Joe and a friend crashed into a mountain in the friend's private plane and both were killed.

There is a lesson involved in this anecdote about Joe and it is one that every player who wishes success must learn and follow. A player must be philosophical. He must not get upset and lose his judgment by a good winning streak any more than by a bad losing streak. He must accept them both as an incident in playing the races.

The secret is to send it in when you are playing with winnings and to be as "tight" as Scrooge when on a losing streak and using your own capital. Lady Luck runs in cycles. When she is with you, send it in. If you lose you are not losing your own capital. Be stingy when using your own capital.

Gimmick Used by the Tout Who Guarantees You a Winner or Returns your Fee Plus Price of Ticket to the Track

There is one prize tout offering that both the suspicious and the gullible are prone to fall for. The tout offers you a sure-fire winner. It is so impossible for it to lose that if it does here is what he will do:

1. Refund the money you pay for the tip.
2. Pay you the price paid for track admission.

And the fee he charges is only a modest $50.00. Only a thoroughly experienced player who knows any horse can lose will pass such an offer knowing there has to be a gimmick hidden some place. The unwary reason that this tout must be sure of himself, and even if the horse loses I have nothing to lose. I can't go wrong. So he sends in the $50.00 fee.

This is how the scheme is worked. The tout mails thousands of circulars and let's say on such an apparent good thing offer he convinces one hundred players. Let's suppose the horse loses and he returns the money paid for the tip. He receives from 100 suckers $5,000. He refunds the $5,000 received plus about $500 admission prices.

He takes in $5,000 and pays out $5,500. So he loses $500 on the face of it. So how can he profit, may reasonably be asked? Here is the gimmick. He gives out some outstanding horse in a stake or handicap race. Nine times out of ten if the horse wins it is at less than even money. The horse can pay $2.20 or $2.40 or $3.80, it makes no matter how small a price. He can't help but come out way ahead of the game.

Anyone who can add and multiply figures has to win with this scheme even if he does not know one end of a horse from another. To prove this statement, I looked at the *American Racing Manual* for 1967 results. Therein is reproduced the charts of every race run that had at least a $50,000 gross purse value. I counted 181 such races. Over 50 percent or 80 of these great races were won by the favorite. Look at these two.

July 4, 7 Aqueduct Suburban Handicap winner Buckpasser paid $3.00.

July 15, 7 Aqueduct Dwyer Handicap winner Damascus paid $3.00.

But consider this: the odds on both these winners was 50¢ to $1.00 and the closest odds next to Buckpasser was $5.30 to 1 or nearly eleven times greater and in the case of Damascus $5.40 to 1, about the same difference. Anyone could pick these horses as winners.

It is enlightening to show how much profit the tout would make if he confined his tips to the favorite in these great races. Here is how the picture looks:

Bear in mind, even if the tout returns the fee plus ticket price, when his selection loses that it only costs him $500.00. He returns the $5,000 fee plus $500.00. So his cost for the deal is only $500 on each group of customers for each race.

Total fees received for 151 races....	$755,000.00
Total fees returned for 71 races....	355,000.00
	400,000.00
Ticket price refunded	35,500.00
Gross Profit....	$364,500.00

The only cost to the tout is postage and printing charge on 5,000 circulars he mails. It only requires a 2 percent return to get 100 suckers. In legitimate mailings the norm is about 4 percent minimum return. With the attractive tout offer it is likely he'll get better than a 2 percent return.

I am showing the picture at its worst for the tout. If he sends a tip only on big purse races and only when there is a wide spread between the favorite and the second choice instead of over 50 percent winners the tout could reach as high as 75 percent. Of course, a tout would not need to send out tips on all these races. He'd make enough to satisfy anyone even if the number of tips was much less. Also there are just as good chances, and perhaps better, in any handicap or allowance and even claiming race when there is a wide spread in the odds between the favorite and second choice.

Another Scheme by Which the Tipster Can't Lose

A prospective sucker gets a telephone call from a person saying he is Jockey so and so, one of the leading jockeys at the time of the call. He has a convincing story about a certain horse that can't lose. He relates that a friend told him that the person he is calling likes to make a good bet now and then when he knows of a good thing. The caller insidiously feels the sucker out as to how much he generally bets. No matter what the size of the amount stated the caller says while it is too small this time he will give the name of the horse to prove how good the information is.

The suspicions of some will be dissipated when the caller tells them to send his fee to Jockey so and so, care of Western Union, Jamaica, New York. Or care of Stable No. ?, Belmont Race Track, N.Y. Any doubt is removed when a stable address is given. The fee is always the winnings of a bet made by the recipient for the jockey.

The tout then proceeds to give each sucker he phones a different horse in the same race. He is almost certain thereby to have at least three of these suckers wager for him the next time he phones them. The one having the winner is sure to bet next time. The one having the second and third horse is likely, especially in a close finish or where the horse closes a gap in the stretch, to bet next time. And among the others if their horse had trouble in the race they will also bet. Also some are ever hopeful and gullible and will again bet when called upon.

It is factual that a tout representing himself as a leading jockey in connivance with an employee of the Telegraph Company in Jamaica successfully worked this scheme until they were caught and sent to jail. The sucker was led on because he figured that if he telegraphed the money it must be the real jockey as no one but him could get the money from the telegraph office. But through chicanery money sent in the name of the jockey was delivered to the tout.

Of course, the tout using a stable address is working in cahoots with a stable boy or other employee of some stable located in the address area. What has been related concerning jockeys applies to touts claiming to work for some trainer or the relative or friend of some well-known trainer or jockey. These boys are tricky and can be real convincing in their approach.

Touting is operated in many different ways, but basically the sales talk is the same. They attempt to convince the sucker to pay all the traffic will bear. When these peddlers have broken or disgusted the suckers on their list they trade it with another tipster in the business. This creates a chain reaction so that in a short time the victim is deluged with tipster mail. It acts like a drug on the victimized and they will try one tipster after another. Some never give up falling for a tout, believe it or not!

I could go on and give you twenty or more different methods touts use but it will serve no purpose. Enough has been given to make you wary.

How I Was Touted on My Own Horse

When I was racing my own horses, it was my custom to attend the track every day. My office for over thirty years is located in the Bronx on East 219th

Street off White Plains Road. Usually I would leave it by automobile, proceed across the Whitestone Bridge and get to the Long Island tracks in about half an hour. However, one day—for some reason I cannot now recall—I had to be in Brooklyn. From there I was on my way to Aqueduct where one of my horses was entered. I had no idea how to proceed and I'd stop at a gas station or bar and inquire my way. In one place the bartender gave me directions and then asked if I was going to the track. When I said yes, he related to me that he knew of a sure winner. I forget the story, something about a friend of the owner, and a regular customer of the bar, had given him the tip which he was glad to pass along since I was going to the track. He said the name of the horse was Dohoev. I smiled and said: "That's funny. I own the horse and it will be trying but it's news to me that it is a sure winner." Dohoev did not win that day!

Not all tips of course originate from a tout or tipster source. Many of them derive from the fact that someone would like you to believe he intimately knows an owner, a trainer, or a jockey, and has been given an inside track. Many other tips are honest and well meant.

Tips I Have Personally Won On

I do not believe in tips. I have never fallen for them even when I first started to play the races. There was a dry goods store near my office. The proprietor operated as a bookie on the side. An ex-jockey induced him to buy a race horse for a few hundred dollars and the jockey was to train it. I'd see the bookie in the grandstand whenever his horse was entered. He'd call me over and never failed to bet on his horse and to tell me to bet on it. I'd laugh to myself and say to my wife this guy must be nuts to think his horse can win. The horse never won a race in its racing career.

It is a puzzle to me how I ever came to actually bet on two tips since I was prone to ignore them. Many times while at the track trainers have handed me money and asked me to place it for them on their horses. The impression I have now is that only one I can recall ever won.

One day I had a horse entered in a race. There were sixteen entries. Because of the width of tracks a limit is established as to the number of horses that can be run in any race. The post positions of horses are decided by lot. First name picked out of the box gets Post 1, the next Post 2 and right down to the last horse's name in the race. Thus, for sixteen entries, there would be sixteen post positions. But if only twelve can run, those horses having from Post 13 to 16 would go on what is called the "Also Eligible" list. Should one of the first twelve horses be scratched, or withdrawn from the race for any reason, the first horse on the eligible list is moved up and runs from Post 12. If two are scratched two move up, and so on.

One day a trainer came to me and asked me to do him a favor. He was

Major somebody or other but I can't remember his last name. He said he had an entry who was first on the eligible list and was sure he could win this race if he could get into it. It just so happens that he was very conservative. Some trainers honestly feel almost every time they race a horse it will win. On the other hand, when others think their horse can win they are mostly correct. It is natural for trainers and owners to be on a friendly basis among themselves. You could not pay them a thousand dollars for a tip on their horse; if offered, they'd be insulted. But if they knew you'd keep your mouth shut they'd pass the word along to you when they expected to win a race. You'd do the same for them, its being a reciprocal arrangement.

You see by this that the word "tip" can have two different meanings. Its nomenclature structure used in racing is a "tip" given for payment of a consideration or a "tip" given out of friendship. Considered in the light of being paid for, it is looked down upon with scorn and a known tipster or tout is escorted out of any race track.

Not all players know that a horse cannot be scratched at the will of the trainer. A very good reason must be given to receive permission for a scratch. This is necessary or otherwise in a small field a scratch might force the cancellation of the race.

Touts often use the fact that a horse has been scratched several times as a potent selling point in their approach. They'll say a horse has been scratched purposely waiting to get in a right spot and "this is it." The fact of the matter is that such a horse was ordered scratched by the track veterinarian or was on the eligible list one or more times.

When there is a field with also eligible horses in it then it becomes a meaningless routine to be given permission to scratch since other horses can replace any that may be scratched.

I agreed with Major X, let me call him this, to scratch my horse, which I did. His horse being first on the eligible list, Post 13 automatically was moved up and ran from Post 12. His horse came from behind and I won a nice bet on it.

Years passed before I ever placed a wager on another horse I had been given a tip on. In this book I am going to give a system that has produced phenomenal winners since 1938. It is called the "secret play" and you'll find it starting on page 159.

I played this myself when I was at the track. This play can only be made at the track. I was at this time playing with a bookie and played on tracks all over the country. So, in order to get the track data necessary to play this system I hired someone at other tracks such as an employee of the mutuel department or people working around the stables. Every season when a track first opened these men would contact me and I'd mail them forms upon which to compile the data I required, which when completed they mailed back.

My man in California at the Bay Meadows track had sent me a tip on a horse named The Whale. Being prone to disregard tips no matter from whom, there must have been some good reason why I gave this consideration. I played it once or maybe twice, I believe, and it lost. The next time it was entered I made a good-sized escalated wager on it. Along with this wager, since it was in the second part of the daily double, I scanned and handicapped the first part of the Daily Double and made another wager on the double tying The Whale up with three horses in the first race.

The *New York Daily Mirror* would be out on the stands the night before its dated edition. Since there is three hours' difference in time between New York and California, this was the only means through which you could get late results.

On the night of the race I was in bed reading a book when one of my brothers came in and said "The Whale won," and handed me the paper. I'll run down to my library in a moment and get the data from the official picture of this race. Here is the data: "The Whale" 2nd race B.M. May 4, 1944, paid $69.30. The photograph shows it winning by four lengths.

Picture shows the winning horse and jockey, the owner, trainer, and two other men. There is an arrow pointing to one of them and the word *me*, so I guess my man was an employee of the stable. It was he who sent me the photograph and this is the only photo of any horse I have in my library aside from my own horses shown winning their races.

I can't recall what the Daily Double paid but by its price of $69.30 you can judge it was a big payoff. It amounted to over 100 to 1 because here is what happened to the payment of my wagers.

The average bookie limits payoff odds to 20 to 1, 8 to 1 and 4 to 1. The big bookies like mine limited winning odds to 50 to 1. Some would allow 50 to 1 only up to a certain amount bet and reduced odds for any sum over that stated amount.

When my bookie's runner came to my office to pay me off, a discussion arose as to how much I was to receive. The sum I won was so large that I had to compromise and settle for less than the track odds called for. I won so much that I was agreeable, as my bookie was tops and did me many favors and took bets from me no other bookie would have continued to take.

I remember these two incidents clearly. In the case of The Whale I made the biggest killing in all my years of playing. One of the greatest thrills of my life was when I returned home after being paid off on The Whale. My wife was sitting on a couch. I entered the room, put my hand in my pocket, took the bills out, threw them at her, covering her and the couch and part of the floor in front of her feet. What a climax and thrill for both of us! Something never to be lived again, as I have never had another Whale since. I remember the case of Major X's horse because of the circumstances of my scratching my horse, which might have won.

As I read this sheet over for corrections it comes to me that the man sending the tip on The Whale was a jockey's agent. It's possible his jockey had ridden the horse and knew it well.

Over the years, I've received hundreds of letters from players asking me to telephone or telegraph them tips on horses. I have had one offer to bet as much as $200.00 for me on each such tip. Others offered to establish a certain bankroll and divide the winnings with me on a daily, weekly, or whatever basis I desired.

My answer was always along these lines: I do not need you to bet for me. I can afford to bet my own money. I have spent the major part of my adult life learning how to play the races. Why should I be annoyed by having to take time to call and reach you by telephone or by telegraph when I go to the track every day to play with my own money? If you are not willing to dig in and learn "racing-know-how" as every successful player must do if he expects to reap the reward in playing the races, then you do not deserve the rewards possible.

It seems to me axiomatic that the voice of reason should tell all that anyone who can consistently predict winners is not going to be bothered selling tips or asking another person to bet for them. I never cease to be flabbergasted when I hear of someone susceptible to the come-on of touts.

The incalculable rewards offered in playing the races will never come to those unwilling to make the sacrifice necessary to obtain them! (Note: The thought comes to me that since I went to the track every day to play, some might wonder why I speak of playing through a bookie. I wagered with one or more bookies every day on races outside the track I attended. The bookie's runner would pick up my bets in the morning and, if I was playing with more than one bookie at the time, I would call a bookie in Las Vegas before I left for the track. And often I would call Las Vegas if I did not go to the track when I did not have a horse entered to listen on the phone to the running of a race I might have a substantial bet on.)

This practice is impossible today as is general playing with bookies as they are gradually being forced out of business and becoming extinct. To sum up about touts it would seem that reasonable intelligence would tell anyone that if a "tout" could successfully continue to give you winners he could do the same for himself. And by betting his own tips he could make more money easier than to have you pay him or place a bet for him.

16

The Art of Wagering

IF IT WERE possible to convince every existent horse player that knowing how to wager is infinitely more important than being able to pick winning selections, and if they would make an effort to acquire the know-how of proper betting, many presently successful players would greatly enhance their profits and many now unable to produce a yearly profit would be able to turn losing into winning results.

I am fully convinced that there can be no real hope of turf success until the art of wagering is mastered. There are innumerable approaches that can be used to produce winning selections. And they get winners—good winners! I feel safe in saying that any system, whether it is based upon solid bases or upon some crack-pot idea such as sticking a pin through a program and betting on the horses whose names are penetrated by the pin, will actually win provided the proper wagering method is applied in connection with it.

Perhaps I can make this statement appear more plausible by explaining it this way. It is a fact that billions of dollars are bet on a single play by life insurance companies each year. Instead of one *entry* in a race there are millions. A man applies for insurance and is quoted odds, these odds depending upon how old he is when he enters the race for time. The insurance company is betting that this man will outlive his competitors in the race and continue to pay premiums. If he does, the company wins. If he loses his family gets paid off, and thus is the winner since premiums cease. The company has gambled and lost on this man! But in the end they are the winner and must always be the winner!

The relationship of the insurance company to an insured person is the same as that of the bookie to a player. The insured is in the same relationship to the insurance company as a horse is to a bookie. If an insured dies within a short time the company has lost a bet and his family collects the winnings. If a player wins a bet the bookie loses a bet. But both the bookie and the company must end up winning because they know and apply the art of wagering. If you grant that what I have said is actually a fact, in reality you must admit that knowing how to bet is a thousand times more important than knowing how to pick a winner.

My reference to insurance companies herein applies to straight life insurance wherein the insured continues to pay a premium as long as he lives and a stated sum is paid upon his death. Definitely, everyone insured eventually must die. But the odds quoted him are based upon his life expectancy. The longer he survives beyond this expectancy period the more profit the company makes because premiums continue. And since new races for time are scheduled by life, new competitors (new insureds) are entered daily thus setting up never-ending chain reaction.

The *tables of mortality* is the magic wand that produces profits for the insurance company. Billions—not millions—of statistics on the life expectancy of men and women give the companies data upon which to quote their odds to the insured. For example, an insured twenty-eight years of age, when he enters the race for time, by taking out an insurance policy, can within a reasonable degree of certainty be expected to die at a certain future age. If he does not, it makes not one iota of difference to the companies.

"Dutching the book" is the secret by which bookies must always win. The bookie balances his book by the limit of the odds he quotes on each horse combined with how much action he will accept on each horse. So, no matter what horse wins he has to win! By balancing his book is meant that he pays out to those who bet on the winning horse some of the money lost on all other horses in the race. But he has more money lost in the race than he pays out. So he must net a profit!

9 race Lrl. Nov. 18, 1968. Winner Winsome Lad

Finish	Horse	Odds	Bets	Pays	Profit	Loss
*1	Winsome Lad	4	10	$ 40	$30	
2	Hath Charms	24	10	240		$170
*3	Long Count	3	10	30	40	
4	Oh Jimmy II	12	10	120		50
*5	Cortex	1	10	10	60	
*6	Great Pacifist	3	10	30	40	
7	Happy Wonder	12	10	120		50

By chance, I picked up a racing paper and am using the above race as an illustration. The headings explain themselves. I placed the finish positions to the left to separate them from the other numerical figures. I am using only the dollar figures disregarding the cents. For example, the true odds of Winsome Lad actually was $4.30 to $1.00 rather than $4.00. The cents only confuse the issue and have no meaning here.

You can see that in a seven-horse race, the bookie would have netted a profit if any one of four horses won the race, viz: Number 1 or 3 or 5 or 6. Without having the slightest opinion as to who could or who would win the race he has nearly 60 percent of the competitors on whom, if they did win, he would make a goodly profit, no matter which one of the four won. The setup is made on the basis of only ten players betting on each separate horse in the race. Naturally, this is hypothetically assumed. In actual practice the number of persons betting on each separate horse would vary. The principal thing to remember right now is that the bookie has six horses out of the seven running for him against the player's one horse. A decidedly big edge, wouldn't you say?

This chart does not show the book being dutched. It is merely to show that even without the magic force of dutching, the bookie has every horse, but one, running for him against the player's one; and to show that even when not dutching the book in this particular race he would win if any one of four horses won, and he'd have lost if any one of the other three won. But this loss is prevented by dutching the book.

The bookie so arranged his book that he controlled how much money he would accept on each separate horse. This control was effected by adjusting, raising, or lowering the odds, to suit his purpose. If he had too much money bet on one horse he would send his runner out who would lay off some of it with another bookie. He could refuse more bets on a horse he was overloaded on, but he wanted to accommodate his customers and keep their trade so he'd accept more than wanted and lay it off. Naturally, another bookie who did not have enough on the same horse "overbet" would be glad to accept the other bookie's money so this worked to the mutual advantage of all.

There is a formula that was used for this specific purpose. The book was thereby dutched so that no matter which horse won the bookie cleared on each race a net profit of 15 percent to 20 percent or more.

Now, of course, the picturesque days when a bookie sat on a stool high above the heads of the crowds, with his slate giving the odds fastened over his head, are gone forever.

There are several reasons why I write about them. One is that I will give you herein a method showing how you can play more than one horse in a race and be able to get the same advantage a bookie had.

"Pittsburgh Phil" tells how the betting commissioners of successful plungers were known to the men he employed to watch their action and now I quote him. "They were always on the watch for some clue to the purposes of persons who might have an important influence on the race. As a result of this, there was a never-ending fight of stratagem and ruse during the day. If I had watched them, I knew they watched me. Many a time, for instance, I have seen a commissioner come into the ring and bet possibly five hundred dollars on a certain horse with a certain bookmaker, after which he would bet $100 or so with other men. Immediately the whisper would go about the ring that 'so and so's commissioner was betting on such and such a horse.' The unthinking and uninformed usually took that as sufficient reason for following the lead. It is here that the fine work began. My man would stand at the book where the commissioner bet his $500 and watch the effect of the wager. He would be able to tell in a few minutes. Many a time the same bookmaker has accepted the money, say at three to one, and immediately laid the top price in the ring against the same horse. That would satisfy me. It was a bet for effect. There was collusion between the bookmaker and the commissioner, which would have to be thrown out of the betting calculation altogether. It was intended to trap the unsuspecting public and I regret to say that it frequently succeeded. Nine times out of ten such horses do not finish in the money."

(Note: Phil mentions "collusion" but does not say what I suspect actually took place. The bookie taking the $500 bet and maintaining his price was let in on the fact that that horse bet on had no chance. This would allow him to take advantage of this in balancing his book and he would later return the $500 to the commissioner.)

"The advantage of this particular incident to me was that it eliminated a possible contender, and in a four- or five-horse race that had an important effect. [Note: In those days three-, four-, and five-horse races were frequent. Fields much smaller than those running today was the norm.] It even helped me at times in beating the race on the *dutch book* system. Knowing that one horse out of four, say, was not good, I would bet on all the others, thus in some cases winning twenty-five cents for every dollar invested. In other words, I bought their dollar notes for seventy-five cents each. I recall, some years ago, seeing the value of close observation in the betting ring. This occurred when 'Mike' Dwyer was the heaviest bettor on the turf. I will not give the names of others concerned for the reason that some of them are now men highly respected, and who have lived down anything that they might have done in days gone by.

"The race I allude to was run at a track in the vicinity of New York City, and it was practically a two-horse affair, one of the horses being owned by the Dwyer Brothers, then partners in the best stable of horses that was ever trained. To hide the identity of those concerned in the affair more thoroughly, I will designate the horse as 'A' and 'B.' I may say that the incident was about the most cowardly piece of highway robbery that ever occurred in this or any other country. The race looked such a certainty for the Dwyer horse, which I will designate as 'A,' that when the betting opened it was a one to four shot. Few cared to speculate at those odds, consequently the business in the ring was light. I never dreamed of making a bet that day and had dismissed the race from my mind, when as I strolled toward the paddock to look over the horses entered in the following race, I met Charley Dwyer, who was then quite a youngster. We exchanged greetings and I said that it was a walkover for his father's horse. The boy replied that his father was of the same opinion and had just given an order that $30,000 be bet on the horse at any old price. I do not know what prompted me to go back to the betting ring. Possibly it was curiosity to notice the effect of a $30,000 commission on a horse already held at one to four. To my surprise there was little or no change noticeable in the odds. The commission had evidently not yet been placed and I began to watch more closely. The horses were called to the post, and still there was no change—one to four was obtainable all over the ring, while the contender showed signs of support from some quarters. In those days, and in these days too, for that matter, a thirty-thousand-dollar commission would or will drive a one to four shot to at least one to seven. There was therefore "a tiger in the woodpile." My mind worked quickly—that commission was being held out. The man, or men holding it out, would do so only with the knowledge that the jockey riding the favorite was in their conspiracy. I may say right here in justice to one of the most reputable men on the turf that this jockey was not 'Jimmy' McLaughlin.

"As soon as I reached this conclusion, I bet several thousand dollars on the horse designated 'B.' The race was run and Mr. Dwyer's horse was beaten. His $30,000 had gone into the hands of some unscrupulous men and a jockey. I never said a word to him and it is possible that he never knew the truth of the affair. A funny part of this whole transaction is that other men, who had caught the drift of things, have since accused me of being implicated in the plot, because my wagers had been heaviest. But the facts are as I have related. *My betting was due solely to my close observation of the ring's proceedings.*"

The words above set in italics is to point out that "Pittsburgh Phil" was acting as a racing detective as you will have observed, as I have mentioned in this book, that I have done. He acted as a detective to detect the secrets that he discovered and applied them to win millions. You have the same material to work with as he had, and as I had with the exception of any secrets relating to wagering with bookmakers at the track, which of course no longer exist.

Knowing the art of wagering and the financing of your money is the high road to success. Again, I quote Phil. "Learn when to put down a heavy wager by picking out an almost sure winner. In a race where three or four horses have a chance to win the odds are much against you, and the wager must be small or pass the race up.

"I have lost as many as twenty-seven straight bets and got even and became a winner on the next few races. The average bettor should always cut his wagers when running in a losing streak and press them when luck favors him. *Doubling bets when losing is ruination to any person.* The time to double is when you have the bookmaker's money in hand. If a bookmaker gets you hooked, try and wiggle off with as little loss as possible, but if you get a bookmaker hooked send in your money, and if your judgment is good and you go at him cold-bloodedly, betting on what appears to be certainties, you have a good chance to win a small fortune."

Substitute the words mutuel machine for bookmaker and you will get the idea conveyed in the preceding paragraph.

Wagering Must Be Geared To Selections!

One of the secrets of success is that any method of wagering must first of all be mathematically sound and designed to produce specific results, and it must be only with the right type of selections. There is no such thing as a single investment method that will fit all types of selections. I say, and I expect to prove to you, that almost any set of professionally made selections can be made to produce profits, month after month, when the correct method of investing is applied. By professionally made selections I refer to the picks of any person whose selections appear in racing papers, scratch sheets, or newspapers.

Around the time I first started to play the races the *Green Sheet* was published here in the East. It was published by Roy Tollison. I suspect that never in racing history was there a publication that made such an impact upon the playing public. His selections were unbelievably fantastic. Horse players who followed Tollison had the heyday of their lives. For a long time the bookies took the most unmerciful beating ever known. Finally, it reached the stage when all the small-time bookies refused to accept any bet that was made on any *Green Sheet* selection. Even some of the big bookies either refused to accept a bet on a *Green Sheet* selection or limited the action thereon. An overloaded bookmaker could always lay off as much of his action as he wanted. He could telephone to Chicago, St. Louis, or to any of the layoff centers and thus spread any action beyond what he wanted for himself. Thousands of players were daily taking the bookies over the hurdles. Eventually, the bookies adopted the most unprecedented action ever known and reduced the price on every Tollison selection so low or refused all action that the "goose that laid the golden egg" was killed and the *Green Sheet* suspended publication. Tollison was probably the greatest of all handicappers.

I notice in a present-day scratch sheet, where the Consensus Points appears, they list a Green Sheet. This is not the same as the original *Green Sheet*. The Tollison *Green Sheet* was not a scratch sheet. It was a turf newsletter similar to a scratch sheet in its listings, but with running comments upon the selections made.

To the proponents of the flat play principle I want to say this: Any method capable of producing flat play *profits* may be made to show much larger profits, far more consistently, and *often on much less capital* than is required to finance a flat play.

Also selections that result in a flat play *loss* on a flat play basis may easily be made to produce *profits consistently*, and because selections that *win* on a flat play may be made to show *bigger profits* more consistently, the art of wagering and financing should be given even more attention than any method of making selections. I can't emphasize too strongly that the method of investing is almost everything. Master the subject of proper wagering and you will have taken your longest step forward toward success at turf speculation. If you fail to master it fully you might just as well abandon any hope of success on the turf.

Now let us get down to "brass tacks." Let me begin by pointing out that there are but *two* basic principles involved where methods of investing are concerned: One, methods that aim to recoup losses incurred since starting operation, plus a profit on a single winner; usually the first winner to come along after one or more losers have been played is the purpose. Two, methods that aim to spread the recouping of past losses, together with a profit, over a series of winners.

All such methods make use of progressing or the increasing of wagers usually after each loser. Some methods are designed to finance the increase with bets out of the operator's own capital; others to increase the size of bets only from winnings.

Speaking of financing, a great many players labor under the delusion that if given sufficient money they can beat the races. Such players are just kidding themselves! It is my contention that if a person cannot make racing profits on a total bankroll of $100 to $500 then he can not produce profits if given a working capital of $5,000. The principle inherent is exactly the same whether the capital be $100 or $500. The only differential is in the units of bets applied.

Consult the chart on page 131 as you continue to read from here on.

Three Basic Types of Progression

If you now have the chart ready, let us proceed. First, give your attention to the method shown, under heading "EXAMPLE A" to the extreme left. Let me explain how the workout is arranged. Numbers from 1 to 36 on left side indicate the number of *plays* made; these numbers, incidentally, indicate the number of plays in *all* of the three examples shown. Thus, if I refer to play number 1, or 7, or 15, you can quickly find the line in question. The figures in the column marked "bet" indicate the size of wagers made at different times. Please note that in *all* examples the wagers are supposedly made at the track; for this reason wagers will jump from $2 to $4 even if a wager of $3 is actually called for. Those who are able to legally place wagers through bookmakers can, of course, make wagers of any size and thereby modify the progression somewhat.

In the column marked "odds" are given the figures indicating the odds a horse will, or did pay. Rather than give the odds as they appear on the odds board, as 8/5, 7/2, and the like, which is confusing to many, I give you the odds in terms of dollars and cents. Thus, the figure 1.50 means 1.50-to-1, the figure 2.00 means 2.00 to 1, and so on. In the column marked "lost" you will find recorded all losing wagers. In the column marked "won" are recorded the winnings on each play that wins. Please understand this: only actual winnings on any specific play ever go in the "won" column, not the sum collected, as such sums would include the wager itself.

Explanation of Example "A"

The method used in this example is the well-known *doubling-up* method, probably the first method of progression ever used on horses, dice, or what

Examples of Wagering Scales

EXAMPLE "A"

No.	Bet	Odds	Lost	Won
1	$ 2	—	$ 2	—
2	(4)	1.50	—	$ 6
3	(2)	2.00	—	4
4	2	—	2	—
5	(4)	2.50	—	10
6	2	—	2	—
7	4	—	4	—
8	8	—	8	—
9	(16)	1.50	—	24
10	(2)	2.00	—	4
11	(2)	1.00	—	2
12	(2)	1.50	—	3
13	2	—	2	—
14	4	—	4	—
15	8	—	8	—
16	16	—	16	—
17	32	—	32	—
18	64	—	64	—
19	128	—	128	—
20	256	—	256	—
21	(512)	1.00	—	512
22	(2)	2.50	—	5
23	2	—	2	—
24	(4)	2.00	—	8
25	2	—	2	—
26	(4)	1.50	—	6
27	2	—	2	—
28	4	—	4	—
29	(8)	1.25	—	10
30	(2)	1.50	—	3
31	(2)	2.50	—	5
32	(2)	2.00	—	4
33	2	—	2	—
34	(4)	1.50	—	6
35	(2)	2.00	—	4
36	(2)	2.00	—	4

		$540	$620
			540
	Profit:	$ 80	

Capital used
  worst period $1,028
Percent Winners 50%
Return on Invest. 7%

FLAT PLAY

$10 Won $137.50
Return on Invest. 7%
Capital used $90

EXAMPLE "B"

Deb.	Odds	Bet	Lost	Won
$20	2.00	$10	$10	—
30	3.00	10	10	—
40	2.50	16	16	—
56	4.00	14	14	—
70	2.00	35	35	—
105	5.00	21	21	—
126	2.00	63	63	—
(189)	1.00	189	—	$189
20	2.00	10	10	—
30	1.50	20	20	—
50	2.50	20	20	—
70	3.00	24	24	—
(94)	2.00	47	—	94
20	1.50	14	14	—
34	2.00	17	17	—
(51)	3.00	17	—	51
20	1.50	14	14	—
34	6.00	6	6	—
40	4.00	10	10	—
50	2.00	25	25	—
75	1.00	75	75	—
(150)	1.50	100	—	150
20	3.00	7	7	—
27	2.00	14	14	—
41	2.50	17	17	—
58	1.50	39	39	—
97	1.20	81	81	—
178	2.00	89	89	—
267	2.50	107	107	—
374	1.50	250	250	—
624	3.00	208	208	—
(832)	3.00	278	—	834
20	1.00	20	20	—
40	2.00	20	20	—
60	1.50	40	40	—
(100)	2.00	50	—	100

		$1,296	$1,418
			1,296
	Profit:	$ 122	

Capital used $2,518
Return on Invest. 6.2%
Percent Winners 16.6%

FLAT PLAY

$10 Lost $175.00

EXAMPLE "C"

Bet	Odds	Lost	Won
$ 5	—	$ 5	—
10	—	10	—
15	—	15	—
(20)	1.00	—	$20
15	—	15	—
(20)	1.00	—	20
(15)	1.00	—	15
10	—	10	—
(15)	1.00	—	15
10	—	10	—
15	—	15	—
20	—	20	—
(25)	1.00	—	25
(20)	1.00	—	20
15	—	15	—
(20)	1.00	—	20
15	—	15	—
20	—	20	—
(25)	1.00	—	25
20	—	20	—
25	—	25	—
(30)	1.00	—	30
(25)	1.00	—	25
(20)	1.00	—	20
15	—	15	—
(20)	1.00	—	20
(15)	1.00	—	15
10	—	10	—
(15)	1.00	—	15
10	—	10	—
15	—	15	—
(20)	1.00	—	20
15	—	15	—
(20)	1.00	—	20
(15)	1.00	—	15
(10)	1.00	—	10

		$260	$350
			260
	Profit:	$ 90	

Capital used
  worst period ...$75
Return, Inv. ..13.4%

FLAT PLAY

Breaks exactly even
with 50% winners at
even money.

have you. Most players have the good sense to realize that a method of this type will break you sooner or later, mostly sooner. But a great many players still feel that they could beat the races with a method of this type. I choose to begin this discussion by using this method as a terrible example of what the smart player should *never* do, not only because the method calls for a very large capital but because it will invariably fail and is highly inefficient as well. Let's quickly run through the workout and see why this is so.

We begin play with the smallest practical wager of $2. It is not important what selections are used in the example; anyone dumb enough to tackle this method should certainly make sure of using a method that will produce at least 50 percent of winners even if the prices should be but slightly better than even money. A lower percentage of winners would invite likely runs of losers that would wreck the operator in no time at all. The odds shown in the odds column represent the kind of odds you would get on strong favorites and, I might add, it would be a good handicapper who could produce the results shown.

Our first wager of $2 loses. Note that we record this loss in the *lost* column. Since the idea is to double the size of each wager after each loser, wager number 2 is $4. Note that this figure is shown in the *bet* column. This wager wins (note the brackets) at odds of 1.50 to 1. We win $6. Note that we jot the winnings down in the *won* column. Since we hit a winner, we now regress to our initial wager of $2.00 for play No. 3. The play wins, at odds of 2.00 to 1. We win $4 and this goes in *won* column. We again play $2 on play number 4. Play loses. Play number 5 is therefore $4. It wins, at odds of 2.50 to 1. Play number 6 is $2. It loses so we play $4 on play number 7. Play loses so we double our wager and bet $8 on play number 8. We lose, so we double the wager and play $16 on play number 9. Play wins, at odds of 1.50 to 1 and the winnings of $24 go in *won* column.

I am sure the idea is clear. Wagers are doubled in size after each loser; they go back to the initial bet of $2 after each winner. Note that plays number 10, 11, 12 all win with a wager of $2 each. Starting with play number 13, we run into a string of 8 consecutive losers; note how wagers pile up, wager number 21 being $512. This run of losers could as easily have been number 10 or 15, in which case some hefty wagers would have to be made. Play No. 21 won at odds of even money; the odds could as easily have been even shorter; of course, they could have been longer too, but things seldom work out that way; at best, this is leaving too much to chance.

From there on, the method keeps clicking on small wagers, due to the exceptional percentage of winners. Now check the results. The method shows a profit of $80. This is a return of 7 percent on all the money risked, or wagered. Not a very good return, but better than losing. Now note this: there are exactly 50 percent of winners; a uniform flat play of $10, with no increase or decrease in wagers, produced a profit of $137.50. This is a return of 38 percent on all money wagered, and the largest capital needed to finance these $10 wagers over the very worst period (plays 13 to 21) was $90, as against the $1,028 needed to carry the doubling-up scheme over the same period.

The main fault of this method is that wagers are pyramided too rapidly during losing streaks; during winning streaks, the wagers are too *small* to produce any real results. As for inefficiency, the idea of any progressive method is to place heavier wagers on the winning plays than on the losing ones; what happens here? A total of $576 was wagered on 18 winners for an average wager of $32. A total of $540 was wagered on 18 losers for an average of $30.

Explanation of Example "B"

The method for which a workout is given in Example B is known to most serious students of methods; it is perhaps one of the first wagering plans perfected and, if the simple principle involved is thoroughly understood, it is a method that is as sure to win as night follows day, if backed by the necessary capital.

Before I take up the workout figures, let me explain the meaning of the figures in the first (left) column which has the heading of "Deb." This is an abbreviation of *debit*; sometimes this column is called a "Due" column, because the figures appearing in it represent the sums that are *due* you—the sums that must be won, usually on the first winner you hit after one or more losers, in order to accomplish what you have set out to do. Generally, with this type of method you set out to win a predetermined sum per race or per day. You may set out to win $2, $5, $10 or any other amount per race actually played; or you may set out to win $10, $20, $50 or any other sum per day. The figures appearing in the debit column, then, represent the sum you have set out to win, plus any losing wagers you may make. I'll explain that as we go along.

With a method like this, there are those who advocate that you set out to win a given amount per day, say $20, and then carry on the play just until you hit a winner after which you are through playing for the day. The idea has something to recommend it.

In Example B, however, we set out to win $20 on the first winner we hit, with no thought of stopping play, continuing to play with the idea in mind of winning $20 on every winner we hit.

We start play, then, with the object of winning $20 on play No. 1. Note that we jot this sum down in the *Debit* column. To determine the amount to wager, we must consult the *odds board* to learn the odds on the horse we mean to wager on; since it is important that we know the probable odds a horse will pay, wagers must be placed fairly late, after the bulk of the money has been wagered and the odds are pretty well settled. A couple of minutes before the horses reach the post, we find that our horse is 2.00 to 1. We want to win $20. At odds of 2.00 to 1 we must wager $10 in order to win $20. Had our horse been 5.00 to 1, we would only need to wager $4. If he were 10.00 to 1, we would only need to wager $2. That's the idea in a nutshell; we wager enough money, at the prevailing odds, to win the amount we seek to win.

Play number 1 loses. Note that we record the loss in the *lost* column. Now, we failed to win the $20 we set out to win; we lost $10. We now add the loss of $10 to the $20 we failed to win on our first try; this makes a total of $30 we must try to win on the next race. Note that for play number 2 we jot the sum of $30 down in the *Debit* column. The odds on our horse in this race are 3.00 to 1. To win $30 at odds of 3.00 to 1 we must again wager $10. Note that we jot down a $10 wager in the *Bet* column and that the play loses, so we put this amount down in the *Lost* column.

Now, we again add the loss of $10, to the figure ($30) in the *Debit* column, making our debit $40. Note that for play No. 3 this sum is shown in the *Debit* column. The odds on our horse in the third race are 2.50 to 1. At these odds, we would have to wager the sum of $16 to win $40. We do this, and lose. We jot the loss of $16 down in the *Lost* column and we now add the loss of $16 to the $40 in our *Debit* column, making the new debit $56 as the amount we must try to win on the fourth race. The odds on our horse in the fourth race are 4.00 to 1; to win $56 at these odds, we must wager $14. Note that this is done and that our horse loses; the loss of $14 is put in the *Lost* column and is added to the debit.

We keep going in this manner for plays No. 5, 6, and 7, which all lose; in each case, we wager enough money at the prevailing odds to win the amount shown in our *Debit* column; when we lose, we add the amount of the lost wager to the sum in the *Debit* column.

As we come to play number 8, our debit has climbed to $189, the odds on our horse are EVEN MONEY, so we must wager $189 in order to win the sum shown in the *Debit* column. This time we win. Note that we record the winnings of $189 in the *Won* column. We have now accomplished our purpose; we have won the $20 we set out to win, plus the losses incurred while backing the first seven losers. If you will add up the figures shown in the *Lost* column, for the first seven races, you will find that they add up to a total loss of $169; we won $189 on the eighth race, giving us the profit of $20 we were playing for.

We now start play anew, with a fresh $20 in the *Debit* column. The procedure from here on is always the same; it never varies; you start play by trying to win $20, wagering enough at the prevailing odds to win this sum, should the horse win; when horse loses, you add the amount of the lost wager to the figure in the *Debit* column, then wager enough money, at the prevailing odds to win the sum shown in the *Debit* column.

As may be seen, this method cannot fail to win. The percentage of winners is unimportant; all the method asks for is just *one* winner, at any kind of a price—before the operator runs out of money, or before wagers get so large that it would be impracticable to get them placed. In theory, this method is a sure winner; in actual practice, however, the method is not a safe one to use on selections that produce winners at *mixed* prices, meaning that prices run from very short to fairly good; this is because the *short* prices force the player to make larger and larger wagers; a relatively short run of consecutive losers, coupled with fairly short prices on the horses played, will pyramid the debit and the wagers rapidly; a prolonged run of losers would run the debit and the wagers up to such sums that only a millionaire could finance the wagers.

If you will turn your attention back to the example workout, and begin following the play down, line for line, starting on line number 3 and going down to line 32, you will see what can happen during a run of just *nine* (from line number 23 to line 31 inclusive) consecutive losers; during this period, it took the sum of $2,518 to finance the play on the nine losers and the eventual winner that came on play number 32. Had the prices been still shorter, an even larger capital would have been needed; if, for example, play number 32 had gone to post at even money the wager would have been $832. You can figure what would happen during a streak of, say 20 consecutive losers; such a run can happen, when using selections that run to mixed prices, such as the picks of public selectors.

All this does not mean that the method is worthless. The facts are that the selections used result in a net loss of $175 on the basis of a $10 flat play, the percentage of winners being extremely low, only 16.6 percent. Still, the method turned in a net profit of $122, and a return of 6.2 percent on every dollar wagered. This form of play has real possibilities; the trouble is that the method is not suitable for a play on selections that run mostly to fairly short prices: The method, if it is used, should be used only with selections that run to *long* prices; with such selections, wagers will increase in size very gradually and it becomes practicable to span tremendously long runs of consecutive losers on reasonably small capital.

I said before that one of the secrets of turf success is that the method of investing must fit the method of selection; this method does not fit selections at mixed prices; true, it may work wonderfully well over periods of time when winners come fairly close together, but the method will get the operator in trouble during any prolonged run of losers.

Now let us consider the workout shown in Example "C."

Explanation of Example "C"

Thus far, we have dealt with two methods that aim to recoup previous losses, together with a profit, on a single winner; now we shall discuss a method that aims to recoup losses and produce a profit over a series of winners.

Please turn to Example "C." With this method, it is not necessary to know the odds on any horse. The progression is mechanical and works as follows: You start with a wager of a given size, $2, $3, $4, $5, or any other amount. Whatever the size of your initial wager is, we shall refer to that as one unit.

After each loser, you increase your wager one unit; after each winner you decrease your wager one unit. In the example, we start out with a wager of $5. After each loser, we shall increase the wager by $5. After each winner we shall decrease the wager by $5.

This particular method was perfected primarily for use on games of chance where the odds are even money, such as craps and roulette. I will use the same odds here, because it simplifies matters and makes it easy to grasp the principle involved. Later, while retaining the basic principle, the method will be changed so as to handle the different odds encountered in horse racing.

Now please follow the figures on the chart. The first wager is $5. It loses. We now increase the wager by $5, making wager No. 2 $10. It loses. We increase our wager by $5, making wager No. 3 $15. It loses. We increase the wager by $5, making wager No. 4 $20. This wager wins, at even money. We now decrease the wager by $5, so that wager number 5 is $15. It loses. We increase the wager by $5, making wager number 6 $20. It wins, at even money. We now decrease the wager by $5, making wager number 6 $15. It wins, we again decrease the wager $5, so that wager number 8 is $10.

This should make everything clear. After each loser, you increase your wager one unit (the size of your initial wager) and after each winner you decrease your wager one unit. If your starting wager is $2, you raise your wager $2 after each loser and you reduce it by $2 after each winner. The same procedure is used for any other size starting bet.

Now please follow the figures in the *Bet* column down, line for line, and note how the wagers increase and decrease depending upon whether we hit winners or losers. Wagers go up slowly during a run of losers and they come down at the same rate during a run of winners.

Now study the results. There are exactly 50 percent winners. At odds of even money a flat play of any amount would break exactly even. By using this method, a profit of $90 is realized, which is a return of 13.4 percent on every dollar wagered. Now please note this: A total of $350 was wagered on the 18 winners, for an average wager on winners of $19.44. A total of $260 was wagered on 18 losers, for an average wager on losers of $14.44. This means that wagers on the winners were 35 percent higher than wagers on the losers. And that's what progression is meant to do; place heavier wagers on the winners than on the losers. This method, albeit in its most primitive form, will do it all the time, with mathematical accuracy—just so long as play is continued until an even number of winners and losers has been played. That is, when taking odds of even money. When getting better odds, it is not necessary to get 50 percent winners; the method, when further details are given, will function with the same mathematical precision on 25 percent, 30 percent, or any other percentage of winners. Further, it is capable of producing even greater profits.

The three hypothetical workouts given indicate the basic principles upon which efficient and winning wagering methods are devised. Using these foundations, I can arrange these principles to achieve any purpose I want. For example, supposing my objective is to always wager twice as much on *every* winner than on the losers in a series of plays. Or suppose the aim is for three times more wagering on winners than on losers. It can be done. There are books on the Art of Wagering. In this book there is only space to give you enough data so that it will whet your appetite, and send you on a profitable search to acquire the "know-how" of proper wagering. The procedure of learning proper wagering is not as complex as it may seem. In fact, once you get the knack of what it is necessary to know you'll find it more interesting and easier than picking winners. Those who take up this subject are going to spend many an enjoyable hour figuring out the correct form of wagering applied to the right selections.

Here is how to go about it. Select charts of any races run and study them. Also select one or more handicappers and devise a wagering method that will positively win if based upon his norm of winners and prices. There are many ways. Here is a simple one. Suppose you establish that the average odds averages 5 to 1.

Bet No.	Amt. Bet	Total Bet	Net Win
1	$1	$1	$5.00
2	1	2	4.00
3	1	3	3.00
4	1	4	2.00
5	2	6	6.00
6	2	8	4.00
7	3	11	7.00
8	3	14	4.00
9	4	18	6.00
10	5	23	7.00
11	6	29	7.00

The columns are self-explanatory. Refer to bet No. 7. Using the exact scale shown under Amount Bet you have lost six wagers for a total loss of $8.00. Remember the odds are always 5 to 1 here. You bet $3.00 on your 7th bet and win $15.00 net. Deducting $8.00 lost on previous bets you now have a net win of $7.00. Any time a winner comes at odds of no less than 5 to 1 we have to have a net profit up to that point of playing. We can continue this on for any number of races, and at any odds. There are innumerable ways in which to get one winner out of eleven picks by your own "know-how" of selecting your own winners or using mechanical means such as some public handicapper. What I am doing is showing you the pattern to follow. Does this seem difficult to you? Well, it isn't, as evidenced by the following amazing play.

I call this the "$17,000 Fool Play."

In checking odds given in scratch sheets I continually noticed that amazing payoffs occurred very frequently when either the third or the fourth horse down on the price line won. Their odds might be 5 to 1 yet $20.00, $30.00, and $40.00 payoffs recurred so often that I started a preliminary research to see if it was possible to promulgate a winning method based upon these facts.

As a general rule the Graded Selections' price line showed the third and fourth choices ranging from 3 to 1 to 6 to 1. Therefore, it hardly appears possible, with these quoted odds, that $20 to $40 payoffs so often took place. My preliminary investigation proved the feasibility of my continuing the research.

Just as I advise you to do, I set about with pencil and paper and experimented with different wagering investments until I found the right one. It is to be expected that it is natural to get long strings of consecutive losers with this loose method of making the selections upon which to wager. I realized that there most likely would be times when large sums might have to be wagered and that with a payoff of 20 to 1 or more placing bets might be difficult. Also, as originally set up, the play was to cease upon hitting the first winner.

Because of these two possible difficulties I contacted my bookie. It was not unusual for my bookie, when I gave him a large wager, to lay off the bet and send some of his own money along with it to bet on my selection. To make a long story short here is what happened. We agreed to go partners on this deal and I started play with $2.00 and won the first bet paying such a price that no more than this $2.00 capital was ever needed thereafter.

Starting with this original bet of $2.00 the accumulated winnings ran up to $17,000, and this is why I named it the "$17,000 Fool Play." We split the winnings and continued to use this method for some time. A $17,000 profit on $2 starting capital was possible because unit bet was increased out of winnings as they accumulated.

Conditions as they exist today will not permit the operation of this system to function now. So I am giving you a slightly changed version of it adaptable for present-day playing.

The $17,000 Fool Play

The first important feature of this method is that for certain you will get amazingly long-priced winners beyond belief. The next important thing is that for certain you have to expect long strings of losers. This is to be expected as it is an essential of racing—just as much as the sun and the moon are a necessary part of the universe.

The idea started to win $2 for every race on a nine-card program. It was assumed that starting with $2 wagers, making $18.00 a day profit, that making larger wagers from winnings would result in tremendous profits. However, it was early discovered that to achieve this objective the risk was too great and the progression required was higher than common sense dictated. After innumerable approaches the plan herein was found to be the *key*.

While it can happen, it should not occur often that you could get 24 straight losers. On the 13th play (shown on this page) a total of $44 has been wagered. As the bet here is only for $6, it takes only a $15 payoff to wipe out this loss. Anything over $15 will show a profit. If a $30 payoff is received for the 24th wager, $150 would come back for a profit of $16. Nothing to rave about, but it proves the safety of the plan. It is unlikely you'll get 24 straight losers often, if ever.

Briefly, here is how you proceed: Play either the 3rd or 4th choice down from the top of the Scratch Sheet. Start the first race with a $2 wager and continue to wager $2 each on the first *six* wagers; then $4 on the next *five* bets, and so on, as shown below.

The Progression

Scale No. 1			Scale No. 2		
Number of Play	Bet	Total			
1	$ 2	$ 2	1	$ 2	$ 2
2	2	4	2	2	4
3	2	6	3	2	6
4	2	8	4	2	8
5	2	10	5	2	10
6	2	12	6	2	12
7	4	16	7	4	16
8	4	20	8	4	20
9	4	24	9	4	24
10	4	28........*10	4	28	
11	4	32	11	4	32
12	6	38	12	6	38
13	6	44	13	6	44
14	6	50	14	6	50
15	6	56	15	6	56
16	6	62	16	6	62
17	8	70	17	8	70
18	8	78	18	8	78
19	8	86	19	8	86
*20	8	94	20	8	94
21	10	104	21	10	104
22	10	114	22	10	114
23	10	124	23	10	124
24	10	134	24	10	134
25	12	146	25	12	146
26	12	158	26	12	158
27	12	170	27	12	170
28	12	182	28	12	182
29	12	194	29	12	194
30	12	216	30	12	216

Stop on the first winner: At the track, win and go home. If away from the track where betting is legal as in Nevada or Mexico, put your slip in marked "Stop at a winner." Often play will stop at a winner paying, for example, $18, and then in a later race will come in at $70. But it works most satisfactorily if you *stop at the first winner!*

After a winner the next play, on the following day, you start over at $2.

If you should have 24 straight losers your total loss can only be $134.00. This represents a few cents over $5.50 as an average bet. Should you ever lose 24 wagers in a row, there are two possible courses to take:

1. Forget your loss and start over with a new bank roll, or
2. wager $12 each on six additional plays, allowing for a total of 30 plays instead of 24.

Should the third or fourth choice be quoted at less than 3 to 1 odds do not play it. Instead substitute for it another horse that is higher up on the list.

To prevent any ambiguity let me say this: Some price lines are given with the choices being placed in rotation like this:

> 1st choice A   2/1
> 2nd choice B   3/1
> 3rd choice C   5/1
> etc.   7/1
>   4/1

Other price lines are given in rotation of post position. All you need be concerned with is to play the third or fourth horse when the names appear in rotation as above shown. Where they are not shown in rotation you know by the odds quoted which is the 1st and 2nd choices, so you eliminate them and play the 3rd or 4th choice.

I strongly recommend that you do not play this method until you first work it out on paper, first using the horse fourth down from the top then playing the third horse from the top and compare the results between the two.

While on this subject let me say that no sensible experienced horse player will attempt to play any new method or system until he has taken the race charts of a substantial number of races and runs a workout on them.

How To Avoid a Run of Consecutive Losers

Here is one method that can be used to overcome the unquestioned primary cause of playing losses. This is *runs of consecutive losers!* The best system in the world may become a loser when subjected to the attack of many straight losers.

One of many ways to stop a run of consecutive losers is the following. Say you have lost ten straight wagers in a row. Before making your next wager, set up a new and *separate* investment account and start from scratch with your new bankroll.

Let us assume you have lost right up to your tenth wager. Go to your next bet, the eleventh, but *at the same time* make a bet in addition, using the new bankroll. Here is how it figures out. On your eleventh wager, on your first scale it calls for an investment of $4.00. At the same time you bet $2.00 as the first bet of your added scale. See chart on page 139.

Let us suppose your $2.00 bet on scale No. 1 wins and pays $24.00. This represents odds of 11 to 1 and is more usual to occur than not with these selections. This same winner comes at play No. 10 on your scale No. 2. The combined bet is $8.00 on scale No. 1 and $4.00 on Scale No. 2 or $12.00. You win a total of $132.00 or a net profit of $10.00. Forget this small win. I am merely using these figures to make the theory easier to explain and easier to understand.

When this happens you have several choices to make.

1. Apply total win to Scale No. 1 and you have a net profit of $46.00. This is figured thusly: On previous losers you invested $86. This deducted from $132 won gives you a net win of $46. Now discard Scale No. 1.
2. Continue along with Scale No. 2 just as if you did not have a win at play No. 10.

Glancing at this printed page will not adequately prove to you the power and effectiveness of this method of wagering. Experiment with it and see for yourself how high the winnings can result from its application.

It will be noted that you can use a third chart with a separate bankroll after you have continued to get straight losers. The sky is your limit if you have a bankroll accumulated from your previous winnings. By this I mean, I frequently start with $2 on this play. Seldom do I ever go without getting a winner within the first three or four bets. Many times this winner's price is so high that it carries me along for many wagers. When I have gained a substantial bankroll—from winnings—I stop play and start all over again with a $2.00 wager or whatever unit of play I feel is sensible to the size of my capital set aside for this particular method of playing. This makes sense to me.

Another Stop-the-Consecutive-Losers Device

In the rolling of dice, or on the roulette wheel, figures run in cycles. Knowing this, I took advantage sometimes in the gambling Casinos in France. I have never visited Las Vegas or Reno so never played there. But I came out a winner every time I visited France. One New Year's Eve at Cannes I played the red all night long and won a respectable sum and the day following, New Year's

Day, went to Monte Carlo and also won there, but it was a very small amount. I also several times played in Puerto Rico but not liking it there risked but a small amount. I played there two or three times but never won.

I tell you this because for a cycle to present itself, the number first has to turn up. Whenever you are in a losing cycle and have a goodly number of straight losers stop play. If the losers continue, it means you are ahead that much since you will not be playing them. Then when your first horse wins, it can mean your play is back to normal. Then resume your regular play.

How To Dutch Your Wagering

As mentioned previously, the bookmakers dutched their books so that no matter which horse in the race won the bookie came out a winner. As I tell you of dutching your play from here on I use the term loosely. The bookies worked to exact figures. It is not necessary that exactness exist for the player now. You of course know that the mutuel payoff window is the bookmaker of today.

Racing Associations require favorable publicity to produce increased earnings the same as any other business concern. Publicity is, of course, a specialized form of advertising. The best advertising a race track can get is the Daily Double payoffs when it runs into hundreds of dollars. This is true also with any of the specialized trick plays conducted. The big payoffs attract the masses, and thus increases track attendance.

One way to achieve this aim is for the Racing Secretary to card the first and second races, so that the entries in these races are the poorest of available contenders. The lower the grade of horses the more difficult it is to pick a winner. They are mostly ailing, inconsistent, or otherwise inferior. Therefore, the harder it is to pick the winners in the two daily double races enhances the chances of getting a Daily Double paying high figures. For example the highest D. D. in 1967 was at River Downs for $6,574.60 for $2.00; for Aqueduct $3,648.20. In the past thirty-five years there have been five D. Ds. paying from $8,498.35 to a high of $12,724.80 for $2.00 occurring at Caliente July 4, 1954. During the 1967 season of racing there were one hundred and one (101) Daily Doubles that paid $1,000 or more for $2.00.

17

How to Win
Playing Daily Doubles

WHENEVER A PLAYER selects more than one horse in either of the D. D. races he is applying some type of dutching. Many times I have won a D. D. by tying one horse in either of the two races with all the horses in the other race. The single horse would be a standout horse and even if it was a very low price or the favorite if some rank outsider won the other half of the double the payoff was certain to be high. This play would cost $24.00. Sometimes, I would try to eliminate some of the rank outsiders in the other race, and thus the play might cost only $12.00 to $16.00. Say the single picked horse was a favorite at 6/5, which means odds of $1.20 to $1.00, what this play actually meant was that by playing from six to twelve horses in the other race, I was gambling for odds that might and could be 50 to 1 or more, which it sometimes was.

I have had many thrills in racing. Not so often because of the amount of money won, but by reason of the circumstances surrounding the winning. One of these was when through a "fluke" on my part, I won the biggest Daily Double that was paid in New York up to the time of this win and the biggest for many years thereafter.

I think relating the circumstances will interest the reader and I will tell about them, but first let me finish on how to play daily doubles.

Very frequently you will see that both daily double races end up having the favorite or one of the three choices win both races. One might expect the payoff would be low commensurate with the low odds on the winners. But often you will find that you get a $20.00, $30.00, or $40.00 payoff. If you had played these horses separately to win, you'd be lucky to collect $10.00 total on both. This has so intrigued me since I started writing this book that I am now having a professional researcher furnish me the data on which I can formulate a sound scientific conclusion.

The best way to play D. Ds. is to pick a *key* horse in either race and tie it up with several of the most likely winners in the other race, and it need not necessarily be one of the choices.

The next best way is to eliminate as many as possible of horses in each race than on the face of it have not the ghost of a chance. You'll have one of these eliminated horses fool you and come in now and then. But in the long run the doubles you do win will more than offset any such losses.

How I Won the First Record D.D. in New York

You'll understand that there was no such plays as Daily Doubles until bookie operations at the track were discontinued, and the parimutuel system of wagering was inaugurated in New York State. It was first activated in New York in 1940. I was always keen for the doubles as they offered a challenge to me which I liked. There are many smart professionals who operate on the track in New York and until 1943 no sensational payoffs took place. Then one day, September 3, 1943, it happened!

The number of horses permitted to race on any track depends upon the width of the track and is determined by each track's officials. I believe I said some place that the limit on New York tracks was twelve horses. If I did it is not true. I've known as many as sixteen horses to run in a race. It may be that I was momentarily confused with the limit of twelve different tickets sold on any race. The reason for this is that the ticket machines have room only for the sale of 12 different tickets. Therefore, any entries in the race exceeding twelve are coupled with twelve and sold as one ticket. When there is more than one horse beyond twelve, the twelfth and all following horses are known as and sold as the Field. Sometimes, you buy a ticket for $2.00 and may have four or more horses running for you so that if any one of the field wins you win nevertheless.

The aim for everything at a race track is to attract a large attendance, and to get the most betting action possible. Making up of the field is handled by the mutuel department. The manager puts in the field the horses in the race that he thinks have the least chance. Many unknowing players buy the field ticket feeling that because they have four to six or more horses running for them they have more chance to win, whereas the field offers less possibility of winning than any single horse in the race.

When the betting windows opened early for the Daily Double here is what I noticed. In the first race a horse was entered by a very smart trainer. When the entries came out around noon the day before, as they do, this horse —Markobob—was about post 14 and on the eligible list. More often than not the mutuel manager used to group the horses on the eligible list as field horses unless it was a favorite. You could ask him, if early enough, to keep your horse out of the field.

When the Daily Double windows opened, I noticed that Markobob was not in the field. I also noticed that there was a change of equipment—possibly blinkers off or on—shown in the program. I immediately became suspicious! I figured that the trainer asked that his horse not be put in the field. I had often made this request because a horse in the field generally will pay less than it will out of the field. So I figured with the change of equipment and asking to be taken out of the field meant this trainer felt his charge was sure of winning.

I used Markobob as my key horse in the first race and bought a ticket with all twelve (including the field of course) in the second race. Therefore, my investment was $24.00. Post time came! They were off! Markobob won!

I forgot to mention that I had also wagered separately in the first race on Markobob as you might suspect since I had so much confidence in my analysis. Markobob paid something like $60.00 odd dollars.

The race was over! I waited anxiously to see what the double payoffs would be on each of the horses entered in the second half of the daily double. It was not long before they were posted. As I recall now the smallest payoff that the winning Daily Double would pay was over $400.00. Players who knew I had the winner of the first race tried to buy my tickets. It is a usual thing that if you hold a ticket on the winner of the first half of the daily double you will be approached to sell your tickets. This then offers you a sure profit as one can't foretell what horse will win the coming second half of the double. Naturally, I refused all offers.

I waited for the coming race. The wait seemed interminable! But at last the race started and they were off!

Hughie Fontain also had his own box at Aqueduct, not using Mrs. Sloan's box. I had my own box at Belmont but not at Aqueduct so I was in his box when the race started. As a rule when a race is in progress I conceal my feelings and no one can tell if I have a bet in the race or not.

Maybe I have witnessed the same kind of a race at other times. But I do not think so. Here is how the race was run. It was a distance race as I recall. First one horse would take the lead. This horse would be challenged and fall back after being headed. Then another would come on and take the lead. From start to finish there were no less than four to five leaders, not to mention the second and third horses, all of which could win the race. As they raced along I was more excited than I had ever been in my life up to then and more than I have ever been since. I howled and was shouting, "Come on something! Come on something!"

The double payoffs for each horse in the race was shown in large figures on a board used for this purpose and set up to the right of the tote board. As each horse took the lead I would glance at this board to see what I would win if the leading horse won. Keep in mind that no matter what horse won, the *least* I could receive was around $400.00. If my glance indicated the payoff for the leader would be less than $1,000, I was hoping for it to lose and I was praying for one of the other horses to win.

Well, the race was over! There was a close grouping of four or five horses at the finish line. Not that it was a photo finish. But they were all grouped together. I thought the horse that won would give me a payoff of about $600.00. I was satisfied and happy, of course.

Then the numbers went up! Lo and behold, the winner was a horse named Spirit, a longshot in the race!

And the payoff? On September 3, 1943, Markobob and Spirit coupled in the Daily Double paid three thousand eight hundred and eighty-eight ($3,888.00) dollars!

Neither this amount of money nor a greater amount could possibly give me the thrill this did. It inflated my ego because acting as a detective I thought I had made a clever deduction. Not even the winning by "The Whale" as previously detailed gave me the thrill this race did. And the way the race was won added immeasurably to the thrill. Had one or two horses been in the lead and stayed there during the race my thrill would have been lessened. Again, I repeat that I never saw a similar race when from start to finish it was likely that any number of horses entered could have won it.

Daily Doubles had been in existence for three years before this day. But there never was previous to this one that paid more than $200.00. This was New York's first record Daily Double.

There is an incident connected with this event I can't resist telling about. In the days of the bookmakers many of the real big time plungers like "Pittsburgh Phil" and Dwyer, hired men called betting commissioners to place their wagers. When mutuel betting came into being, the tracks hired what is known as "runners." They are stationed all about the grandstand and you can keep your seat, give one of them the money and tell him what horse you want to play. He will proceed to the betting windows and bring back the ticket you want.

You can't own a racing stable without being known to all regular followers of the track, and without being approached and asked for tips or your opinion. When the crowds were great on Saturdays or holidays, I would sometimes give a certain runner my bets to place. We became friends and I was accustomed to mark up his wife's program every day. By this I mean indicate on her program what horse in each race I thought would win. She had already won several doubles on my advice and had great confidence in me.

On the day I have been talking about I told her to buy a ticket on Markobob and key it up with every horse in the second race.

After this race was over, I went down to the payoff windows and saw her waiting for me. She was leaning up against a post and her face was as white as a piece of paper. I asked her if she had played as I told her, but she could not speak. Instead she showed me *two winning tickets* calling for a total payoff of $7,776.00. In a few moments she had recovered herself and asked me what she should do and I told her to give the tickets to her husband to cash.

There is an aftermath to this event. Listen to this for a climax! Several weeks after this race, I was speaking to the trainer of Markobob. I related what I have already told was the basis of my conclusion concerning this horse and asked him if he had requested that the horse be taken out of the field. He said no he had not and that he did not bet a dime on his horse as it apparently had no chance of winning.

I was deflated and hit the earth as a tire experiencing a blowout will do. Here I was patting myself on the back as having made a most clever and profitable deduction to find it was purely a matter of luck that I had wagered on this Daily Double.

Here is a method of play that any knowledgeable player should be able to utilize to profitable advantage. I have said that the two races of the Daily Double are generally made up of the scum of the horses at the track. Aside from the double, frequently both races have winners paying in the high four figures. Incidentally, as a general rule these two races have more entries than do the other races and this is one reason why extra large payoffs are prevalent.

I would study the two races and eliminate as far as possible as many horses as my judgment told me had no chance of winning. I would also discard the first and second, and sometimes the third choices. The reason for this was that I was not looking for just a winner. I was seeking a winner at longshot odds. I would purchase a ticket on each of the remaining horses in these races. Some of the payoffs I received on these plays were amazing, and many who knew I played the winning horse would say they could not understand how it could be figured. I am going to be honest about it, and tell you I never let on that I had played as many as five or six horses in the race in order to get the right one. This method of playing is, of course, a minor dutching of the play.

Most players are able to get two to three to four horses in every race that comprises the real contention. Their greatest problem is to eliminate all but one of these. There are a number of methods published that are exceptionally effective in this respect. But I am herein going to give you a method that any one can use with profit. If you can't decide the contention yourself use a good public selector or the picks of a scratch sheet to do the spade work for you.

Again, it calls for playing more than one horse in a race, and thus it is a modified form of dutching your play.

First of all glance at the following table. For lack of a better title I'll call it the Dutching Table. This represents what percentage each odds represent. I am not giving the precise odds as this serves no purpose in this illustration, nor does it in actual play. For example, the precise percentage for odds of 10 to 1 is 9.09 percent. Using the figure 9 percent is close enough, etc.

Dutching Table

Odds	%	Odds	%	Odds	%
1–1	50	5–2	29	7–1	13
6–5	46	3–1	25	8–1	11
7–5	42	7–2	22	9–1	10
3–2	40	4–1	20	10–1	9
8–5	39	9–2	18	11–1	8
9–5	36	5–1	16	12–1	8
2–1	33	6–1	14	13–1	7

Let us consider an actual race. I will list only the four contenders as the others are inconsequential. The odds actually paid are given in dollars, the cents skipped to make for quicker comprehension.

2 Race, GP, April 5, 1969

Horse	Finish	Odds	Percent	Bet	Won
Evade the Law	1	4	20%	$20	$80
Gondolier	2	6	14%	14	84
Yoga	6	4	20%	20	80
My Advice II	8	3	25%	25	75
			79%		

Of course, the *Won* column means that is what would have been won if each separate horse won. Evade the Law won the race at odds of 4 to 1.

You simply add the percentage for each contender you play, and deduct it from 100 percent and you have the amount you won. You won $80.00 on Evade the Law. From this you must deduct the total bet on the three losers, which is $59.00, or net profit of $21.00 for each $1.00 wagered. If My Advice II won, you collected $75.00 and after deducting $54.00 the total bet on the three losers you'd net $21.00.

Anyone who does not know a public handicapper that can spot the three or four contenders can by attending the race track get this data from the tote board.

Obviously, if the total percentages for all the horses you play in the same race equals or excels 100 percent, the play cannot be dutched.

I most highly suggest to readers that they take the selections of the "$17,000 Fool Play" given on page 139 and dutch the third, fourth, and fifth horse down from the top of the scratch sheet, then take fourth, fifth, and sixth down and do the same thing and compare the two results. After this research, you can detect the better of the two ways for use hereafter. You'll find these selections showing odds of 4 to 1 and 5 to 1 and coming back with payoffs of $30.00 and $40.00. It was because of these unusually high payoffs that my attention was first attracted to the Fool Play.

Playing From 2 to 5 Horses in a Race

Many players over the years have asked me if it is possible to win by playing more than one horse in a race. I think the question has been answered with what I have written in this chapter. I will now give you proper wagering methods to use when playing two, three, four, or five horses on the same race. A different wagering method must be applied in each case. As you read consult the charts pertaining to this multiple wagering.

Please look at chart for two horse method. The idea is to play to win a given amount per race; in this workout it will be $2.00. To determine amount to wager, divide the *debit* (Deb.) by *eight* and wager the resultant sum on *two* horses in the same race. Note that under the *Bets* column heading we put down *two* $2.00 wagers, assuming that we are at the track and making the smallest practicable wager. Both our horses lose. We add the loss of $4.00 to debit, plus $2.00 to be won on next race, the debit, making it $8.00 for play number 2. We divide debit by *eight* and get $1.00 as our wager to be placed on each of our TWO horses; since we cannot wager $1.00 at the track, we wager $2.00. We lose play number 2. We add the loss of $4.00, plus the usual $2.00 to our debit, making it $14.00 for play number 3.

8-1
(Two Horse Method)

No.	Deb.	Bets		Odds	Lost	Won
1	$ 2	$2	$2	—	$4	—
2	8	2	2	—	4	—
3	14	2	2	—	4	—
4	20	4	4	—	8	—
5	30	4	(4)	2.00	4	$ 8
6	28	4	4	—	8	—
7	38	5	(5)	5.80	5	29
8	16	2	2	—	4	—
9	22	4	4	—	8	—
10	32	4	(4)	9.00	4	—
					$53	$73
						53
						$20

In other words, we proceed dividing the debit by *eight* and wagering the resultant sum on *each* of our two horses, adding losses plus the $2.00 to be won on each race to the debit.

When we win, as we do on play number 5, and fail to win enough to cancel the debit, we simply deduct the winnings from the debit and continue right on, wagering one-eighth of the debit until we hit a winner that pays odds of 9 to 1 (that's right, 9 to 1) when we will fully cancel the debit.

Let's go over that again, starting with play number 5. The debit is $30.00. One eighth of this would call for a $4.00 wager on each of the two horses. One horse wins, at odds of 2 to 1. We win $8.00. We lose $4.00 on the other horse, giving us a net winning of $4.00 on the race. We deduct this $4.00 from the debit, making it $26.00 and we add the $2.00 to be won on the next race making this debit $28.00 for play number 6. The play loses. Play number 7 wins, at odds of $5.80 to 1. We win $29.00 on the winner; we lose $5.00 on the loser, giving us a net profit of $24.00 on the race; we deduct the $24.00 from the debit, making it $14.00; we add the usual $2.00 and the debit is $16.00. Plays number 8 and 9 both lose. For play number 10, debit is $32.00; one-eighth of this is $4.00; we wager this sum on each of our two horses; we win, at odds of 9 to 1. We win $36.00; we lose $4.00 on the losing horse, making for a net profit of $32.00 on the race; this exactly cancels the debit and play will now start over with a debit of $2.00.

If you will now add up the amounts in the *Lost* column and in the *Won* column, you will see that there is a net profit of exactly $20.00, which is pre-cisely what we set out to win on the 10 races. Of course, had the winner in play number 10 paid odds of, say 15 to 1, then the profits would have been $24.00 larger. But it takes a winner at odds of 9 to 1 to cancel the debit. Using the figure *five* (instead of 8), playing one-fifth of the debit, a winner at odds of 6 to 1 would be needed to cancel the debit. When playing one-third of the debit, a winner at odds of 4 to 1 will be needed to cancel the debit.

When contemplating a play of this type, the idea is to find out which figure to use to divide the debit by. If your selections produce only very occa-sional winners at odds of 9 to 1, remembering that you are playing two horses, then go to a lower figure so as to cancel the debit oftener; on the other hand, if your selections produce winners at higher odds then use a higher figure, dividing the debit by 10, 15, or any such figure, provided that you get such winners often enough to cancel the debit fairly regularly so that wagers will not get out of hand.

If you've been handicapping horses for any length of time, you've had the aggravating experience of seeing your second choice win a race, at a price of from $10.00 to $30.00, more than once. This method enables you to take advantage of such fine prices, while at the same time, your winners at shorter prices act to keep the debit from getting too large, thus keeping down the size of wagers.

On page 151 is a workout showing how things work out when playing *three* horses in the same race. Procedure is identical to the one that is used when playing two horses, the only difference being that you make three bets instead of two. You divide the debit by 8 and wager the resultant amount on each of three horses. You add all lost wagers, plus the $2.00 to be won on each race, to the debit. When you hit a winner, you deduct the money lost on the two losing horses from your winnings; you then deduct the remaining profits from the debit, add the usual $2.00 you are playing for and then divide the debit by 8 again. When it happens that you win less than the loss incurred on the two losing horses, you simply figure the net loss on the race and add this loss to the debit. For example, suppose the debit is $40.00. One-eighth of this is $5.00; you wager this sum on each of your three horses; one horse wins, at odds of even money; you win $5.00; you lose $10.00 on the two losing horses; you have a net loss of $5.00 on the race and you add this loss, plus the usual $2.00, to the debit, making it $47.00.

There is no need to explain the three-horse workout in detail, other than to say that a winner at odds of 10 to 1 is needed to cancel the debit. You need

8-1
(Three Horse Method)

Deb.	Bets			Odds	Lost	Won
$ 2	$2	$2	$2	—	$ 6	—
10	2	2	2	—	6	—
18	4	4	4	—	12	—
32	4	4	(4)	2.50	8	$10
32	4	4	4	—	12	—
46	6	6	(6)	3.50	12	21
39	5	5	(5)	2.00	10	10
41	5	5	5	—	15	—
58	7	7	(7)	6.00	14	42
32	4	4	(4)	10.00	8	40
					$103	$123
						103
						$ 20

odds of 8 to 1 to take care of the debit; you need odds 1 point higher for each of the two losers. Go over the figures, line for line, to make sure that you understand everything clearly.

Go to the next workout. This is a workout for playing *four* horses in the same race.

8-1
(Four Horse Method)

No.	Deb.	Bets				Odds	Lost	Won
1	$ 2	$2	$2	$2	$2	—	$ 8	—
2	12	2	2	2	2	—	8	—
3	22	4	4	4	(4)	2.75	12	$11
4	25	4	4	4	4	—	16	—
5	43	6	6	6	(6)	2.00	18	12
6	51	7	7	7	(7)	2.00	21	14
7	60	8	8	8	8	—	32	—
8	94	12	12	12	(12)	4.50	36	54
9	78	10	10	10	10	—	40	—
10	120	15	15	15	(15)	11.00	45	165
							$236	$256
								236
							Net Profit:	$ 20

This procedure is identically the same, except that you play four horses and it takes a winner at odds of 11 to 1 to cancel the debit. Bear in mind that when you play four horses in a race then you have every right to expect an extra high percentage of winners, if your selections are professionally made.

A competent selector should produce around 70 percent of winners among his first four selections so a player should not miss having the winner in too many races in a row. Of course, when odds are less than 3 to 1, then a player would lose a little money on a race even when he plays the winner; on the other hand, he breaks even on a winner paying odds of 3 to 1; he makes a little profit on a winner paying odds of 4 to 1; the debit will be reduced on a winner that pays odds of 5 to 1 or better, keeping the size of bets down and the debit will be canceled on a winner at 11 to 1.

Below is a workout on a play of *five* horses in the same race. Procedure is the same as explained, the only difference being that you need a winner at odds of 12 to 1 to cancel the debit. Please go over this workout, line for line, doing all figuring and making each move as explained.

8-1
(Five Horse Method)

No.	Deb.	Bets					Odds	Lost	Won
1	$ 2	$2	$2	$2	$2	$2	—	$10	—
2	14	2	2	2	2	2	—	10	—
3	26	4	4	4	4	4	—	20	—
4	48	6	6	6	6	(6)	3.00	24	$18
5	56	7	7	7	7	(7)	2.00	28	14
6	72	9	9	9	9	9	—	45	—
7	119	15	15	15	15	(15)	6.00	45	90
8	76	10	10	10	10	(10)	3.10	40	31
9	87	11	11	11	11	11	—	55	—
10	144	18	18	18	18	(18)	12.00	72	216
								$349	$369
									349

Net Profit: $ 20

A while ago I said something about playing *all* the horses in certain races. I imagine that by now you are far ahead of me. Sure, the idea would be to play every horse in races with only five starters. You could not miss having the winner. Of course, you would lose a little money on some races, break even on others, make a profit on some races and eventually cancel the debit when you hit a winner paying odds of 12 to 1 or better. So, assuming that you do not hit a tremendously long run of winners paying around $3.00 or $4.00, which could shoot the debit up pretty high and use up some capital, again assuming that you hit your 12 to 1 winner before you run out of money, I don't see how this method can fail to beat the races.

When playing two or more horses in the same race, it is best if it is confined to races in which the favorite is 2 to 1 or better. Such races have more upsets than races in which a strongly backed favorite is present.

I feel that the majority of readers have hitherto never given a thought to the art of wagering. I hope that this chapter has demonstrably proved that proper betting is more important than to be adept at selecting winners. If I have encouraged anyone to decide to make a deeper study of the subject, I will be well rewarded. There are methods available for this purpose.

There are more unlimited potentialities of getting out of the rut of mediocrity in playing the races by learning how to bet. Acquiring the art has many advantages over the usual method of playing when no attention is paid to wagering. Most important of all, it offers no such dilemmas as is present in handicapping. There are innumerable ways to get selections to bet on. You save time.

18

How to Play—
Daily Double, Exacta,
Twin Double, 5-10

I HAVE ALREADY discussed at length in the preceding chapter the method to be used in playing the Daily Double in order to obtain the best results. In this chapter, I shall not only amplify upon this highly popular type of race, but also touch upon a number of similar or "gimmick" races.

The inauguration of parimutuel wagering in this country started an entirely new trend in horse betting. Starting from that date, racing became really big business for horse tracks and the tax authorities. Its advent was like the discovery of a new gold field and, as natural, the prevailing authorities set about to make the best of it. Their main purpose was to increase the volume of wagering at the tracks.

This culminated in newly discovered forms of play. These are variously known under such titles as multiple wagering or gimmick wagering. All of these new forms of special play offer astronomical payoffs for only $2.00. The publicity contingent upon the winning of thousands of dollars for $2.00 increases the patronage at the tracks and thus achieves the purposes of these new types of betting pools.

The Daily Double was the first of this nature and has continued to be the most popular form of "trick" or gimmick betting. It also offers players more of a chance to cash in than any of the other forms. Frankly, it is the only form of gimmick betting that I ever indulged in or would ever consider.

The three highest Daily Double payoffs for $2.00 in 1967 and in 1969 were as follows:

1967	1969
$6,574	$3,728
$4,553	$3,279
$4,202	$3,100

The three highest Twin Doubles for 1967 and 1969 were:

1967	1969
$36,998	$26,030
$35,628	$13,311
$31,805	$12,994

I understand one 5-10 payoff was $80,000.

I will first enumerate the various types of multiple playing pools and then proceed to indicate methods that have proven successful by enabling players to participate in the winnings of such pools.

The Daily Double

The way to play Daily Doubles is given in Chapter 17 under How To Win Playing Daily Doubles. The Daily Double part starts on page 144. I will not therefore again cover the playing action in this part.

The Exacta

In general, the rules governing all of these gimmick plays are the same wherever the plays are used. Any slight variation will be shown in the program of the track involved.

The object of the Exacta is to select in order of finish the first and second place finishers in the designated Exacta race or races. The Exacta pool is held separate from all other pools and is in no way a part of the Daily Double, or win, place, or show pools.

Every separate type of multiple play has its own pool and has no connection with any other pool at the track.

The rules controlling the Exacta is that if a horse is scratched or excused from racing, no further tickets shall be sold designating such horse. All tickets previously sold naming such horses shall be refunded and the money deducted from the gross pool.

Dead Heat. 1. In the event of a dead heat for win, the net pool shall be distributed to each combination of winners separately as in a win pool dead heat; for example, in a dead heat of two horses there are two winning combinations, in a dead heat of three horses there are six winning combinations. 2. In the event of a dead heat for second the net pool shall be divided as in a win pool dead heat among the holders of tickets combining the winner with each second place horse.

Coupled entries and fields are not permitted in Exacta races, as they are in Daily Double selections.

If no ticket is sold on the winning combination of an Exacta pool, the net pool is distributed equally between holders of tickets selecting the winning horse to finish first and/or holders of tickets selecting the second place horse to finish second.

The Twin Double

The object of the Twin Double is to select the winners of four (4) races in advance. The Optional Twin Double selects the winners of the two designated first races involved, say, for example, the fourth and fifth races. After these two races are run the holder of a winning ticket has the option of using the winning ticket to then pick the winner of the next two designated races, or to play safe and cash in on the already winning ticket.

At the time I am writing this, a change has been made at Lincoln Downs in the Twin Double.

They are returning to the Straight Twin Double (as contrasted to the Optional Twin Double). This will set the stage for sensational payoffs, which resulted in past years when this multiple wagering was in vogue. On February 19, 1966, there was a payoff of $54,838 and on December 9, 1965, the return was $42,268, two of the large payoffs made at Lincoln.

In the Straight Twin Double there is no cashing in of tickets after the first half as is the case with Optional Twin Doubles. The player must select all four winners, with the exchanges being made after the first two horses win.

The 5-10

This 5–10 play, as far as I know, is played only at the Caliente track in Tijuana, Mexico. It is not unlikely that some day a payoff of around $100,000 for $2.00 will occur.

The object of the 5–10 is to pick the winners of the 5, 6, 7, 8, 9 and 10th races each day. Thus it gets its name—"5–10." It seems preposterous to bet against such odds of winning. But hope is ever eternal and it is a most popular play where it is played.

Fundamentally, there is no difference in making selections for these gimmick plays than there is for making the selection for any single race. You "dope" or handicap each race for the objective in view.

The only opportunity available to offset the odds presented in each type of play is to make more than one selection for each position.

In any type of doubles combination, whenever you can find in any one of the races involved an outstanding possible winner there are two good moves available:

1. Use the "sure winner" as a key horse and couple it with every other horse in the other race or races involved.

2. Use the key horse, and from the other race eliminate as many of the contenders therefrom that you can safely figure has no chance.

Under the Daily Double playing in Chapter 16, this use of a key horse is more explicitly explained.

When it comes to playing the Exacta, where you have to pick the horses to run one-two in the same race, here is how to proceed: Consider the first and second position as *two different races*. With that as a start, you then try to eliminate as many horses as possible that do not seem to have a chance. And treat each position the same as a Daily Double race.

I am sure that you never try to pick a horse to run last. Will it surprise you when I tell you that it is *more* difficult to pick the horse that will run last in any race than it is to pick the winner? I want to modify this statement a trifle and say this is true in 98 percent of all races. You won't believe this statement until you try it for yourself. Try it and see and then try to answer what the reason for this is!

When it comes to playing the 5–10 my judgment (remember I have never played or researched this type of play) would be as follows:

By handicapping or "doping" each of the six races involved, try to bring out the two or three top contenders in each race. Then buy tickets by criss-crossing all picked in the six races so that no matter which one wins you'll have it.

Naturally, this is going to require quite an enhanced investment each day over trying to win by selecting just one horse in each race. But this cross-crossing in the races involved is the *only* way by which you can increase your chances of winning.

There are untold thousands of players that can get the top two or three contenders in every race they consider. This is no dilemma for them. Their problem is to get the winner of the two or three possibilities.

Some Interesting Facts About Gimmick Plays

You would suspect that because of the million-dollar pools and many thousands of attendance that the major tracks would be the source of bigger payoffs on gimmick plays. But such is not a fact.

For example, here are the six top Daily Double payoffs for two years.

1967		1969	
River Downs	$6,574	Portland	$3,728
Thistledown	$4,553	Aqueduct	$3,279
Lincoln Downs	$4,202	Evangeline Downs	$3,100
Aqueduct	$3,648	Bay Meadows	$2,796
Lincoln Downs	$3,260	Detroit	$2,529
Lincoln Downs	$2,666	Arlington	$2,486

Of these the only track of major proportions is Aqueduct.

To conclude these observations it should be mentioned here that the play at certain tracks known by the name of Perfecta is identical to the Exacta. Also, the play called Quinella selects two horses in Quinella races. To win, these two horses must finish one-two. It makes no difference which is first or second as long as they are the two front horses.

19

The Secret Play—The Best Play in Racing

WHEN YOU ENTER the race track you will find boards placed in different locations displaying names of entries and price line of the first and second races on the card. These comprise the two races of the Daily Double. The inclination of the unknowing public in playing the Daily Double is to use these two price lines as a basis for selection. The size of the Daily Double payoffs is closely related to the choices. In other words, the three or four lowest-priced horses in the first race are tied up with horses in the second race. As might be expected invariably the payoffs closely follow the odds as shown.

Perhaps I can best explain by asking you to refer to the next chart, which is headed *Record Sheet "A."* Again, I draw your attention to the fact that the race shown is dated 1941, a matter of 30 years ago, to prove that the length of time element has no bearing in playing the races. If any method of play is sound it will never cease to function exactly as it did when it was originated because the conformation, temperament of the horse, and the conduct of racing is exactly the same today as it was 30 years ago.

The figures listed under column 3 represent the *Opening Track Morning Price* or *Odds Line* (OTML). The table shown is for the second half of the double. Post position No. 9, Thrift, is favorite in the race at 8/5 odds. If it was coupled with the winner of the first race of the double it would have paid $9.30. The second choice is the Field, comprised of horses at post positions 12, 13, and 14. The odds were 2 to 1 and if any one of these three horses won the payoff would have been $13.20. It is most unusual for any horse in the field to be good enough to result in such low odds. It very seldom happens.

The third choice in the race at 10 to 1 is Horticulturist and the fourth choice, Pompier at 12 to 1. Since the odds on the third and fourth choice are five and six times greater than for the first two choices you will realize that the latter must have been outstanding choices. Keep this in mind for what is to come.

Record Sheet "A"

Wednesday, July 16, 1941—Empire

Col. 1 No.	Col. 2 Horse	Col. 3 OTML	Col. 4 Daily Double	Col. 5 Proportionate Odds
1	SPRING AWAY	30	91.10	3
2	Davitt	15	64.40	4
3	Javert	20	405.00	20
4	Second Best	30	357.60	12
5	Storm Orphan	20	220.30	11
6	Pompier	12	367.20	31
7	Amerosa	30	411.00	14
8	Who Reigh	20	196.70	10
9	Thrift	8/5	9.30	5
10	Horticulturist	10	136.30	14
11	Swamp Fire	30	245.80	8
Field				
12	Tellevane	2	13.20	7
13	Periover			
14	Scauch			

Spring Away won this race and paid $28.90 to win. It paid $91.10 in the double.

I had noticed a few times that a long-priced horse won the second race of the double, which is contrary to what usually happens. I started an investigation and finally came up with what in my opinion is one of the two best secrets of getting winners that exists.

Here are the lines along which I reasoned out this "inconsistency." The masses buy their D. D. tickets along normal lines, most of them tying up their selection in the first race with at least the first three or four choices in the second race. How come Spring Away, showing odds at 30 to 1—indicative that it did not have the ghost of a chance in this race—would pay only $91.10? Look at the other horses whose odds were 20 or 30 to 1. Note if they won they would have paid from over $300.00 each to over $400.00 each. Observing this, would it not have made you suspicious?

It just so happens that this particular race offers the most perfect example for me to explain the play. The reason is that the two choices were so much lower in price compared to the next highest priced horse. Ordinarily, you don't find such a wide spread. Therefore, the unusual double payoff is not so easily discerned.

The past performances of Spring Away must have been terribly bad in order for it to be quoted the longest odds given of 30 to 1. This horse might have been a 50 to 1 in the pricemaker's mind, but his limit on paper was 30 to 1. I repeat that especially in daily double play the selections are based upon two factors: the odds quoted and the past performances. On both these factors this horse did not stand the chance of a "snowball in Hades." Yet, a ton of money had to be played on it in the race itself to cause the odds to drop from 30 to 1 to only 13.40 to 1—won at $28.90, which is $13.40 to $1.00.

I feel sure that you will agree with me that this money could beyond doubt have been bet only by the horse's connections. What happened was this. These people invested plenty of money playing it in the double and also bet a ton when it ran in the second race. No matter how secret they were about it—no matter if they did not tell a single outside person—I had discovered a way to detect their hidden intentions, you might say almost being able to read their minds.

Before I give you the secret of this play and show how you can put it to real practical use, and win many a four-figure wager—both for flat racing and even more so for harness racing—I shall digress for just a moment.

In the heading of this chapter appear the words "the Best Play in Racing." It is one of the two best plays in racing, which I did not say, not wanting the heading to be too long. One of the best players I have ever known is a man by the name of Robert Rowe. He devised a different way of reading the minds of inside bettors when they are out for a real killing. His method can, with reasonable certainty, detect from tote board action when a "good thing" is being bet by its connections and his method can do it in any race on the card where there is such a hidden play. It works equally well on any type of wagering where the mutuel machines operate. And it works even better with harness racing. His play and this Daily Double play are unquestionably the two best plays ever known.

Now I'll get back to this Secret Play. Consult the chart or table as you read. It is possible with this particular race of Spring Away to detect this secret from reading the double payoff. You can see Davitt at 15 to 1 pays $64.40. Therefore, if no extra large sum had been played on Spring Away, since it was 30 to 1 or double 15 to 1 for Davitt, the payoff instead of being $91.10 should be $182.20. But this is seldom possible. A more insidious way of going about reading the secret must be applied.

Under normal circumstances all double payoffs would conform reasonably close, comparatively, to the odds quoted before the race was won. Naturally before, since the double tickets must be bought even before the first race. Note Column 5 on the chart. Proportionate odds means this: If you divide the OTML odds into the double payoff the resultant figure will positively disclose the Secret Play if there is one present. Naturally, there is not a ton of money bet on some good thing in every race. And incidentally, the secret can be exposed only in the second race of the daily double.

Spring Away's odds of 30 to 1 divided into the payoff is 3. You never bother with cents. Storm Orphan, Post 5, at odds of 20 to one when divided into the payoff gives 11 as its proportionate odds.

Note that the favorite Thrift was 8/5, which is $1.60 to 1 divided into the payoff of $9.30, giving an approximate proportionate odds of 5 or 6. The second choice field horses have proportionate odds of 7. Observe how close these two figures are. It proves what I claim that the bulk of the play is based on the odds quoted.

It is not too often that a race stands out like this. Mostly, the proportionate odds are closer together.

It will help greatly to prove the soundness of this reasoning to compare what Spring Away would have paid if it had been played in the same proportion as the other long priced horses in the race.

Study the following chart.

A	B	C	D	E
Second Best	12 to 1	$357.60	Spring Away	$360.00
Storm Orphan	11 to 1	220.30	" "	330.00
Amerosa	14 to 1	411.00	" "	420.00
Who Reigh	10 to 1	196.70	" "	300.00
Swamp Fire	8 to 1	245.80	" "	240.00

Under A appears a list of horses with the longest odds in the morning line. Column B indicates what their proportionate odds were. Column C gives the payoff related to them. And Column D and E show what Spring Away would have paid if it had been played along normal lines. It is quite illuminating how the special heavy betting can be easily detected.

After giving the following examples of winners, to build your confidence in this play, I will summarize the rules of play and add a most important feature.

December 26, 1941. Tropical Park

Col. 1 No.	Col. 2 Horse	Col. 3 OTML	Col. 4 Daily Double	Col. 5 Proportionate Odds
1	Out Front	10	$ 669	66
2	Grenadier	15	535	36
3	Peace Puff	10	669	66
4	Wise Colonel*	1	49	49
5	Guile	15	1147	79
6	Gay Chic	30	803	26
7	JACK K	30	573	19
8	Stueben*	3	170	57

* Wise Colonel and Stueben eliminated as being 1st and 2nd choices, see later rules.
   Selection: Jack K won, paid $57.70.

Miranda Z won the following race paying *$107.70; $48.90* and *$21.60.* As clear as if it happened yesterday I can visualize myself running into Francis

Dunn's office—he was Racing Secretary at the time—and excitedly showing him the tickets I had on this nice "juicy winner."

May 8, 1942. Jamaica

Col. 1 No.	Col. 2 Horse	Col. 3 OTML	Col. 4 Daily Double	Col. 5 Proportionate Odds
	Miranda Z	30	$294	10

	Horse	Odds	D.D.	Prop. Odds	
8/29/46 G.S.	Country Dude	20	254	12	won paid $56.20
9/ 3/46 Nar.	Domestic Blend	30	427	14	" " 85.00
9/ 9/46 Haw.	Appetizer	30	397	13	" " 72.60
10/ 1/46 At.	Soup and Fish	20	304	15	" " 41.30

Thursday, July 17, 1941. Empire

No.	Horse	Odds	D.D.	Prop. Odds
1	(Ariel Toy)	10	228.90	23
1a	(Bright View)			
2	Drudgery	3	158.30	53
3	Shadows Pass	15	270.00	18
4	Marogay	7/5	47.40	34
5	Shortstop	12	183.10	15
6	Straight Load	5/2	228.90	91

Selection: NO PLAY

Shortstop had lowest P.O. but there was not at least (4) four points difference from Shadows Pass, who had 18—see rules later.

Rules For Secret Play

1. After the first race has been run, you consult the board on which the Daily Double payoffs for all horses in the second race will be run.
2. Divide the OTML into these payoff prices and the result will give you the proportionate odds.
3. Play the horse in the second with the lowest proportionate odds after these qualifications:

A. Disregard the field and the first and second choices. They have no significance, since they always will be played by the public.

B. Do not play the race unless the lowest odds showing is at least four (4) points lower than the next closest odds.

4. Do not play if the lowest proportionate odds is twenty or more. In such an event, it means there has been no special inside betting in the race.

It is important to remember that you pay attention to only two sets of figures and no others. These two contain the secret. Do not pay any attention to the odds as flashed on the tote board for either the first or the second race. The only figures you consider are the Opening Track Morning Line, which you get before the running of the first race, and the Daily Double payoff figures which are posted before the running of the second race. As soon as the payoff figures for the double are posted you get the proportionate odds as explained. Then and *only* then can you determine if you have a play in that second race.

Better Yet To Come

It would be unrealistic to suppose that you will find a play every day. Nor is it possible that a well-intended coup for a killing does not fail in its objective at times. But here is where the real beauty of this Secret Play comes in.

You may recall that in Chapter 15, when telling about a tip on "The Whale," I remembered that the person giving me the tip was employed by me. I had an employee at all the major tracks sending me in daily reports on the Secret Play horses that lost.

We know that only stable connections and insiders wager on these Secret Plays. So when they lose we have preknowledge that this must be a good prospect to bet in its next race or so, more especially if it ran an irregular race or if it had interference, or if it had a bad post position in relationship to its mode of running. I had these employees send me the reports because the plays that lost were ideal for future play. So my advice is for you to list these losing Secret Plays and follow them a race or two.

Simplification of Secret Play

Make no mistake about it. This Secret Play is, in my opinion, the best play known to racing. It may require several readings before its simplicity is realized and its power appreciated.

Turn back to page 160 and consider the horses listed under *Record Sheet "A."*

The morning odds of Spring Away was 30 to 1 and the Daily Double payoff if Spring Away was coupled with the winner of the first race of the Daily Double would be $91.10. 30 to 1 divided into $91.10 is roughly 3 to 1, which represents proportionate odds.

Now Second Best was also 30 to 1 on the morning line, and it would have paid $357.60 if coupled with winner of first race. Its proportionate odds is 12 to 1.

Amerosa was also 30 to 1 with payoff of $411.00, or proportionate odds 14 to 1.

There is no need to consider other horses. These three are enough for illustration.

Obviously, if all horses were equally bet all three of the Daily Double payoff would show the same payoff. All would pay either $91.10, $357.60, or $411.00.

But of the three Spring Away was bet more heavily than the other two. And this betting had to be done before either race of the Daily Double was run.

It is evident on the face of it that Spring Away was wagered upon not by the public but by "smart money" that knew something about this horse that the public did not.

20

How Important Is the Jockey in Racing?

IN THESE ENLIGHTENED times, it becomes a little tiresome to be approached by horse players with a request for an unbeatable method to beat the races. There is no such thing and the very thought that there might be is indicative of a person incapable of reasoning power. As a matter of fact, there is no approach to life itself or anything in it that is "unbeatable," much less so in any endeavor where the element of chance is predominant, such as in horse racing. History shows that in normal times, even in the soundest type of businesses, each new one started operates under difficulties and a small percentage of them succeed.

If the reader imagines that herein he is going to find a sure and certain way to better his horse playing then I say to him right now, don't waste your time reading further. But if the reader is willing to read this treatise with the thought that if he salvages even one single idea that is new to him or may be used to advantage, then he will be well repaid for the little time required to complete the reading.

There exists in horse racing more absurdities that are generally accepted as sound reason than in any other sport of which I know. Men will believe the most fantastic and unadulterated claptrap imaginable when it comes to the Sport of Kings, even though these same men will approach any other subject with a high degree of common sense and logical reasoning.

For instance, here is a classical example of what I mean: Warren Brown, writing memories of his reportorial days, tells this story: In speaking of the different types of reporters he said that some people are suspicious from birth of everyone and everything. He tells of a certain reporter who was trying to get up enough courage to play the *outstanding favorite* in the 1936 Santa Anita Handicap. The horse was Alfred G. Vanderbilt's mighty Discovery, quoted on the boards at odds of 8/5. This reporter approached another reporter and asked if he knew Vanderbilt personally, and when queried why he asked, said: "I'm thinking of making a bet on his horse. I'd like to know if he is 'shooting,' with the price as low as 8 to 5."

When racing my own large stable of horses I had a casual acquaintance with Vanderbilt, having claimed the horse Be Prepared from him after I had been unsuccessful in getting Vanderbilt to sell her to me at a private sale. To my knowledge he seldom bets even on his own horses, and in a few instances he may wager only $10.00. This is true of most of the millionaire owners, like the late Mrs. Dodge Sloan of Brookmeade Stable fame, who never made more than a sentimental wager of $10.00 at most.

Now just try to imagine *anyone not trying* to win a race with a purse of $100,000 as the reward. Incidentally, the same goes for $2,000 or $3,000 purses, no matter what people with suspicious minds may imagine. The average owner can't afford to take chances betting money in amounts large enough to win $2,000, $3,000, and $5,000 which they earn when their horses win.

Jockey fees are established by The Jockey Club. The maximum fee is $50.00 for a winning mount and for a losing mount $25.00. When I raced my stables there was a flat fee of $10.00 for any sized purse. This $50.00 fee is for races having a purse value of $2,000 or over. The fee decreases for races less than $2,000. These fees apply only to a jockey when he rides a horse not owned by his contract employer. Those stables that employ a contract jockey pay a stated salary. However, a jockey is always paid 10 percent of any purse earnings in addition to his fee or salary. Some owners, as I did, will place a bet for the jockey on the horse he is riding and say "Jock, I have placed a bet for you so do your best."

So if a purse is for $2,000 the owner bets $50, by paying the fee, and gets back $2,000 so that in reality he is getting odds of 40 to 1 whereas, if he bet this sum with a bookie or the mutuel machines he'd be apt to get odds of 2 or 3 to 1. For a $3,000 purse the odds are 60 to 1; and for a $5,000 purse they are 100 to 1.

I am referring here to claiming, allowance, and handicap races wherein no entry fees are called for. The classic races require entry fees to be paid, but even with them the odds the owner-nominators get run 200 to 500 to 1 and more.

These odds should be enough to make any reasonable person realize that, even in small purse races, it is lunacy for any horsemen not to make every effort to win any race in which he has a horse entered. Since cheating is done for the gain of money no cheating devised can offer the gain possible by simply winning races.

Say you are an owner, and you enter a horse in a race for a $5,000 purse. The odds on your horse are 2 to 1. You would have to wager $2,500 on your horse at 2 to 1 to win $5,000, whereas you would have to bet only $50 by paying a rider, to win the same amount of money. And your chances of winning are exactly the same under either situation. I am sure you would do what I would do and what every owner does. He makes every effort to get his horse to win.

The unbelievable stupidity of this reporter's attitude will be realized when you stop to consider that in order to win $100,000 at odds of 8/5, which is $1.80 for each $1.00 wagered, Vanderbilt would have had to bet $55,500. This is a classical example of why there is a belief in chicanery where racing is concerned. The truth of the matter is that such beliefs exist only in the minds of those who, being inherently dishonest themselves, cannot believe that anyone can act without seeking immoral advantage. True sportmanship, for its own reward, does not exist in the minds of those so readily prone to accept as truth any accusation detrimental to the honesty of racing.

I am merely giving you the above story to show how asinine otherwise intelligent people can be where horse racing is concerned. This is, of course, a glaring example. But, let me tell you that there are thousands of such ridiculous instances every day of racing, that may not stand out as clearly.

The attempt to gain financial profit in horse playing by following a jockey or certain jockeys is not new. But, as ordinarily practiced it is but another form of madness that predominates the sport. Jockeys come and go. Just how they can do such excellent work for one spell, and then fail so wretchedly at another seems to be quite beyond explanation. Often, the leading jockeys will go into a slump and fail to bring in a single winner out of 20 to 40 mounts. The reason for their failure to score cannot be attributed to the inferiority of their mounts, because frequently every loser they have may be a logical contender.

I have never once in all my playing career played or stopped from playing any horse because of the jockey who was riding. It is my firm conviction that given exactly the same mounts, any one of a dozen riders would have won the same races and equaled the record of any jockey. My reasoning is that it is the four legs of the horse that does the running and not those of the jockey. It is only once that I ever knew of anyone thinking along the lines that I do.

The *Thoroughbred Record* is a magazine devoted to horsemen such as owners, trainers, breeders, and the like. Therein Mr. John Hennessy, who is a trained management consultant, wrote an article. He had done research of hundreds of jockeys' riding records and concluded that the leading jockeys and the average or mediocre jockeys performed on a par, all things being equal. By this he meant what I have said, that give to a mediocre jockey the same horse to ride as the top-string jockeys and there is little to choose between them.

A writer in *Turf and Sport Digest* interviewed both trainers and jockeys after this article appeared and here are some of their opinions. Trainer Hirsch Jacobs said in substance that if he has the best horse in the race there are plenty of riders that will win riding it. Trainer Johnny Nerud said he never saw a jockey win without a horse and that the horse carries the jockey. Trainer Buddy Jacobson said that only rarely can a jockey make a contribution to a horse winning. Trainer Eddie Yowell said that only a horse that can run is needed, next a really competent rider and 75 percent racing luck. Trainer Allen Jerkens said that there are horses that can win but certain jockeys help a horse a little. Do you, reader, remember the riders saying you could tie a bag of *oats* on my Jim's Niece and she would run and win her own race?

Now a word from the jockeys. Bill Boland said if you have a class horse that runs freely, if you tied a bag of *mud* on it it would win. But if a bad-mannered horse, it would be different. Hedley Woodhouse sensibly compares the question to automobiles and says it's like driving a Cadillac compared to a jalopy. You must have the horse in order to get anywhere. Braulio Baeza says that if a rider does not have a good and right horse under him there is little he can improve upon.

Now I think anyone who rides horseback will admit that for some unknown reason a horse will function better with some riders than with others. I attribute this in part to pressure. A horse is most sensitive to pressure. There are different pressures exerted in riding and it varies with people and also with the sensitivity of the horse. There is a different pressure when a rider's weight is in front in the saddle or in the middle of the saddle or back in the saddle. There is a variance in pressure applied by riders in the thigh, in the knee, and in the calves of the leg.

However, as you'll recall from our discussion of the jockey's present-day position on a horse, no pressure is exerted on the race horse as it is on a saddle horse. The jockey's thighs and his calves are in the air. Therefore, I do not consider pressure valid in this respect. Undoubtedly, though, some horses will run more willingly for certain riders. But I do not believe this willingness affects a horse's speed. Therefore, any competent jockey can get the same speed out of a horse as can any other jockey.

There is overwhelming credence to the idea that a jockey may make a horse win a race, and therefore the jockey is important. I think this idea can best be exploded and proved untrue by the consideration of apprentice jockeys. You know that a weight allowance is given a new rider until such times as he graduates out of the apprentice class by riding a certain number of winners.

Hardly a season passes without some new apprentice jockey failing to gain the racing headlines. He is "hot," as the saying goes, and wins race after race, becoming a real sensation. He rides his quota of winners and then loses the weight advantage and rides on equal basis with all jockeys. After staying in the limelight he performs with mediocracy. Why is this? What has happened?

My own reasoning on this is as follows. I told you previously the question of weight is a fetish with owners and trainers and most handicappers. A new rider appears on the scene. He commences to ride winners. This is noticed by horsemen and because of the weight allowance they start engaging this boy to ride their horses. This sets up a chain reaction and in little time the jockey's agent is deluged with requests for his client's services. He receives more offers than he can fulfill. This permits him to be selective, so naturally if he can accept a mount on a horse that is short odds—even odds on—he will accept this mount in preference to any other mount in the race. In other words, he is being offered, and accepts, mounts only on the most likely winners.

Then the day comes! The honeymoon is over for this apprentice! He rides the required winners necessary to become a regular jockey and thereafter competes with the regular jockeys on an equal basis.

Now here is an important consideration. I have never known of two such sensations to appear on the scene at the same time. There are over 1200 members in the Jockey Guild—the Jockey Union—and many other jockeys that are not members. Only about nine races are run daily, and not too many tracks are in operation at the same time. Consider, then, the competition when over 1200 are daily seeking to get mounts. It is terrific. That is why they need a good jockey agent to go out, like a salesman, and drum up trade. The big-name riders making the headlines make the big money. The average jockey has a hard time making a little and many of them engage in additional work, such as exercising horses, to sustain themselves. So you see all that glitters is not gold.

Once the apprentice loses his weight allowance horsemen no longer are anxious to engage him. His agent is not having trainers begging for his rider's services and has to go out and sell his client to prospective customers. Instead of having his choice of the best horses in every race he has to take what he can get. So his winning average gradually descends the scale, and he gets the average run of horses to ride and levels off as a mediocre jockey.

He is the same lad that got the headlines! He rides no differently now! His winning declination is caused by one thing, and that is that he must now ride average horses and not those of the class of Damascus, Kelso, and others. *It is the horse that wins the race and not the jockey.* And don't forget it!

The most absurd of racing hocus-pocus is the judging of a jockey's real ability by the number of races he wins. Yet, of the dozens and dozens of experts with whom I have discussed racing—and they include professional horsemen of all types and outstanding private and public handicappers—not a single one questioned the effectiveness of judging a rider by his percentage of winning races. Many players rate jockeys and use their rating figures as a basis on which to favor or disfavor a selection.

Great horses at odds-on prices are frequently defeated. In the Barbara Fritchie Handicap, 7th race at Bowie, February 25, 1967, with a gross value of $59,900.00, the odds-on favorite Moccasin ridden by Brussard was defeated by a neck. The winner was Holly-O mounted by Lovata at odds of $5.70 to $1.00. Moccasin went off odds-on at 60¢ to $1.00. Now, is it reasonable to credit in a jockey-rating scale Lovata with one win to add to his average when he brought in an outsider against the favorite? Does he not deserve a better rating than Brussard would have received had Brussard won the race on the outstanding favorite?

Let's take another example—7th race, Aque., July 22, 1967, the Brooklyn Handicap with a gross value of $106,700. Baeza rode Buckpasser, one of the greats who went off odds-on at 70¢ to $1.00. The winner by 8 lengths was

Handsome Boy ridden by Belmonte. Should not he have been given more credit for winning than Baeza would have been given had he won?

Then too, there is this to consider. The jockey on a winning horse that is odds-on or even money wins by one length. The second and third horses finishing within three lengths of the winner went off at odds of 6 and 8 to 1 respectively. On the basis of the odds these two losing horses should have been beaten by much more than they were. Let me put it this way, if either of the jockeys of the second or third horse changed mounts with the winner is it not likely they would have won the race?

For a jockey rating scale to be reasonably accurate it would have to be promulgated along these lines: It is my opinion that it is not winning that deserves the credit allowance percentagewise but on what horse the performance was made. In other words, a rider on a rank outsider at long odds that rides that horse in the money, especially if close up to the winner, deserves as much if not more credit allowance than the rider of a winning favorite. The same applies if the outsider wins the race.

Obviously, the only sensible way to rate a rider is to credit him when he does *as well or better than expected*, and charge him when he fails. Credit for success and demerit for failure is a common sense law of life and nature and it is amazing to me that no one ever thought of it before in connection with jockey ratings, especially among those who claim, or are supposed, to know something about horse racing.

Under present conditions a jockey who loses on a 1 to 10 favorite is assumed to have done no worse than a jockey who loses on a 100 to 1 shot; and a jockey who wins on a 6 to 5 favorite is assumed to have accomplished a riding feat equal to a jockey who wins on a 50 to 1 shot. I am sure you will agree with me that this just does not make sense. Since present-day jockey ratings are based upon the relation of winning mounts to the total horses ridden, it is clear that each race ridden influences the rating figure. No distinction is made upon whether a jockey is riding a Man O' War against an ordinary handicap horse, or a $2,000 claiming horse.

For a guide as to what we have a perfect right to expect in rating jockeys, there is nothing that will prove better than the odds at which a horse goes to post. Admittedly post odds are *not* an *infallible* guide to what a horse may do. But there is no other guide that for better approximation can be used. In theory, a favorite should be brought in first, a second choice should be brought in second, and a third choice should be brought in third. Horses of greater odds than the choices naturally are expected to be out of the money. Of course, errors are made as to the form of horses, but the prices reflect what we have a right to expect frequently enough to gauge the jockey intelligently by this method. At most, this method should surpass any method that has hitherto been known.

However, the line of demarcation cannot be drawn too fine. When a horse is a favorite and finishes in second place, instead of winning, the benefit of a doubt must be given and credit allowed just as if the horse had won. The reason for defeat need not of necessity be the fault of the rider. It could be due to an improper price or to the fact that a better horse in that particular race beat it. One cannot be too arbitrary in racing.

It follows, therefore, that when a horse finishes in the position expected, or finishes better or finishes only one position worse than expected, the rider must be assumed to do what was expected of him and he is credited therefor. For example: A horse that is second choice may finish 1st, better than expected, or 2nd, exactly as expected, or 3rd, worse than expected but for which allowance must be made, and the rider of that horse should be credited accordingly.

The most absurd of all racing hocus-pocus concerns jockey ratings and the judging of a jockey's ability based upon the number of winners he rides. Yet, of the thousands and thousands of men with whom I have discussed racing, and these include professional horsemen of all types and outstanding private and public handicappers, *not a single* one ever questioned that the existing way of rating a jockey is anything but the best method known.

It is not my purpose here to tell how to formulate good jockey ratings. It would require a book by itself. The rider of a horse has never influenced any wager I have ever made. I believe it is the horse that wins the race and not the jockey!

Let me give you another example to support my opinion. I am not sure it is the exact race and correct names of the horse and rider. However, this is not important because the incident actually did take place although the names may be different.

The late Max Hirsch was, in my judgment, and I am sure in the opinion of all horsemen, one of the most capable, shrewdest, and successful trainers ever to appear in the racing scene. In 1936 he entered a horse named Bold Venture. To the surprise of all, the rider was a boy who had never ridden in a race. Mind you this was the first time this boy ever had a mount in a race. The value of the Kentucky Derby for 1967 was $162,200. But the glory of winning this oldest race in America means more to the millionaire owners than the money. The name of this first-time rider was I. Hanford and he won the race on Bold Venture in 1936.

The ambition of every living trainer is to saddle a Kentucky Derby winner.

If Max Hirsch believed that a jockey exerts so much importance in a horse winning a race, is it likely that he would have taken the chance of mounting a first time untried jockey in the stirrups? Think of this!

Please do not misunderstand me. It is not my intention in any manner or form to deride the ability of jockeys. My purpose is only to express my opinion that a great many horse players attach too much importance to the jockey. A competent jockey can upon occasion make an error in judgment but that does not mean he is not a great craftsman at his trade. The thought I want to leave is that you can't judge the ability between two jockeys as you can in other competitive sports. How can it be done since no two horses are alike? Golfers use the same shaped clubs, skaters all use the same type of skate, baseball players use the same type of bat and ball. All except the jockey competes upon equal terms.

The jockey of today is a perfect gentleman of honesty and character and is welcomed into all circles.

21

How Tod Sloan Got
His Chance for
Fame and Fortune

I AM GOING to relate some facts from the "Pittsburgh Phil" book to show the acumen and astuteness of "Pittsburgh Phil," and to urge the horse player to emulate him in seeking out the answers to every problem that confronts him in playing the races. Following are some excerpts giving you the facts as written by Mr. Cole, authorized author of the book containing "Phil's" secrets.

"Many stories have been written as to how 'Tod' Sloan became famous as a jockey and many have been told as to who it was that gave him his first opportunity. All reports to the contrary, it was 'Pittsburgh Phil' who gave him his real start and it was an upright beginning.

"It was in the late 'nineties' that 'Pittsburgh Phil' happened to be in California while racing was being conducted at the old Bay District track. It was a prolonged meeting, and for some cause, which Phil attributed to a few of the conniving element then rampant, he found himself a loser on the meeting to the extent of about $50,000. He had made up his mind to quit speculation, knowing that he could not succeed when there was so much in-and-out running, and where inconsistency in the handling of horses predominated. He was inclined to believe that several of the jockeys were pulling horses in the interests of their employers. Many times one owner did not know what his neighbor was doing, and inconsistency was so pronounced that sometimes three and four horses in a race were being taken care of by their riders, and a horse would win that should have finished out of the money. The racing was so mystifying that a cold deliberating handicapper, who depended upon form for his deductions, was a victim at almost every turn.

"While 'Phil' was sitting alone in the grandstand, the day before he had decided to leave, Sloan happened to be not far away, having no engagements to ride that day, and when he noticed 'Phil' in solitude, went over and sat beside him. In those days Sloan was hustling his way through the world as best he could, putting a bet down for himself when he had the money, and when he was without, doing his best to get someone to make a wager for him.

"When Sloan was seated he began a conversation. 'I think such and such a horse will win this race sure,' said he to Phil, naming the horse to which he referred.

" 'What makes you think so, Tod?' returned Phil. 'You rode him the last time he started and he finished away back.' Phil knew what Sloan was driving at and was gathering such information from him as he could. 'If he could not beat the lot that he met a few days ago, he cannot beat the field that he meets today.'

" 'Well,' said Sloan, 'I'd like you to put a bet on him for me, he is as good as 7 to 1 in the betting. He'll win sure, Mr. Smith.'

" 'Don't talk nonsense,' returned Phil. 'Why didn't he win the other day? Tell me why you think he can win today.' Though Phil asked these questions, he knew what the trouble had been in the previous race and merely wanted to learn what information Sloan would give.

" 'That horse was short the last time out,' was all that Sloan said in answer to Phil's direct question.

" 'Well, I'm not going to bet any more on the races here,' said Phil, 'so I don't care to put a bet down for you, but sit here and we will watch the race and if this horse wins I will make you a proposition.'

"They sat together while the race was being run, and just as Sloan predicted, the horse won in a common gallop.

" 'Didn't I tell you he would win?' was Sloan's first remark after the horses had passed the winning post. 'He was a good horse the other day but he met with a lot of interference, as well as being short of work.'

" 'Say, Tod, why don't you make up your mind to be thorough in your work,' asked Phil, 'and ride from the drop of the hat? You'll make plenty of money and be successful. I will give you a start. I'll make an agreement with you if you will abide by it strictly and confidentially.'

" 'What will you do?' asked Sloan.

" 'What will I do?' returned Phil, repeating the question, while he gave himself time to think, 'Why, I'll give you $400 every time you ride a winner at this track. It will make no difference whether I bet on it or not. If you win a race you can go to my representative every Saturday night at the Palace Hotel and collect $400 for every winning mount you have had during the week. That is more money than you can make mixing up with 'sharps' and you will get your money. There will be no standing you up for it and paying off in promises but it will be in good solid gold coin. There is one thing I shall want you to observe and that is secrecy. Upon no consideration must this interview be mentioned or even intimated. I do not wish to see you, or be recognized by you. The only two things that you have to think about are winning a race and collecting $400 for so doing, and if you win ten races next week you can go direct to my representative and he will have instructions to pay you $4,000. Do not let your valet or anyone else know that you and I have had this conversation or that we have made an agreement.'

" 'I'll do it. I'll put all I know into every race that I ride. You can bet on me every time,' was Sloan's decision.

" 'Oh no,' replied Phil, 'I am not going to bet on you every time you ride, but I am going to bet when I think you are riding the best horse. But that will not make any difference in the fee part of the proposition. You will get your $400 if you win whether I bet or not.'

" 'It's a bargain. When does it begin?' said Sloan.

" 'Tomorrow, and next Saturday if you have ridden any winners go to Mr. ....' [Phil was always discreet about letting the world know who was working for him and though he gave Sloan the name of his representative he did not divulge it to the writer when telling the story] 'and collect whatever money is coming to you. He will have full instructions to pay, no matter what the amount.'

"It was only a person with turf wisdom such as Phil possessed who could see his way clear to make such a proposition payable. But he knew what it meant to have a jockey trying to win every race against a half a dozen who were manipulating horses at the dictation of unscrupulous owners and trainers. There were many times presumably that Tod would win races through such manipulations, being 'shooed in,' as it were, and there was no question that some of his winning mounts would be quoted at ridiculous prices by the bookmakers. All these things had been well thought out by Phil, and he laid his plans accordingly.

"To keep the matter as quiet as possible he employed several persons, whom he trusted implicitly, to execute his commissions in the ring. These men were never seen with Phil. In fact, they were practically strangers to the bookmakers but it was a band of well-versed and thoroughly educated employees, who learned signs and signals perfectly, which were directed from Phil while he sat apparently unconcerned in the grandstand oblivious to what was going on in the betting ring. At the same time, he was kept well posted as to the prices and who was betting on horses by his messenger who was employed for such a purpose.

"It was not long before Sloan began winning race after race and upon nearly every occasion Phil's agents made some good-sized collections. All the wagers were made with cash, and to blind the operations each agent took a different section of the ring daily, so that the same bettor would not be so familiar to the bookmakers.

"Before every race Phil's commissioners would be at several points of vantage, where they could catch his signals. Then they would go into the ring and fulfill his orders. Many of these commissioners were not known to each other, so secretly and systematically were the speculations accomplished.

"In less than three weeks Phil had recovered all his previous losses and was a good winner, and at the end of the first month he was between $70,000 and $80,000 ahead. The bookmakers were confused. They did not know where all the money was going to. None of the regulars seemed to be making any headway, and yet money was being taken out of the ring by strangers, whom no one knew, except in a betting and collecting way.

"It was common to hear conversations between the bookmakers, as they returned from the track, asking each other what they knew about that clerical looking fellow, who beat three or four races that day, or that country-looking chap, who thought nothing of betting five or six hundred on a 3 to 1 shot, and collecting four times out of five. Sloan was becoming so popular at the end of a month that he was a public favorite and the rank and file would have nothing but Sloan.

"One day going home in the street car Phil happened to be seated beside John Coleman, one of the most prominent and gentlemanly bookmakers in the business, when the conversation turned to the doings in the betting ring. 'I can't understand who is getting all the money,' said Coleman. 'In the last month I have lost over $10,000 and it has been split up into a thousand parts. No one man has got it, but it has been divided between half a dozen big bettors whom nobody knows. They come along and bet two or three hundred in cash and invariably get away with it. There must be some big combination somewhere that is getting a lot of money. It reminds me of the "Little Pete" episode of a few years ago when he had all the jockeys in the business on a string. The strangest part of the thing is that in nearly all cases they play Sloan's mounts just as if he had been nominated to win every race no matter what horse he rides.'

"Phil smiled and intimated that Sloan was a good rider and no one could be blamed for following him.

" 'Well, in the future,' replied Coleman, 'if Sloan is on a natural 3 to 1 shot they won't get better than 6 to 5 for my money. I think I will string with them, instead of going against the deluge of Sloan money, and there is many another bookmaker will do the same thing.'

"This was the beginning of the end of the successful campaign of the Phil-Sloan combination at Bay District track. When Phil saw that he would have to take such short prices against Sloan's mounts he knew that the odds were somewhat against him, and that it would eventually become unprofitable to accept even money against a horse, which, under normal conditions, would be quoted at two or even three to one.

"It was only a matter of a day or so when Phil settled up his affairs, paid off his commissioners, and packed his grip for the East, taking Sloan with him. Not until after he was gone did the bookmakers awaken, rub their eyes, and gradually grasp the fact that they had been outwitted by 'Pittsburgh Phil.' In argument some said that Phil had only just engaged Sloan to ride for him in the East on account of his good work in California. They were loath to believe that he had been in his employ for a month, and it was not until the story was told by Phil himself that the skeptical could be made to understand that such a clever yet honorable system could have been employed to 'separate them from their bankrolls.'

"Sloan had to thank George E. Smith, 'Pittsburgh Phil,' for his rise in the turf world."

22

Anecdotes About Famous Plungers on the English Turf

THE ENGLISH SCHOOL of Plungers in the Victorian Era may be divided into two classes. First was the amateur or patrician plunger, who was usually the owner of a large and influential stable, and who employed the most talented trainers, the most fashionable jockeys and the most astute watchers of horses, or, as they are styled in England, "touts."

These owners necessarily had great wealth at their command and the majority of the great plungers of this era had inherited their tastes for racing and gambling through a long line of ancestors. Many of them had stables of racehorses while yet in their teens and though most of them ran their horses under assumed names, or the name of some willing relative, the rosters of Oxford and Cambridge Universities and even the public schools of Eton and Harrow had many winning owners yearly among their students. Up to 1860, when the Gambling Act went into force, betting lists of the prevailing odds on all the more important turf events were openly posted. Yearling Books on the Derby were common, 100 to 1 on the Field being the usual quotation, and it was an easy matter for the owner of a promising yearling to back his horse for a small outlay to win him any sum he might desire. At the time that he made the bet, which was always play or pay, the race would be some eighteen months in the future, but that did not deter him, and almost invariably the makers of the larger books on this race had to cover at a loss.

The Cheshire Cup was a favorite race for early speculation. This was, and is still, a handicap at $2\frac{1}{4}$ miles, and it was possible to back a horse for a large amount before the entries closed, and necessarily long before either the weights or acceptances were declared.

In those days, information was not so readily obtainable by the racing public as it is today. Stable works were most jealously guarded. The majority of the horses outside of those at Newmarket, Epsom, and Malton were trained at country villages, away from all railways and on private grounds, to which access by any unauthorized stranger was not only a difficult but a dangerous matter. All employees were under the strictest surveillance, letters were scrutinized by the trainer, and telegraph offices were only in the larger towns. It was very difficult to convey any stable secrets to the list-keepers, who were always willing to pay high prices for information as to a prominent stable's intentions in important races.

Horses for the leading events were dispatched to and from their training vans, accompanied by prize fighters, and were never left unguarded a single instant. All the hay, oats, and water necessary were taken from home and were under lock and key.

The return home of the winner of an important race was the occasion of a great jubilee. Bonfires were lighted, the church bells pealed, and the poor of the neighborhood were feasted to their heart's content. Even Ministers of the Gospel owned and raced horses. As late as 1874 the winner of the St. Leger, Apology, was bred and raised by the Rev. J. S. King, though she ran as being the property of "Mr. Launde" his registered and assumed name.

Queen Victoria maintained a large breeding farm at Hampton Court, the yearlings of which were disposed of annually at auctions. Both George IV and William IV owned and raced large stables and all the more important race meetings such as Epsom, Goodwood, and Ascot were invariably graced by the royal presence. Under such mentorship racing speedily became the fashion and, thanks to the sportsmanlike efforts of His Majesty, King Edward VII, is now on a higher plane in England than ever before.

He was the breeder and owner of two Derby winners, Persimmon and Diamond Jubilee. Whenever his state duties permitted, His Majesty journeyed to the course for recreation, where he mingled with the crowd especially at Newmarket, as democratic and unguarded as an ordinary citizen. King Edward formerly dearly loved to "back his opinion" and while he would not bet personally, the royal commission was executed by Capt. Batchelor.

Among the plungers in the "60's" that of the Marquis of Hastings on his mare, Lady Elizabeth, was by far the most gigantic. It was an ill-fated one as the mare showed nothing like her two-year-old form. Mr. Henry Chaplin, who owned Hermit, the Derby winner of 1867, is credited with winning the largest amount on that race of any individual, his winnings totaling $900,000 to which amount the Marquis of Hastings largely contributed, as, in addition to being a backer, the Marquis made a large book among his friends on the race in question. As Hermit started at the remunerative price of 66 to 1 the initial outlay to win this large sum was not so great.

The race in question was a memorable one, as it was run in a blinding snowstorm. The Marquis considerably overlaid his book against Hermit to Chaplin, a matter of sentiment being the cause of the bitter feeling between the men. It was generally believed that the trouble between them was caused by a love affair. In order to meet his losses the marquis had to invoke the aid of Mr. Padwick, the fashionable money lender of the day. His losses on this race probably equalled $600,000. He died at the early age of twenty-four, presumably of a broken heart. Outwardly cool, but with an intensity of purpose that would not be denied, on several occasions he made the leading bookmakers top-laying against his own horse or that of a friend.

Lord Dupplin, who owned Petrarch, the winner of the 2,000 guineas, was a very heavy plunger in the early 70's. His horses were trained by the shrewd Captain Machell, who probably brought off more coups than any of his professional brethren. Among the patrons of his stable were such plungers as the late Duke of Beaufort and the late Duke of Hamilton, the latter of whom is credited with losing over $5,000,000 on the turf.

The Duke of Beaufort confined his operations to flat racing only, and during a turf career of forty years was only fortunate enough to own two really good horses, Ceylon and Petronel. The Duke of Hamilton maintained two large stables and was possibly more fond of a huge speculation on a steeplechase, or hurdle race, than on a flat race, especially so when the King's present trainer, Richard Marsh, was wearing the ducal livery of "Cerise and French Grey" sleeves and cap. His turf losses became so excessive that he was compelled to dispose of the wonderful collection of pictures and objects of art in Hamilton Palace. This was a most remarkable sale, lasting four days, and realizing some $2,500,000. The catalogues of the sale cost each intending purchaser five dollars. Over six feet in height, with broad shoulders and a very red face, the Duke was easily distinguishable at most meetings. He invariably wore a blue shirt, which earned for him the sobriquet of the "Butcher Duke." "Jack" Watts was his favorite flat-race jockey, and possibly no incident of the great rider's turf career, outside of his victory in the Derby of '96 on Persimmon in the royal livery, gave that jockey half the satisfaction that he experienced when he beat Foxhall on the Duke's Fiddler at Ascot, the Duke winning very heavily on the race.

An enormous amount was taken out of the ring when the Duke's horse Ossian won the St. Leger of '83.

Sir George Chetwynd and Sir John Ashley were the owners of large stables from 1870 to 1880. Both of these baronets had calls upon the riding services of Charlie Woods, and many a successful coup was landed by the confederacy until the jockey lost his license, through complicity in the ownership of horses in conjunction with Sir George Chetwynd and Sir John Ashley. The latter was the patron of all manly sports and was the owner of Peter, and other celebrities. Thanks to the wonderful efforts of Archer, who persuaded that erratic horse to try again when he stopped to kick during the race for the Royal Hunt Cup, eventually finishing first, the owner won an enormous sum on the result.

Sir John also won a tremendous amount on Scamp when the latter won the International Hurdle Race, one of the then leading cross country events.

This horse won a Goodwood Cup as well, and was sent to Australia, where he sired some good winners. Always cheery, with his broad-brimmed derby hat on one side of his head, a huge cigar in his mouth and wearing the invariable red necktie, his advent at the rail of Tattersall's ring was always the prelude for some heavy wagers to be recorded well up in the thousands. He had a large stable in training and the somewhat doubtful distinction of winning more selling races than any other owner in the course of the year. Sir John was an athlete of no mean ability and on one occasion took the law into his own hands and administered a severe beating to Plunger Walton, the American turf speculator, whom he accused of seeking information from his jockey.

Two young Hungarians, the brothers Baltazzi, flashed upon the English turf in 1875 and soon had a stable upon which great plunges were made in 1876. They had a very promising colt unnamed, which throughout the winter betting on the Derby had occasionally received support. Finding themselves in financial difficulties they had to apply to the late "Sam" Lewis, the great turf money lender of Cork Street, Piccadilly, for assistance, giving as part security for the loan a bill of sale of their horses, among them the horse in question known then as the "Mineral Colt." Failing to meet their obligations with Mr. Lewis, the latter sent for Mr. Baltazzi to ask him for a delivery order for the horses. The latter was willing to turn them all over except the "Mineral Colt," and tried hard to get Lewis to agree to accept him. The latter said the particular colt was the only one that had any pretensions to class and he must insist upon receiving it.

Baltazzi then signed the order and hurled it at Lewis bursting into tears as he did so. Lewis looked askance for a moment or two, and then said: "What's the matter?"

Baltazzi replied: "I had set my heart upon winning your English Derby and now the colt is yours, there is nothing to prevent your going to Tattersall's and scratching him."

Lewis thought a moment and said: "Do you really think the colt has a chance to win?"

Baltazzi replied, "Yes, a great chance."

Lewis reached into a drawer, pulled out a cheque book, wrote a cheque to Baltazzi's order for a thousand pounds, handed it to him, and at the same time tore up the Bill of Sale, saying: "Well, if you really think he has a chance, put that on him and if you want any more come back."

The colt did well and, as history records, in the hands of Custance won the Derby of 1876, being named "Kisber" on the morning of the race after the Baltazzi Estate in Hungary. This victory well replenished the Baltazzi exchequer and needless to say, "Sam" Lewis got more than his own. Unfortunately their turf speculations were unwise and they returned to their native land, where they still operate a small stable.

Ernest Benzon, the only son of a Hebrew iron founder, of Birmingham, flashed on the turf in 1887 and while not a patrician had something like one million and a half dollars in ready cash at his disposal. He first startled the turf world by betting fifty thousand dollars on Bendigo for the "Jubilee Cup" at Kempton. This plunge was successful and speedily earned for him the title of the "Jubilee Plunger." As the young man's dissipations speedily became notorious, it was changed to "Jubilee Juggins." He paid large prices for horses, but his stable was notoriously mismanaged and eventually he finished penniless and was sent to jail for debt.

While in prison he amused himself by writing a book of his life which he entitled *My Fortune and How I Spent It.* It is more than probable that he lost more at cards and dice than he did on the turf. His other extravagances were numerous. One of his fads was never to wear the same shirt twice.

Of the professional plungers of humble origin, and who were in no instance helped by rich relatives, a few may be mentioned.

Principal among them must be included John Hammond of Newmarket, who as a boy polished shoes and sold shoe laces in the streets of London. He next held a humble position in a stable and became eventually the owner of a large string of horses and the heaviest speculator whose operations were conducted upon a businesslike basis. At one time a tout, Hammond naturally had a good eye for a horse, and through doing Fred Archer a slight service, eventually became that famous jockey's great friend and, no doubt through Archer's information about the horses he rode, profited largely.

Hammond owned St. Gatien, who ran a dead heat with Harvester for the Derby, and the great mare, Florence, by whose Cambridgeshire victory he is credited with winning $500,000. Eventually Archer and he had a quarrel and the jockey transferred his friendship to Arthur Cooper and Joseph Davis, the latter of whom was wealthy and who raced a stable. Eighteen months later Hammond became penniless and again sold shoe laces. Davis won a large amount when his horse Fortissimo won the Goodwood Stakes. In this event, he was fortunate enough to secure Archer's services. Mr. Davis, who is the principal owner of Hurst Park, one of the most profitably run courses near London, never plunges now. Arthur Cooper, after amassing much wealth, was stricken with consumption and died some years ago.

"Sam" Lewis, when he found time to attend races, was a very large operator and would think nothing of betting from ten thousand to twenty thousand pounds in an afternoon.

There are hundreds of racegoers in England, who make good incomes yearly by backing horses, and this despite the increased cost of attending the meetings. Traveling and other expenses there are much higher than in the United States. It is by no means impossible to make money on the races, but to do so it is certainly incumbent that common sense, sobriety and a strict attention to every detail must be followed.

Unnecessary extravagances are the rock on which so many race track ships are shattered. The prices quoted against horses' chances seem to have a tremendous effect upon the average bettor. For instance, if the horse upon which one intends to place a wager is quoted at even money, 6 to 5 or 7 to 5, he says, "Too short a price for me," and places his capital upon possibly the longest-priced horse in the race.

On the other hand, when a horse which a bettor thinks should be 4 to 1 or 5 to 1 is quoted at 8 to 1 or 10 to 1, he turns to the favorite, and in both instances probably has the mortification of seeing his original choice the winner. "The chalk hurt me," has been the refrain of many a backer and is one that should never be allowed to influence an individual who has a good reason for making a wager. "Any price is a good price if it is a winning one," is an old adage and it is not the bets that win but those that lose that "hurt."

23

How to Play the Harness Races

ACTUALLY, THERE IS little basic difference between playing the harness races or the flat races. In either case, the star performer is the horse. And the horse is not different in conformation, temperament, or running ability in either type of racing.

If a player chooses the path of winning money through a mechanical wagering method, of which many are available, then playing either type of race is about the same.

If you will get together a number of race charts for the trots, you will note that the principle of the irregular race is present. A horse will fall back and come on again, the irregularity being caused by the same reasons as present in a race on the flat. These irregular races are productive of many future winners.

This irregular race method plus the Secret Play, given in Chapter 19, are the two most potent factors I know for beating the races. There is one other method I use and without being egotistical I do not believe the average player can utilize it, since it is based upon the running action of a harness horse and it is so insidious even when explained few will be able to recognize and use it profitably. I'll relate the details later in this chapter.

As you will recall, the Secret Play is supposed to detect the horse that the smart inside money is placed on. You also know that I do not believe in tips. But when it comes to harness racing, I want to modify my conclusions about tips. I do believe when it comes to harness racing a tip is more apt to be productive than it is in thoroughbred flat racing, and here is why.

A workout for a thoroughbred means nothing except to indicate its fitness. But it is different with the harness racing breed of horses. They will generally run more true to a fast workout. What has previously been said about trainers and stable help being close to the horses in training and are able to detect a possible future winner is more true with harness horses. In the first place, there are considerably fewer horses stabled at a harness track than on a thoroughbred track. So the opportunity for observing each other's horses is much greater at harness tracks. To this is added the fact that harness horses run truer to workouts than other horses, enhancing the chances of men in the stable area to be able to spot a potential winner. And it is for this reason I believe a tip from a knowing harness horseman is worthy of consideration.

Many players are given tips that win on harness horses, and this is well known, so those not fortunate enough to be the recipient of winning inside information conclude that harness racing is many times more crooked than flat racing. I do not believe there is any more chicanery involved in either type of racing, but the reasons are as I explained above.

In any event, the Secret Play will work well no matter what type of racing is involved—flat, harness, quarter-horse, dog, and so on. For the reasons I have given above, the Secret Play works better at harness racing that at flat racing and you are apt to get more playing days.

Hundreds of times I have gone with my son to the harness tracks just for the purpose of playing the second half of the daily double if a horse qualified. The play has always intrigued my son.

The other play is this. It is a little difficult to explain to other than thorough horsemen, but I'll try my best. Those horses entered in later races come out on the track for a "blow-out," which means they are run around on the track to loosen them up for their coming contest. Sit in the stands and note how when running fast they operate their front legs. I refer *only* to trotters —ignore pacers. Notice the position of the knee at its highest point in running. Then look at that portion of the leg below the knee including the hoofs. You will note, if you are observant enough, that some horses run with their legs straight out, including the hoofs in a sort of bow line. Or, in other words, from the knee down the leg stands out as straight as the conformation will permit. Contrasted to this, other horses will pull up that portion of the leg below the knee, the cannon, in a curved line under the forearm.

If you will closely watch a pacer you will note very slight bending of the knee, compared to a trotter, when its leg is stretched out in stride. Now compare this with a trotter's running action, and I am sure you will know what I mean. The trotter that does not bend his knee as much as the usual trotter gains from three to six inches in every stride. When you figure how many strides are taken running a mile, you will appreciate what a difference this can make. Just keep studying this difference in action and it will become obvious to you.

As I stated, this is a thick thing to observe. However, should you be able to spot it, play this horse in its coming race, especially if you do not observe any like horse in the same race. If there are more than one, then base your selection on the odds and horse's record.

From my observations of written material it appears to me that there is a prevalence of belief that it is better to wager on trotters than on pacers. I am assuming that readers know the difference between the two. The basis for this idea is that pacers are more apt to break their stride, and by this reason eliminate themselves from the contest. Based upon my own playing this is a theory that I do not subscribe to. It has been my experience that trotters run out as often as pacers lose their pacing stride.

Harness racing rules require that each type of horse conform to its established type of racing. Once a pacer or trotter breaks its gait and starts to gallop, it must immediately be pulled up before it gains any headway. If it fails to do so, it is disqualified. In my own personal playing, I have found both gaited horses are equally amiss at times so in the end it equalizes itself.

There is one system that I know of that as far as all reports I have heard on it has never been known to lose at any full meeting covered, if all playable races are wagered on. I can't reveal the system itself, because it is copyrighted, but I can tell you that it is based on playing horses to show. But it is played *only* in specified races and not all races. One of the several reasons for its success is that harness racing show prices are much higher comparably than those for flat racing. I doubt if show betting can make you a winner, unless it is used in the specified races of the system.

Here is another little tip that has occasionally been profitable for me. After I have determined upon a selection to win, I look over the past odds of the horse. If it has been a favorite or has been running at very short prices, it is a sign that the horse was well regarded in those races, and that there may have been good reason for it. Other things being equal, I sometimes have used it to balance the scales in its favor.

24

A Potpourri and Medley of Racing Wisdom

THIS IS MY next to last chapter before I tackle the final one and relate my day's work in going about playing the races. It can be skipped if wished. But heed my advice. You'll learn about the game in many ways from this chapter. I'll relate about great plungers, tricks of the trade, and interesting facts that are dear to the hearts of all true horsemen. Well, here goes.

Every breeding establishment is presented with a problem each year. This is the naming of their yearlings. The name must meet certain rules of The Jockey Club and often three or four names must be submitted before one is acceptable. Alfred Vanderbilt is known for the ability to select suitable names. For example, I claimed from him Be Prepared, so named because one of its progenitors was Bugle Call.

Needles won the Kentucky Derby in 1956 for my friend Hughie Fontain and was most appropriately named. When a yearling, the animal was constantly under a veterinarian's care. It had been medicinally injected through a needle hundreds of times—hence the name.

I am about to relate an incident that occurred early in my racing career. Unquestionably, it taught me a lasting lesson that saved hundreds of dollars for me.

It was at Saratoga. The track was muddy. A featured race was coming up. The favorite was held at odds of 1 to 15. I think there were three, possibly four horses in the race. Jim Dandy a rank outsider had odds of 100 to 1.

I was in the box section as the horses were parading to the post and heard a Mr. Levy comments on the race. I have never forgotten them and they have influenced all my future activities. In substance, here is what he said:

"Here is a chance to make the quickest and easiest thousand dollars possible. Put up $15,000 on the favorite and in less than two minutes see it grow into $1,000 profit."

Not being very knowledgeable at the time, this statement did not seem unrealistic and had I had $15,000 would have bet it. In business billions of dollars are invested or used with but a small return of less than 1 percent. So no matter how small the odds wagers are made on horses.

The horses lined up at the barrier! There were no starting gates in those days. Instead horses were led up to a barrier of three or four webbings. When touching the webbing a lever was sprung and the barrier raised over the heads of the horses.

The barrier went up! They were off! The favorite at odds of 1 to 15 and Jim Dandy at 100 to 1 fought it out down to the wire. Jim Dandy won and paid $100.00 to $1.00! Yes, 100 to 1, and all old timers will recall this incident.

For the life of me I cannot recall the name of the favorite so dramatically defeated. I seem to have a recollection that its short drive of 1 to 15 was because it had, up to this time, never been defeated.

I relate this as an interesting incident and also because it reveals several most important racing maxims that have remained with me all my life. 1. There is no such thing as a sure thing. 2. Any horse can lose as well as win. 3. No matter how certain it appears a certain selection will win, it is not worth the risk unless the price is right. 4. No horse is worth a wager at odds of 1/to 3 or less.

I claimed a horse, Who Calls, from the Boeing Stable, owned by the airplane manufacturer of that name. My stable was located at Jamaica and the airplanes from the nearby airports would frequently pass over the stable area. When Who Calls was being walked in the space adjoining my stable and a plane passed overhead it would stand still, look up and follow it with its eyes. I have never seen any horse do this, not even to glance up when a plane passed. It made me curious and I thought about it. One day it came to me that the Boeing plant is located in the State of Washington, I believe. And that it was a possibility that Boeing's breeding farm was located in an area over which the testing planes passed over. This undoubtedly went on several times each day. I visualized Who Calls as a yearling grazing in the field acquiring the habit of watching these planes as they passed by. Just a supposition in my mind and I wish I could verify my conclusion.

This brings to my mind that Who Calls was claimed from me. Shortly thereafter the new owner entered Who Calls in the Kentucky Derby. Now this horse had as much chance of winning the Derby as you or I would have.

The claimant was not insane. Why, then, was the nomination made at a cost of $100 to enter? There are only two probable reasons. One is it inflated his ego to see his name in print as nominating a horse in the Derby, the world's most sought-to-win race. The next is the possibility that the claimant would be able to secure a box or reserved seat for the Derby. It is impossible for the average person to get a good place to witness the Derby. But of course accommodations must be provided for owners whose horses are nominated for the event.

The reason I relate this is that you have seen horses in these big races that do not have the remotest chance. Some players figure that since the owner paid entry fees the horse must be O.K. Not so! The entry is made for the glory of an owner's name to appear as the owner in a classic race.

How I acquired my first race horse and got into racing as an owner is interesting because it teaches why there are horses on the track that never come near to earning their feed bill. One day a visitor was announced and brought into my private office. He said he was a horse trainer and he knew where he could buy a very good racehorse. He made me a proposition. He would train the horse without charge to me. His remuneration would be 10 percent of all purse money earned. This same approach is being made all over the country today, and thus new owners come into the fold.

Now it so happened that his horse, named Dohoev, had been running in Florida and had run an irregular race, and I had been watching for it to run in New York. I had never given a thought to owning a racing stable and had this trainer mentioned any other horse, I never would have acquired a racing stable. I had this horse on my list to play. I figured this trainer must know his business, otherwise he could not be willing to train without a salary, so what had I to lose. We approached the owner, Willie Martin, from whom I subsequently bought Jim's Niece, and I negotiated and bought Dohoev.

It did not take me long before I knew that I'd have to take over all but the physical training of the horse. As to placing and entering and figuring out races for it and how it was to be ridden I would have to make the decisions. During the time I raced my stable I had three different trainers. In all instances I performed all functions, except the physical training of the horses. I remember one of these trainers getting "high-hat." Every time he won a race he was telling me how clever he was and how he knew just what to do to make a horse ready and win a race. I said to him then if a horse winning a race is evidence of your ability and credit is due you, by the same token when it loses a race it is your lack and your fault. If a win is due to a trainer then a loss must be due to him likewise. That's fair isn't it? I do not mean a trainer is lacking in ability because a horse loses; the thought I am trying to convey is no trainer should go "high hat" because his charge wins. As noted previously, anyone could win with Jim's Niece and many horses like her. All three trainers won with her. If both trainers and jockeys want the credit when they win, they should be willing to take the blame when they lose. They should not expect to have it both ways. All they have to do is do the best they can within their own degrees of competence and not look for credit where it is not due.

I am going to relate some experiences and maxims of "Pittsburgh Phil" either verbatim or in substance and some of my own maxims. In them will be many secrets and advice that should help every player along the road to success. Also will be related experiences of others if they teach worthwhile lessons. And some of my own!

Here is an experience of Robert Rowe and it is verbatim.

"Have you ever heard of a 'build-up' at a racetrack? A build-up is usually pulled off at a small track that receives a comparatively small mutuel play. About eight years ago, we happened to be in a board room [betting room]. The sixth race at Charlestown was scheduled to go off. The favorite was quoted in every scratch sheet and Morning Line at 4 to 5 (4/5) or less. We thought it should be 2/5. A more likely 'surething' just could not turn up any time, anywhere.

"Even at 2/5 this horse was an overlay because actually the other horses did not belong in the same race with it. We were winning at the time, and decided to bet our $80 profit on this odds-on favorite—a practice we might mention we seldom engage in. But, we wish to emphasize, it would have been insane to bet against it. The only alternative was to lay off the race.

"Anyway the results came over the wire. The payoff was not $2.80 or even $3.60, as might be expected. This cinch bet paid the astounding odds of 6/1 for a $15.40 mutuel. The bookie turned green and refused to pay off until he had completely verified that the odds as given were correct. This vast overlay was the obvious result of a clever build-up. This is *not* unusual, as you will frequently see a logical 6/5 or 2/1 come back paying in the four figure payoff. Here is how it is done.

"A group enters a 'sure thing' or a 'shoo-in' in a race consisting of as few horses as possible. It also has to be done where the play is comparatively small. The group take possibly $15,000 and if it is a five-horse field they spread the $15,000 *among the four other horses* (the fifth horse being the favorite). $15,000 wagered at a small track in a small field can create havoc with the odds. It forces the odds down on every other horse and the horse they are manipulating has its odds go sky high out of proportion.

"Now let us assume, that as a result of this action, they have driven the odds on the favorite up to 4/1; 5/1 etc. *just prior to post time*. They then, by careful prearrangement, call up their operators scattered in various book rooms and possibly bet $25,000 away from the track on the favorite. They spread it sufficiently and bet it late enough to prevent money coming back to the track. In other words, they do not give the outside bookies a chance to lay off the money if they have any suspicion of what is going on.

"Let us examine the result of this action. The syndicate invested a total of $40,000. The sum of $15,000 was invested for the purpose of a build-up. The actual amount wagered on the winner was $25,000. Now, if the total of $40,000 had been wagered on the winner at the true, legitimate odds (that would have prevailed provided this build-up had not taken place) it would have earned a profit of $20,000 so they would get back $60,000 for the $40,000 wagered.

"By creating a build-up they 'wasted' $15,000 but got 6 to 1 for their money instead of 1/2 for the $25,000 wagered on the favorite. They thus got back a total return of $75,000 compared to $60.000 the other way. This is slick manipulation and I doubt if there is anything illegal about it, aside from betting outside the track."

Of course, the above example is extreme, but it does illustrate what an actual genuine overlay really is. In lesser and undramatic ways these overlays occur every day, at every track in operation, everywhere. Watch the Morning Line or Scratch Sheet lines and you will often see a short-priced favorite come back with a payoff in four figures. When this happens check its past performances and you will wonder *how* it could be possible for the betting public at the track to pass up such an overlay. If you will personally make such observations you will never again underestimate its importance.

The player with the know-how to spot these overlays *must* win if he continues to play long enough to allow the law of averages to start rolling in his favor. Before you read another word, let me say that you are going to learn herein something entirely different concerning this subject that has never before appeared in print.

Let us assume that a tight race comes up and that two horses are evenly matched. (This situation most frequently creates overlays, since the reasons for overlays or underlays are varied.) In this instance the newspaper selectors must pick one of these horses to be on top. Let us further assume that by coincidence most of the selectors of the *Racing Form, Morning Telegraph* or Scratch Sheet, settle on horse "A." The public, which is 90 percent influenced by these selectors (together with those on local newspapers) thus might be prone to wager on horse "A"—install him as a heavy favorite—and make horse "B" an overlay at 9/2 or even better! This despite the fact that both horses have nearly equal chances of winning!

Or, again, let us assume that some wealthy person puts up $2,000 (at a small track) as the result of drunken foolhardiness—and don't think for a moment this does not frequently take place—and thus starts a betting trend. This too, often creates an overlay. The public has been taught (and most often improperly and not based upon sound logic, but upon some "crack-pot" theory) that when such a large single bet turns up to follow, like sheep, and rush to the slaughter.

There are many, many reasons why overlays are created and there is no need to elaborate further about it. Suffice it to say, as all seasoned players know, *that overlays and underlays do exist! If you as an individual aim to win you must learn to understand and spot overlays and underlays and know what to do about them.* Failure to do so, no matter how many winners you may be able to select, will eventually cause failure.

This is actually another way of saying that you must learn when and when *not* to wager, you must learn when you are getting the best of the odds and when you are not! The deadly track-percentage take, of approximately 15 percent, will ordinarily bankrupt you soon enough without adding to the difficulties by increasing the percentage against yourself.

To do his best work a horse must be contented in its surroundings just as humans. If not contented it will fret, lose weight, go off its feed, sulk, stall-walk and be unable to race at its best. Go around racing stable areas and you'll see a multitude of small animal pets. Dogs, a tame crow, kittens, ducks, geese, a turtle, a small pony, a chicken, goats, and what have you. Those who might be considered the pets of the stable help are in the big minority. These pets are mostly kept as the best-known methods adopted to keep a horse happy and contented.

"Pittsburgh Phil" says: "Belmar was a horse that was very hard to please. I knew he was a very good horse, but I knew that there was something wrong with him. He never seemed to run the race that I believed he could run. I bought this horse from Mr. Galway, thinking I could manage him and bring out his best qualities. Almost every moment I had to spare I would spend around Belmar's stall. I told my brother, William, that if ever we could get at the horse's disposition he would win a lot of races. We tried to please him by putting a companion in his stall in the shape of a rooster. He did not seem to take to the rooster and we tried a cat and a goat. Finally, a little fox terrier playing around the stables ran into the stall and Belmar seemed to take to him at once.

"After this, if the fox terrier was away from Belmar, the old horse would sulk and whinny for him to come back again. When Belmar was lying down the little old fox terrier was always lying on his shoulder and the two always slept together. It got so that the fox terrier could be placed on the withers of Belmar and he would trot around the shed with the dog on his neck. No sooner had Belmar become contented with his surroundings then he began to run good races. If I remember rightly, Mr. Vosburgh, unquestionably one of the few high-class handicappers this or any other country has ever seen, had Belmar handicapped at 95 pounds in races before I got him. So much did the horse improve that he won seven straight handicaps without being defeated, and each time his weight was increased until in the last of his winning series he carried 128 pounds. In other words, he had jumped from the bottom to the top of the ladder in the handicap division."

Horses love to roll on their backs. Invariably after they have exercised or worked and are washed off, if they are permitted, they will lie down and roll over from side to side. Knowing this, whenever I was racing at a new meeting the very first thing I did was to have a load of sand dumped close to my stable to add to my horse's comfort of rolling in the sand.

I have had at various times as pets of the help and companions to the horses two or three goats—one at a time, of course—and a boxer dog named "Pete." This recalls one of the funniest (to some but not to me) incidents that ever happened. I was entering the gate to the stable area one day when Pete dashed out of the gate going like a streak of lightning. When I arrived at my stable all the stable help were convulsed with laughter even to the extent that one was lying on the ground helpless with laughter. I asked what was so funny and here is the story they told. At that time my stable was close to the railroad track in its rear. The rails were enclosed with a high wire fence. Pete had dug a hole so that he could crawl under the fence and cross the tracks. This day Pete had entered upon the tracks and urinated against the third rail. The electricity ran up the stream to his body and shocked him and he took off "hell bent." I can't understand why he was not electrocuted unless it is because a dog urinates in spasms instead of a steady uninterrupted stream. Pete was smart enough never to even go near the fence after that!

All the horses liked the goats and Pete. But Pete was the special favorite of Jim's Niece. He wore a collar three inches wide studded with brass nobs. During the warm days stall doors are kept open with a webbing stretched across the open doorway so the horses can hold their heads out and still be confined in the stall. Pete was always either in Jim's Niece's stall or sleeping stretched out at the doorway. Jim's Niece would lean her head down, separate her lips and grab Pete's collar in her teeth. She would raise her head four or five inches and lift up Pete's head and gently lower her head and release the collar. Each time Pete's head was raised he would open one eye and look up and close it when his head was lowered. I have sat for as much as a half hour watching this picturesque and interesting event go on.

Jim's Niece was stabled at Empire City racetrack for the meeting. One day she took to stall-walking, which is the bane of a trainer's life. A stall-walker without cessation walks around its stall, sometimes night and day. It is fretful and in most cases goes off its feed and loses weight. We did not know what to do. Her stools were examined but indicated her stomach was in perfect condition. She was the mainstay of my stable and we were in a quandary. My trainer, at the time, had spent his life from a small boy around race stables and really knew how to care for horses. He suggested something that would never have entered my mind. This was to cut a square space in the adjoining stall so that Jim's Niece could fraternize with its occupant. We changed the horses who occupied this stall several times until we located the horse most acceptable to her. Horses are much like humans in some ways, one of them being they make friends with certain of their kind and dislike others. It is almost universal that if you put a group of horses in a field to graze they will pair off and seek a constant companion. Once found the two will graze side by side. Hang their heads over the neck of the other and when one moves even a foot or two will follow it. When another horse gets too close they will bare their teeth and chase the intruder off.

After we had found the right friend for Jim's Niece, she started to settle down, depleted her feed box, and returned to normalcy. This is the only time that this horse ever showed the least temperament and I never could figure out its originating cause.

The less one thinks of crookedness and trickery in racing the more successful will be his winning selections. Even if there is such a thing, which I cannot impress too strongly upon you there isn't—so what? Suppose there is some crookedness in a race, you are just as apt to be betting on the horse involved as to be betting on any other horse in the race, therefore the crookedness would be to your advantage. So on the whole you would not be the loser thereby. Look for your own defect in your calculations rather than the cheating of others. The fairy tales of crookedness in racing derives from the days when chicanery of this sort did exist. But those days are gone forever, since racing became organized and The Jockey Club became arbiter of racing regulations. The stakes are too high in these days for crookedness to have a part in it. The indulgence in sharp practices derives from the motive of gain.

From what I have previously written about how much anyone would have to bet at much less odds to win a purse, it should be beyond any question of doubt that it is more profitable to follow the rules than to attempt, and nine times out of ten without success, to evade them. Racing is the most strictly regulated sport there is. Under such strict supervision as is current today there is not a chance in a hundred of succeeding with sharp practices. I wish I had time to enlighten you on what I know as an owner. If I did, you'd forget that there might be crookedness in racing. And if in one instance out of many thousands, it is attempted you'll note that it is detected and the culprits severely punished for their misdeeds.

I have won innumerable wagers in this fashion. When a new meeting opens, watch for the first few weeks of the meet. Notice the first time any horse races since the start of the meet. If it runs in the money or shows any type of a good race, play it the second or third time it runs. If it performs well first time out you know it is in its own class, and all other things being equal will win.

Learn to finance your money to advantage. Know when to put a good bet down and when not to. Send it in only when you are ahead of the game and retrench when using your own capital. Learn the best ways of wagering. Learn never to be swayed by the odds quoted and that no bet is worth making unless the odds quoted are in proper relationship to the chances the horse has of winning instead of the odds established by the unknowing public.

It is easier for a horse to run on turf than it is on an earth track. Its hooves sink into the soft few inches of top surface on a track. But on the turf its hoofs stay on top of the surface. Compare it to running a thousand feet in sand on the beach to negotiating the same distance on a baseball or football field. You can appreciate the difference.

Therefore, look for a horse that is starting the first time on the turf. A lot of them win and at good prices. But if it runs a reasonably good race, watch for it to go next time at a longer distance. A horse can maintain its speed farther over the turf than it can on a dirt track.

One night I attended the Harness races at Yonkers Raceway. I bought a $50.00 ticket to win on a horse. As I walked away from the window I saw that I had the wrong numbered ticket on a different horse from the one I wanted to wager on. I can't recall whether the error was my fault or the ticket seller's. I returned to the window and asked him to try and sell the ticket which he accepted and agreed to do. I remained alongside the window hoping someone would buy a ticket on the horse. There are few buyers of $50 tickets at the harness races and waits between buyers. It finally got close to Post Time and I was about to request the ticket back when a buyer came along and to my elation bought the ticket. I went out to see the race.

What do you think happened? You guessed it! The horse I had turned down won the race! If that wasn't enough it paid over $50.00 to $1.00! So you see luck is present in racing.

Before Ted Atkinson became the contract rider for Mrs. Dodge Sloan's Brookmeade Stable, trained by Hughie Fontain, Alfred Robertson, another great jockey was the rider. Any time Hughie saddled a horse I was in the saddling paddock with him. One day after Robby rode the first race and won it, I went into the winner's circle and walked back to the jockey house with Robertson. I said to him, "I just bet on your horse and I have a feeling this is your lucky day so I am going to bet every race you ride in." I was not serious, but only joking with him. Later that day I wished I had been serious and not being jocular for here is what happened.

The day was October 9, 1941. "Robby" had a mount in each of the seven races on the card. He finished as follows:

1st race	Sorgho	won	Paid $15.80
2nd race	Running Lights	won	Paid 29.30
3rd race	Sun Galomar	won	Paid 23.40
4th race	Grand Party	won	Paid 20.80
5th race	Horse lost		—
6th race	Paul Pry	won	Paid 12.70
7th race	Starlike	won	Paid 46.30

Not only riding six winners out of a seven-card day was remarkable, but the prices were extraordinary. Figure a $2.00 parlay on all winners and you'll see some real astronomical figures. Not that any sane person would parlay so many horses, of course. But it's interesting. I have a composite photo of these six races in my library now, that Robby sent to me.

Short Maxims

It is not always the heaviest wager that is collected. The weight of the bet does not make a horse win. A poor man's horse and his $20 speak as loudly as a $10,000 wager from a millionaire or a plunger. It is the horse that must be considered.

You cannot be a successful horse player if you are going to get the worst of the odds all the time.

A workout fast or slow has no value in pointing out a prospective winner. The best a workout can do is to convey to you and the trainer that a horse is in condition.

It is my firm conviction that a horse is better raced once a week. My basis for this belief is that the percentage of winning horses decreases the longer the time lapse between its last race. One race does a horse more good than any workout.

It is a good bet to pick out two or three sure-looking bets and parlay them.

Condition has more to do with a horse winning or losing a race than the weight it carries. A horse in poor condition cannot beat one of its own class. The highest class horse cannot win a race with a feather on its back if it is not in condition. It is well to play horses that are in winning form. A horse in winning condition generally repeats, especially if of same class, or runs in the money. The closer its time is to its last race the better the prospects.

With so many animals becoming extinct through their inability to adapt to new surroundings as evolution advances, it has been wondered how the horse ever survived. Fierce fighting creatures, well supplied by nature with fighting tools, such as the saber-tooth lion with its teeth and claws, have disappeared from the earth. The horse with no fighting defensive weapons is still here. Many of the extinct animals were most prolific in producing young. The horse gives one birth at a time and once a year.

My opinion and the opinion of many is that the curiosity, the speed, and alertness of the horse has been the sole reason for survival. Watch a field of horses. Stand at the gate and hold your hand high waving a handerchief and call or whistle and see what happens. Horses will lift their heads and a few will start off at a gallop toward you, then slowing to a canter and then to a walk come near and examine you. This curiosity made the horse alert upon the earth it roamed. This alertness and its speed getting away from any danger present resulted in its survival.

These conclusions are not mine alone but generally recognized. Thinking about it one day I asked myself. This is all well and undoubtedly true. But what about the nighttime? Lions, tigers, all members of the cat family, as well as other predators can approach within leaping distance without alarming its prey since nature has provided them for this purpose. I thought about this for a long time and came up with what I believe is the answer.

I recall in the army that the majority of horses never lay down to sleep. Nature has provided them in the structure of their legs a mechanism that permits them to lock their legs in a position that supports them without effort while they sleep standing upright. You can realize what an advantage this gives the horse when threatened by danger. Instead of losing time to raise itself from a lying-down sleeping position, he can spring immediately into a fast run. The only other creatures that I know have this locking device are birds. They too lock their claws around a branch to sleep.

25

A Working Day of
a Turf Operator

DURING THE TIME I raced my stable, when I entered one of my horses to run the next day, I was most anxious to check the horses with which it had to contend. The *Morning Telegraph* would be available at all newsstands the following day. But I could not wait until then to see what I was up against. Here again I want to point out how utterly ridiculous it is to pay any attention to "inside information" or "tips" given in advance of any horse running in a coming race. Here is the situation.

The *Condition Book's* races for tomorrow has a race suitable for one of my horses. I have up until closing entry time to enter my horse, which I do. Then about 11 A. M. that same morning I get from the Secretary's office a mimeographed sheet showing the entries for all races scheduled for the following day. Until I read this list I have no idea, nor has the trainer or owner of any horse, what other horses my horse will have to compete with. There might be a horse in the race that has beaten mine a number of times against which my horse has no chance at all. And I just can't scratch the horse. You have to have a *very* good reason to persuade the Stewards to allow your withdrawal. So, on the face of it, even if an honest owner or trainer really wanted to give you a tip on his horse he could not do it until he had seen the entries and knew what the competition would be in the race.

Being anxious to see the past performances of the horses in the race with mine I would drive to some downtown section where an all-night newsstand was located at some prominent subway station and wait for the *Telegraph* to arrive by truck about 10:30 P.M. Picking it out I would go home and study the race.

My preliminary work started from the time I reached my home. Records being kept at my office, I could only partially proceed at home. Of course, if I had entered the first thing I would do was to study and analyze that particular race.

Then, my next procedure was the study of every race chart in the paper.

199

I played at the track and with bookies and so covered every major track in the country. But this is no longer possible today, since bookies are gradually disappearing from the scene. Unless the reader can bet away from the track where it is legal such as in Nevada, he will confine his study of the charts to his local track.

I cannot impress too strongly upon the mind of anyone looking for success in racing the primary importance of studying these charts. This is a necessary part of the business of winning at the races. Tons of dirt, sand, and stone must be worked over in order to find a single ounce of gold. The same applies to finding diamonds. The race charts are identically the same in this respect, as the stone and earth. They simply must be worked over in order to produce the diamonds or the gold which in the case of horseracing appears in the form of a winning mutuel ticket.

I do not now know, and I have never known, a single horseplayer who consistently beats the races who does not make advance study of race charts as I have explained in this work. Aside from the fact that such procedure is absolutely necessary it has advantages for players. There are many who are unable to obtain a *Racing Form* or a *Morning Telegraph* in their locality in time to use to play the races. The best they have is a list of entries given in a newspaper. Many who are in a position to get these racing papers in time, have to get to work early and have not the time necessary to study them. As it stands, they have an insurmountable problem that can be solved in only one way.

Players who cannot get the paper at all can subscribe and get it by mail; those who can only get it too late to play with and those who do not have the time can eliminate the dilemma by studying the race charts of past for future play. Then when a sifted-out, prospective winner is qualified it is a matter of seeing its name in the entries.

And the charts can be studied leisurely at pleasure, at night, on weekends.

I diligently scan the charts, principally searching to spot horses that show an irregular race pattern. I read the running comments of the race to spot any horses that unquestionably would have run a better race, except for some incident in the race that may have retarded its running. Being blocked, crowded, struck by another horse or who because of interference of any kind was prevented from showing at its best.

When I first thought of writing this chapter I had in mind at this point to list everything you should look for in these charts. Then I asked myself what is the purpose of my writing this book. Certainly not the expectation for large monetary reward. My purpose is to leave to posterity wisdom and secrets that have enabled me to be a happy, contented horseplayer.

Unfortunately, you cannot be carried along the road to success in a purely mechanical fashion. From the first chapter to the last, the pages are replete with aids that actually have produced winners over the years and will continue to do so as long as horses run. Unless you have a miraculous memory, at this

point you'll have to go back and slowly read what those secrets are and because
I give the reasoning upon which they are based, you'll appreciate them more
fully. They will stick in your memory and you will be able to use them more
productively. The same applies to when we come to examining past experiences.
Certain patterns can be discerned only in the race charts such as for example
irregular races and interference. Other patterns can be gleaned only from
a study of the past performances. For example, only the past performances will
disclose an imported horse and its earnings. The required data for a claimed
horse is only useful when observed from past performances. The race charts
show when a horse is claimed out of each race, but this means nothing; it is
only when this horse is later entered that it can be considered. Then, in the
pattern of a first time starter, a consultation of both the race chart and the
past performances is required.

Here is a suggestion that I am sure will make the absorbtion of the
"racing-know-how" expounded throughout the book easier and more efficient.
*I am going to ask the publisher to put into the back of the book a few blank
pages.* Start reading the book from the beginning and concentrate deeply.
Whenever you read a sentence that contains any reference to a winning factor,
put a note on these blank sheets and the page on which it is printed so you
can easily refer to it thereafter.

After studying the charts I had finished my work for that day and retired.
The racing day in the stable area begins at dawn, at which time the horses
are fed, after which they are taken out to exercise or be worked out. I have
always been an early riser. After an early breakfast I proceeded to the track,
arriving just about the time the horses were beginning to work out on the track.

I would leave the track to reach my office when it opened at 9 A.M. Attending to any matter requiring my personal attention, my day commenced by
handicapping the races to decide upon my wagers for that day. The first thing
I would do was to get my card file of all horses that, for the reasons I have
given all through this book, I was waiting for to run. I would place a check-
mark alongside their names in the races they are individually entered in. Then
I would proceed to analyze these races. If I did not like the chances of any of
these horses, I'd attempt to see if I could find another likely winner in that
race worthy of a wager. The scratch sheet was delivered to me upon its arrival
and with this and the *Morning Telegraph* I consulted the prices, the comments
and the placement they give to any horse I am interested in. I would do this
with every race all over the country in which one of my file-recorded horses
was a contender.

In those days I played on every major race track. I would prepare my
betting slip to be picked up by the bookie's runner when he called. I then went
to the track and had my lunch at the track restaurant after which I picked up
at the Secretary's office entries made that morning for the following day.

I then played the daily double if I felt that I could pick a winning ticket.
If there was what in my judgment was a sure winner, no matter how small

its odds, I would couple this horse up with all horses in the second race. I would then go to the grandstand and watch the first race. If I had the double winner in this my day started off well because no matter who might win the second race I would most likely be a winner unless the double should pay less than the $24 the play cost me. Invariably there are twelve tickets available in the second half of the double, so these coupled up with one ticket in the first race cost $24. I would then just wait and hope that some longshot would win in the second race. If it did, and the payoff netted me a profit of a few hundred dollars (I mostly bought more than one set of tickets) I might call it a day and not play another race, unless it appealed extra strongly to me.

Activity becomes more rapid immediately after the second race is over. Action required has no time to waste. It is most important that as soon as the first flash of the odds for the second race occurs that I place these figures down on my program. I believe all tracks have the Opening Price Morning Line printed to the left of the horse's names on the program. If they do, it is not necessary to consult the board for the opening line, unless there has been a late scratch, in which case the flashed odds will be different from the ones printed in the program.

The most important thing of each day at the track is to watch for the appearance of a Secret Play in the double. If there is, I have a most probable winner possible to find in racing and if it does not win, which of course it does not every time, I have the best kind of a future play, as previously explained.

This is how my day ends and the thrills, happiness, and contentment are such that I would not change places with anyone in the whole world!

Anyone who will read this book with care and who will absorb its contents, and apply with a modicum of common sense the things he has learned herein, is beyond any question of doubt going to get more enjoyment out of playing the races than he would ever get if he had not read it. If I were not as sure of this as that night follows day, I would tear it up now.

From the time I first started to play the races I always helped myself by digging in and searching out every facet that might enhance my chances of winning. So I would like to complete the work by quoting a maxim learned at the knee of my mother. I so well remember her advice to me. "Always be a good boy, Albert; be sure to go to church every Sunday, and remember the Good Lord Only Helps Those Who Help Themselves."

Bye

A "Special Bonus" From the Author

To show his appreciation to the readers of this book, the author will send free of charge his *Vital Statistics That Win* to all who will write for it. Address your request to A. G. Illich, 697 East 219 Street, Bronx, N.Y. 10467.

notes

notes